SUPRARURAL

Preface

Suprarural: Atlas of Rural Protocols of the American Midwest and the Argentine Pampas presents an alternative approach to existing models of relationship between the urban and the natural based on palliative, decorative, or hygienist ethics. Against the grain of these models and overcoming their nostalgic frameworks, the notion of Suprarural seeks to reframe, systematize, and empower the architectural forces latent in rural organizations, focusing in particular on those relating to agricultural production and livestock farming. Rather than naturalizing nature from a functional perspective of the urban, the intention is to develop techniques to straightforwardly urbanize with and through the rural.

The Atlas is structured along nine systems of organization: transport infrastructure, land subdivision, agricultural production, irrigation and fumigation, water management, cattle management, storage, inhabitation, socialization. Each of these systems possesses a number of organizational types, material components, normative relationships, and spectrums of performance, which become available through a manual of instructions for a Suprarural environment. The research is based on a realistic ethics towards design, which operates by abstracting and intensifying unexplored territorial phenomena with the purpose of developing new territorial models by nurturing them from currently operating ones.

The design research was developed simultaneously in studios and seminars taught at the School of Architecture and Urban Studies of the Universidad Torcuato Di Tella in Buenos Aires and at the School of Architecture of the University of Illinois at Chicago by Ciro Najle and Lluís Ortega. Together with abstract protocolar descriptions of the systems and the exploration of the potentials lying behind the organizational logics of these two parallel territories, the Atlas collects a series of voices by practising architects, architectural theorists, critics, and historians, agricultural engineers, critics, and philosophers, and a photographic survey that expands the investigation under different perspectives and insights.

Towards a Suprarural Architecture

Ciro Najle, Lluís Ortega

Suprarural claims a new domain for the practice of architecture. By turning the discipline's dysfunctions vis-à-vis the urban and its systematic oversights regarding the countryside into a new set of opportunities, *Suprarural* issues an urgent call for a theory that can overcome both of these in the name of extending the spectrum of capabilities by engulfing the ordering systems of the territory. The project is carried out via a program of investigation that takes the know-how embedded in the rural—its organizational protocols, its synchronicity with the natural, and its often disregarded technification—as the raw material for a new form of architectural expertise.

The opportunity provided by the investigation is not to be confused with simple convenience at a practical level. Neither is it meant to develop a new rhetoric of punch lines and improbable statements that are merely ironic or amusing in nature. Instead it involves an earnest plea, mobilized by playing, in virtual terms, with the territory itself. The seemingly ordinary scenario of this game—that is, the fundamental operative failure of the rural domain in the face of the ubiquitous forces of urbanization, and what appears in principle as a thematic outmodedness—is reversed here into a panorama of unprecedented potential, and embedded with straightforward techniques and vibrant new organizations and figures.

Suprarural's call for the rural, that marginal, enigmatic, and apparently minor territory of discussion, is directed to challenge and problematize the condition of the Suburban by turning its ubiquitous model inside out and threatening it with the dark side of the commodification of the territory. The Suprarural is the underside of the myth of endless urban expansion. It involves the intensification of the rural into architectural singularities, rather than its annihilation by the urban, and calls for extreme exposure rather than refuge, engagement rather than retirement, radical technification rather than primitive form, and for the sophisticated wilderness of post-urban uncertainty rather than the domesticated mildness of pre-urban nostalgia.

In past decades the discipline has gone through a triple displacement. To begin with, it has moved from satellite representation to the simulation of systems that manage the complex fluidity of territories beyond political, social, and cultural boundaries.

The ethics and tone of this development have also gradually shifted from different versions of landscape urbanism to various ways of appropriating ecological models for a wiser understanding of the urban. It has thereby established an array of roles for the ecological condition as part of a wider geopolitical project directed at integrating contemporary processes of urbanization in a single inevitable trend by using the metaphysics of survival and the myth of sustainability as its perfect vehicle.

Secondly, the discipline has displaced its focus from the object to the ground by engaging geographic positioning systems, renewing its forms of mapping, and refining its procedures through the popularization of field and systems theory. This shift has recently flipped back into the vertical, with the ground itself becoming the new condition of the architectural object: monumental, geomorphological, post-utopian, and figural. It also converts the organizational potential of the dynamic complexity of the territory—multi-scalarity, multi-temporality, trans-specificity, and pre-urbanity—into cartoon-like figurations that now promise to provide architecture with a solution to the conundrum of its orientation towards service through a renovated palette of persuasion.

Thirdly, a cultural shift has taken place from the general idea of practice as a meta-domain that integrates different disciplines to a polarization between the inter-disciplinary ideology of climatic change and the regressive ethics of the old notion of autonomy, clear expressions of the rapid consumption of ideas and cultural constructs at work in contemporary culture. It seems that the expansive role of the architect as a mediator operating within the systems—an agent installed half-outside of them and an artist working through them—has declined into a model in which the modern notion of the architect as a former ideologue, now expatriated to a post-postmodern, retro-ideological, pseudo-political scenario, has taken over design research, turning it into an enemy to be obliterated from the firmament of serious architectural thought.

In this context, *Suprarural* aligns itself with systemic thinking and its persuasive promise of empowering the architectural project with robust structures. But this alignment is performed amorally, and with an important dose of lightness. Its protocolar machine is not conceived as an ideal means to something else, like a manual of instruments waiting to be used for the right purposes, but as a constitutional state of the in-between, which, like it or not, does not close the perfect circle of the traditional typological manual. Thus the work is not a body of research that operates within the scientific tradition without friction. Even though characterized by identifying territorial conditions and configuring the distinguishable organizational models through which they can be competently directed, on a more basic level it endeavors to open up new spaces of imagination.

The Suprarural is, in this context, regarded as a medium of design operating through a standard that develops a focus through and by the means of production, allowing external inputs to constantly force the re-description of its models. Its methodology is thus directed at progressively constructing relevance in iterative loops, not through sense but through reverberation. The Suprarural is a platform that constitutes meanings of a kind, singularities through consistency, order through resonance. It seeks to deploy power by formulating new questions, without necessarily answering them. Similarly, the notion and the figure of the rural protocol is not to be seen as an instrument for arriving at a Suprarural status, nor is it assumed to be good per se. Instead the rural is the device through which the Suprarural, that blurry vision, can perhaps be instilled into our worldview and enticed into the real.

Diagram as recursive model

Suprarural consists of a set of informational regimes that index the existing formal organization of the rural. This set involves diagrams that collect intelligence from rural systems and integrates their rules into abstract models. The construction works as a design platform through the actualization of territorial latencies. Constituted by protocols made up of different ranges and scopes of performance, the Suprarural allows them to be redefined by various forms of feedback with each other, displaying them and making them perform against one another. In that sense the Atlas of Rural Protocols is not so much a set of components whose instrumentality is external to their form as a fluid medium that establishes continuities between potentials latent in the material world. Traditional representational logics, in which drawings refer to external forms of meaning that engage existing cultural narratives, achieve a status that takes the post-representational nature of the diagram to the level of an abstract register in a territorial model. The systemic condition of this diagrammatic form conducts the rural material to a plane where action and representation are one, operating together by making their relational structures explicit and constantly refining their protocols of description. The Suprarural diagram is a recursive model amongst rural protocols.

Normally, organizational protocols operate through the definition of constraints and the recognition of performances with various levels of redundancy. There is no requirement, in principle, to model them in the direction of the construction of ideals, nor is there a will to design idealizations, but rather an immanent desire to mobilize reverberations through design by intensifying them as instances in larger processes of differentiation, magnifying attributes of the organizations to a point where they are no longer efficient in their original terms, and launching a wider range and higher level of performance, now charged with a broader agenda. This lack of idealization of the rural does not mean that there is a similar loss in the legibility of its character.

Only that it is forced, here, to become operational and forward-looking, referring more to a form of imagination grounded in stimulation and a sense of opportunity than to a figural resemblance to past references. The opportunity for these actions is guided by the proximity of usage and contiguity of different figures, and evolves through perpetual refinement in lending as much attention to the progressively emerging target as to the gaps lying or arising in between. The gaps between protocols have, so to speak, a life of their own, and themselves become the engine of potential constructs, thus blurring the boundaries between sources and meanings, and revealing a deeper passion for the leaps embedded in continuities than a loyalty to conserving them as they are. The ideal within the Suprarural operates as a sort of shadow or, better yet, as a fog of indistinguishable grays, enigmatic in-between states, slippery nuances, and smooth edges. Ideas flicker within this fog, sparkle and become sharper at times, and proliferate in an endless game of readjusting targets and alliances.

Technification as differentiation process

Apparently bare and devoid of architecture, the American Midwest and the Argentine Pampas are highly technified territories that constitute, virtually or actually, consistent forms of extraordinarily large architecture. While in the industrial era the local was merely a by-product of a larger production system at work invisibly across regions, its post-industrial technification operates as the condition of possibility of a global dynamics. The mechanical process was, in modern times, transversally isolated, functionally specialized, technically optimized, and driven by single-minded forms of efficiency, for the most part alien to the multivalent potential of material systems. Currently, it is the material systems themselves that are becoming machinized and made time-efficient, multi-purpose, distributed, and therefore highly volatile, configuring an ubiquitous architectural project that resets, each time and by means of local protocols, the normative conventions by which generic structures operate.

This peculiar coexistence of bottom-up self-organizing processes and top-down territorial design strategies implies both a threat to and a challenge for architecture: either it is swiftly left out of any influence at a geopolitical level, or it is compelled to function as the sine qua non mode of control of territorial form as transformative device. The shared know-how and ownership system that is embedded in local processes commands the globalized dynamics of technification without even noticing it. And, in this context, the discipline is confronted by the possibility of constructing new and expansive forms of knowledge by simply articulating local organizations and nurturing their outcomes from within, and yet exceeding the rationality of their production frameworks. The particular and the generic are enabled to perform not merely as polarities in a process of mutual feedback between local events and global conditions, out of reach for the architect and exclusive of other forms of expertise—geopolitical, geological, ecological—but become the matter of an architectural project themselves. Architecture now has the opportunity to unleash singularities that can become generic systems of a second order: the territory as the ultimate form of architecture.

Furthermore, rural organizational techniques working at a local level exhibit the capacity to not only articulate global processes at a territorial level but, more importantly, to change them from within and transform vast territories along the lines of increasingly convoluted and yet extremely simple patterns. Architecture can take on board this expansive capability, not just by contributing to the organization of the local performance of these patterns but by intensifying them in a symphony of redundancy at various scales, allowing generic territorial structures to be differentiated on the basis of manifold local, regional, and global inputs, rather than operating within the range of encapsulated forms of material efficiency alone. If we read the globe as a single yet multiple informational model, productive in nature, neither urban nor natural as such, the redundant structure that this model embodies allows any form of know-how to be integrated and creatively synchronized, rather than disappearing as mere background noise in the sea of global-local efficiencies. Rural patterns can thus be said to operate as the basic organizational matter in a broader scheme of redundancy management, absorbing, with material directionality, information coming from a wide range of inputs, from the hyper-local, accidental and contingent situations of the farmer to the homogenizing tendencies that are linked to large-scale corporation logics. As a consequence, these patterns should not be understood as averages or as mere negotiations of existing conditions but as incomplete collective constructions that deal with various modalities and intensities. Catalysts of a functioning world of simultaneous processes of differentiation, rural protocols are the ultimate triggers for the constitution of global orders, megalomaniac and yet inherently architectural, self-alienating and self-transforming at base. Architecture is the ultimate and most appropriate means for the world to problematize its comfort zones of territorial efficiency through an artistic model. Inputs of extremely different kinds and degrees can be integrated within such ultra-large fluent structures, where systems provide feedback for one another in loops of proliferating or balancing patterns.

Assemblage as formal technique

How do we work in a context where systems have an open logic and are robust enough to adapt to contingency yet still operate within a narrow range of performance and a very limited world view? How do we expand the narrow-minded, inward-looking scope of performance of rural systems into broadminded, generalist ones, and do this from within, rather than from without? In other words, how do we move

from the local-global dichotomy based on the opposition of rural versus urban to the ubiquitous-singular multiplicity-based level of the Suprarural Cosmopolis?
The convention of constructing hybrid or counter-intuitive figurations by articulating fragments through montage has been the customary formal technique to decontextualize typologies in patchwork-like or field-like landscape proposals since the 1990s. However linguistically curious, formally poignant, or conceptually innovative, these techniques proved to be limited to the rarifying capabilities of formal disruptions or the collision of opposites. By and large they operated within the boundaries of the architectural object, no matter how expanded in scale. And by solely referring to the traditional representational conventions of architecture, frequently based on dichotomies like natural-artificial, inside-outside, rural-urban, full-void, ground-object, soft-hard, open-closed, among others, these techniques lack the organizational effectiveness that they promise and the formal fluency that give them significance. They are there to help evoke a world project by imitating ecologies through static representations of complexity, often metaphorically, but failing to respond to the challenge of constructing the material means of a geopolitical model that might integrate dynamic attributes in forward-looking simulations. By working with static assemblages of objects, these lineages fail to root themselves in the more abstract register of the protocolar and are therefore unable to technically lead a rigorous design process and a greater capacity for establishing supple and adjustable relationships. By being focused on immediate figurations and on the mediatic impact of the rhetoric of form rather than on dynamic organizational capabilities and on the potential of form to have an actual influence over the processes, they fail to recognize the very basic transformational capabilities of architecture that lay not only in persuasion but also in maneuvering performance. The notion of dynamic assemblage, based on the organizational latency of protocols, relational and relative in nature, is conducive, instead, to the integration of subsystems and to the creation of expansive trans-scalar figures, legible within the global continuum at many scales. The local becomes, in this context, not just a figure operating at a discrete scale, but an index of larger systems, whose organization it contributes to at a deep structural level.

This second order of assemblage is constructed by means of two levels of operation: one that recognizes systems, breaks them down into the smallest protocolar relationships, and constructs a manual of variations of those broken-down attributes, and another one that puts these attributes and relationships together and builds up progressively robust assemblages. However, the logic is not linear, as if moving from unit to set, but rather circular, for as the resulting assemblages feed back the systems break down, altering the original protocols and endowing them with renewed potential. In a way this circular process works like an endless dice game which constructs ever-higher forms of chance. Far from being consecutive steps in a traditional deterministic process, these iterative throws of the dice operate as forcefully deterministic actions, where everything is necessary and actually wished for retroactively. The process is not just a way to justify the outcome but rather the opposite: it is the outcome itself that constructs legitimacy in reverse, or better still, both process and outcome keep the feedback loop they partake of in motion, as a motor of determinacy. Global design thus becomes relevant and persuasive not through the artificial magnification of localities through fields or patchworks that extrapolate and generalize effects, but rather as the intentionality in-built in a feedback process that transforms itself en route, setting constantly new agendas and altering the directionality of the forthcoming ones. Such a process works as a sort of vibrating machine, overcoming the segregated condition of protocols by escalating and looping back their abstract regimes.

Protocols as abstract regimes

For this dynamic assembly loop to be possible, there must be a set of inner regulations that can both build the coherence of the particular subsystems and trigger their self-transformation. Rural protocols are not just formal rules that determine relations in an absolute, permanent manner in the direction of the making of closed, descriptive procedures, but are instead relational logics of performance that connect with others and are capable of setting a generative engine in motion. This is one of the main purposes of the iterative use of protocols: to develop a successive mediation directed towards an increasing and progressively expansive form of abstraction. Once the embedded efficiency of systems is released from its restrictiveness to other systems, often assumed to be necessary, protocols become a potential part of a larger synthetic machine, in which the evaluation of performance is set free from its single-mindedness, unfolding and multiplying effects in their context. Designers become complex-system-designers and construct conditions for architectural inventiveness through the abstraction of protocols that, in turn, start operating in directions which diverge from the original instructions. The inner material logics of protocols are therefore not simply removed in a process of abstraction but rather the opposite: they become intensified and freed of the consecutiveness of the linear processes they take part in. Material logics transform differentiation processes in convoluted patterns that contain a manifold of potential actualizations that circulate in constant feedback, oscillating between an inherent abstraction and a progressive charging of meaning and sense. This oscillatory loop promotes the engagement of the unknown as if it were known in advance, encouraging invention and operating as a rigorous but open-ended game of managing potentials.

There is a form of vitalism embedded in such a circular design process, but it is a circular form that embraces chance, intense counter-intuitiveness, and radical arbitrariness as a condition of existence, performing through the mutual adjustment of the outcomes and the protocols that set up the game structure. There is no such thing as an idealized form of efficiency, nor is there a vector of progress which can be claimed in advance or demonstrated as being necessary, not even in a nonlinear version. Instead it is the ongoing convolution of expertise in the systems of rules and the precision of the outcomes which go on continuously nurturing the game, taking its intelligence and playfulness to a higher plane. Far from operating as rules of the sedimentation of know-how, and farther still from defining a coherent model of increasingly refined efficiency, protocols assume the role of being the dischargers and the receivers of a design machine that works by ceaselessly shuttling back and forth between the constituency of rules and the organization of by-products. The Suprarural is a source of protocolar intelligence in that respect, and rural protocols the transitory sediments of an unending game. A protocol-based system of rules is therefore not just a system of nonlinear control but a system of interferences that, depending on the moment, may behave as a driving force, a source of restriction, a resource of conceptual construction, a vehicle of disciplinary problematization, a device of performance evaluation, or a reserve of cultural value. Here, techniques, figures, norms, references, and forms meet in a medium that changes register when necessary. The Atlas embodies just this multivalent medium.

Atlas as political engine

The Atlas is traditionally an instrument of territorial design. The very rationale of its format consists in being able to hold and navigate across the most diverse types of information in a systematic way, the ambition being to create the conditions of a comprehensive totality. However, the Atlas not only works as an all-inclusive mechanism that serves as a passive instrument for fixing and arranging different points of view, but also as a biased platform that redefines perspectives, facilitates novel worldviews, and activates the configuration of new questions and the transfiguration of what is taken to be a given. The Atlas is a plural, multidirectional diagram, a multiplicity of blueprints that forces the user to formulate questions; it is a transformative tool, not just a compilation of inert conditions systematically displayed and made available for the increasing knowledge of an impersonal reader located at an abstract infinite point, fully detached from the real and rendered ever-conscious. Through its systematic structure, it traces the preliminary conditions for new organizations to take place through an active interaction with the reader, an interaction conditioned in turn by its content and techniques. Its drawings create a nature of their own, its techniques construct an operative language, and its chapters structure new frames of mind. The Atlas is an aggregation of voices that expand a spectrum of interest, a multiplicity of images and autonomous documents that proliferate in an open-ended series of collections, a set of captions that multiply the links between artifact and potential. Its objecthood coalesces the disparity and incompatibility of things in a multitude of provisionally coherent systems of relationships. This simultaneous ability for of endlessly incorporating, possessing, and sustaining the world in a limited space is accompanied by an equally fluent capacity for spinning this material around itself to create new worlds. Its diagrammatic nature is there to catalyze otherwise disconnected and senseless information, and purely out of reverberation works as a tabula for the development of consistent design strategies.

Far from wishing, then, to provide a fixed portrait of a territory, made transparent through a precise system of coordinates and a coherent set of instructions to understand and use it judiciously, this Atlas defines the conditions for a series of active relationships that oblige readers to take alternative positions within the territories under question. In other words, it is not a means to safely locate the reader in an otherwise unknown territory—that is, an apparatus of knowledge that preserves the subject's prudent detachment from the real—but a weapon to empower action on the real and engage with the potency of the unknown. The Atlas is a political engine, and requires of the reader an equally earnest will to become an agent of information management. It is a means of unscrupulous resourcefulness, not just a means of disengagement and comprehensiveness. Manifold actualizations that are imprudent, blunt, forceful, and unnatural are embedded in its pages. And yet these actualizations are neither infinite nor gratuitous. They demand projective reading. An Atlas is not a means of indifference but a vehicle for differentiation. Its pages are not flat screens that make knowledge available, but unforgiving sheets that only open themselves to the playful reader who can work transversally in relation to their sequences, submitting to their rules of thumb in order to play a game with them.

The rural as pre-architectural condition

The organization of the rural in an Atlas is regarded as a pre-architectural condition whose pattern is embedded with dynamic intelligence and can foster different urbanization processes. The rural is not presented nostalgically as an inert or obsolete organizational condition waiting to be transformed by urbanization, but rather as a particular structure within which latent architectural systems are ready and willing to be intensified and equipped with prospective properties. The rural works as a set of subsystems operating simultaneously, partly in consonance, partly in parallel. Its substructure is grounded on natural systems dynamics: seasonal to daily weather variations, various conditions of topography and water flows, animal behavior, a limited array of ecologies supported by different technological regimes, artificial drainage systems, infrastructural systems, land division systems, animal management systems, sow and harvest systems, storage systems, which are activated and determined by a range of economic forces, mostly concentrated around agricultural production and cattle, and permeated by habits, rituals, routines, and various cultural traditions, historically characteristic of the prairie and the flatlands. The formalization of those systems and their performance gives a clear identity to the landscape of the Midwest and the Pampas and builds up conditions of possibility for urban organizations to happen. In other words, the Rural Atlas is not simply the result of stabilizing rural culture by capturing it in poignant images but the raw organization of a prospective capability to create unprecedented urban-territorial cultures. If the rural is a matrix of preliminary inputs in a potentially evolving system rather than a given state of things, and if the transformative propensities that develop within these inputs is forced to configure questions which can surpass their status quo rather than be assumed as self-explanatory frameworks, the logics of rural production can be said to already contain logics of urbanization, as if on hold.

The substructure of the rural is differentiated through a series of evaluations that drive the feedback of its current situation with new principles, thus intensifying or modulating its embedded architectural attributes. The outcome of this process is an in-between condition, neither rural nor urban, or both, performing simultaneously at different registers that evolve in time and are fueled by architecture. In other words, the Suprarural does not bring any stabilization or consolidation into the rural, nor does it bring an imposed kind of change into it, but recognizes and upgrades its in-between condition and takes it to another level of complexity, a higher cultural standing. Some of these actualizations work as material sets in evolution, in the sense that they nurture material organizations that already have their constraints and regulations inscribed within regimes of equilibrium or diversification. They can be regarded as entire cultural mindsets in their own right, in the sense that they operate at an abstract linguistic level, in reframing systemic correlations by re-conceptualizing their territory of pertinence. The dual material-mental condition of the rural is integrated within the two simultaneously multifarious and dialectic layers of the Suprarural, where the design of material organizations requires a new conceptual apparatus that can channel its potential, and vice versa, a whole series of material-based routines that can implement such forms of knowledge. The complex loop established between the two layers, each of them inherently multiple and convoluting, is seldom smooth and linear. Instead it is able to generate manifold tensions and disruptions, which oblige the notion of the Suprarural to be permanently provisional and subject to definition.

Supra as meta-authorship

Supra, as in *Suprarural*, is the default condition of meta-authorship. The Suprarural constructs an abstract machine for overcoming the dichotomy between subject and system by means of the internal differentiation of regulatory norms into creative guidelines; that is, of norms that are capable of challenging their own range and mode of variation, paradoxically unfolding their expansive power by accumulating and integrating specifications and various forms of know-how. The Suprarural configures a pre-architectonic ground, from which many, albeit not infinite, architectures are possible. It abstracts, organizes, coordinates, and integrates the latent architectonic potential contained in the rural and, through iterative processes of intensification, actualizes their urban power. If the systemic non-author, fully embedded within systems, was capable of transcending systemic logics by managing their potentials from within, the Suprarural meta-author designs systems of systems, operating from both within and without, making sure not to patronize the outcome as a superior, seemingly natural state that follows on from the threshold of nonlinearity. Instead the meta-author assumes this extra-threshold state as something entirely artificial, and regards its construct as nothing other than his artistic duty, going beyond the intra-systemic notion of the in-between and overcoming the natural-urban opposition implicit in its ethics. This movement that actualizes the intra-systemic fable of self-organization into the supra-systemic artifice of localizing architecture both inside and outside of systems makes use of the circular loop of feedbacks between rural normative intelligence and urban restrictions as the basic definitions of an ubiquitous urban/territorial model. The practice of architecture overcomes the inter-disciplinary myth and ceases to be a mode of transferring knowledge between fields in order to become a mode of unfolding consistencies across fields, precisely through architectural expertise.

Meta-authorship overtakes both the representational traditions of authorship based on ideas, concepts, narratives, or commentaries, and those that either refuse them by recourse to a politics of anti-authorial critique or bypass them by means of an ethics of systemic integration. It involves the blunt differentiation of existing orders—and orders of orders—without falsifying them. The rural, a virtual datum within which this differentiation is developed, is not a tabula rasa and it does not allow creative narratives to be projected or instilled without grounding themselves in its normativity. Rather than discouraging creativity, this void-like inertia encourages authors to engage with extremely slow and at times dumb and pointless processes, with particular design operations that, in the midst of the more intense homogeneity and indifference, differentiate the nuances and hidden striations of this apparent nothingness towards a new status of organization. The subtle legibility of the systems of the rural does not merely call for a subjective projection on the part of the author onto what is regarded as sheer emptiness, but is the most fertile medium for the construction of meta-authorial practices that nurture systems, inherently banal and often insipid, and cause them to collide with each other. The Suprarural is, so to speak, the odd state of the art of the rural, both constraining it anew and upgrading its operations into unforeseen design actions. The figure of the author is not repressed here by superficially heroic but deeply authoritarian single-statement propositions, which arbitrarily and suddenly change the conditions of the land for a more efficient urban usage, nor does it celebrate the multi-statement or the anti-statement-type proposition of the post-authorial. Instead the Suprarural opens up a whole new set of authorial forms. It calls for a collective form of authorship, not in the sense of an interdisciplinary or participatory ethics that dissolves design expertise via politically correct committees, technocratic think-tanks, and paternalistic systems of participation, but by putting authorship under a high level of stress, and by consciously misusing the deceptively indifferent organizational forms of the rural.

Midwest-Pampas as geopolitical project

The Midwest-Pampas is a dual geopolitical arena that articulates cultural, economic, historic, and technological determinations in a plane of consistency running along a north-south axis, parallel to that described by the two American metropolises, New York and Buenos Aires, major trading gates between Europe and America, through which the mainstream flows of immigration of peoples, goods, and civilizing drives has taken place during the 20th century. Ingeniously synthetized by the bifocal map of Le Corbusier in *Precisions* (1930), this axis of the continent's unavoidable destiny grew weaker as the metropolitan model of huge capital cities and hinterlands was replaced by the distributed model of regional networks, installing a new form of geopolitical life. The north-south Midwest-Pampas axis runs today in a precise longitudinal parallel to its metropolitan predecessor and articulates not a model oriented by the inward-outward relationships between the continent and the ocean but one where interior and exterior coincide and pulsate from the two largest agricultural plains. By means of this displaced centrality, the Suburban model, dominant expression of the decaying megalopolitan stage of those two major urban centers, encounters now its antithetical reversal, the Suprarural, expression of an upcoming urban territory, alternative to the regional network model in which it allegedly takes part. With the fundamental capacity to carry the production of a concealed quantity of reserves at the verge of an age of acute lack of resources, this post-sustainability model promises to articulate the potentials of a production map that transforms the outdated model of the rural into an over-technified form, overwhelming the urban as we know it.

It is in this context that the massive monotony and ruthless insipidness of the Midwest and the Pampas build up a new form of cultural prosperity based on the economics of the countryside. If observed with low-resolution lenses, its principal attributes have the aspect of a brutal, crudely homogenous and straightforward territorial archetype, almost dull in its formal frankness and aesthetic earnestness. The prairie is a childlike territory, immature in its form, and candid in its organization. And yet its flatness, figural manifestation of an uncompromising mindset, unveils a landscape of nuanced differences. As its vastness cannot conceal its richness, lying a meter down, far from cancelling differences, it makes them all the more evident and auspicious. The Midwest and the Pampas are fine-resolution fields capable of responding to almost any action, no matter how tiny, casual, or irrelevant. The prairie is a field where any action gets effortlessly escalated to extremes, and immediately projected onto a firmament of hope, imagination, myth, and vision. Laid-back investment, prolific production, and fast development are all proof of the simple theorem of this magnifying plane. Notwithstanding its calm, tranquil appearance, its responsiveness to stimuli is unexpectedly excessive, engendering uniqueness and otherness through sheer quantity and density. The Suprarural becoming of the continent calls for a refocusing on the ground, now in a paradoxical role: to be both the support of a highly rationalized mechanism of capitalist production and the nurturing nature of a machinic sublime.

Three attributes are the expression of this splendor. The first is the non-horizontal property of flatness, and unfolds as the natural manifestation of how an opulent field reacts to simple actions of colonization, namely through sowing and harvesting, triggering convoluted design loops and spinning formal patterns that literally cause the ground to revolve. The second attribute is the historical evidence of the fact that the vertical elevation of anything working anti-gravitationally against the dominance of flatness becomes a figure of praise and glory, no matter how banal. Sources of landscape legibility, rhythm, depth, and orientation, such emergences in elevation—machines, trucks and vehicles, abandoned tools and objects, giant trees, medium-size forests, raw constructions and industrial naves, infrastructural ruins, silos and windmills, animals, and even human figures—distinguish themselves as the sudden heroes of the expansiveness. Finally, a spherical flatness, fashioned by the extreme proportions of the plane, resulting from merging the 360-degree horizon with impossible swelling curvatures. This traveling horizon is invisible in other types of fields, except perhaps for the oceans. Curved horizons, rasterized soils that curl-in-flatness, spherical skies that surround the space with explicit, often poetic, meteorological and astronomic processes bring the earthy constitution of the rural to an oceanic perspective. The ruggedness of the populated horizon and the mirage of the atmosphere give the flatland a dense character. Horizontal, passive, homogenous, endless, universal from one perspective, vertical, revolving, unique, counter-intuitive, singular from another, and curved, surrounding, encompassing, exposing, from a third point of view, the flatland portrays an active three-dimensional field that builds up design actions as if naturally, from the tiniest stimuli and constraints, becoming a territory of clever navigation and expansive differentiation. Le Corbusier's map, that megalomaniac enterprise across the unexplored edges between oceans and continents, operating within the two-dimensional framework of the modern universalizing ground, is now flipped by its parallel counterpart, the intensive consistency of the Suprarural, that ubiquitous biological machine of the impossible escalation of minor actions through the revolution, verticalization, and curving of the flat by means of rural protocols.

The art of territorial activation

Grounded on the nuanced uniformity of the flatlands and nurtured by its inexhaustible plane of consistency, the Suprarural defines the territory of a ubiquitous practice. It adopts the formal norms and informal routines of the rural, reframes them in an Atlas, and sets up the rules of a game of feedback loops that integrate manifold capabilities in a collective development that largely exceeds the communitarian. Without softening the powers embedded in the real, but instead furthering their subtleties, it boosts the sensibility of the rural with an open-ended spectrum of architectural imagination. The techniques of this Atlas are organized according to a series of rural systems: transport and infrastructure, land subdivision, soil management, water management, irrigation, socialization, storage, human inhabitation, animal management. These systems are described as protocols, that is, as rules of engagement with other systems. These rules are defined as simple variations of a series of variables, which, responsive to the variation of other variables, connect systems with one another. Variables synthesize the behavioral regime of systems, often obscured under the guise of habits, routines, and rituals, and only in particularly industrialized cases considered as intelligent, determinable, and predictable. However, these variables, mechanized or not, constitute one of the clearest procedural bodies in the world, consisting not only of mechanisms and instruments of territorial determination, but also of devices, tricks, and trickeries to adapt to the manifold contingencies and accidents that such prolific territory can bring about. Sensible, sensitive, practical, down-to-earth, sequential, astute, prudent, tactile, simple, economical, these rules construct the machine of sensibility of the flat plain. They regulate processes of high efficiency and adaptability with low cost and energy. They are transmitted through the generations without ambiguity, or better yet, with exactly the necessary ambiguity to enable change under unusual circumstances. If anything, rural protocols show that sustainable architecture lies in the methods more than in the artifacts or the materials, and that there is no higher-end technology than an advanced system of abstract intelligence, simple in its instructions and sensible in its performances.

Suprarural has a main structure based on the integration of these rules in a loop-based model that moves back and forth between systemic protocols and articulated projects. If rural systems are described as a detailed taxonomy of existing principles of organization, Suprarural projects are made up of the ways in which these principles distance themselves from the systematic documentation of the catalog through its intensive differentiation. Suprarural Architecture is no more related to the specificities of the original framework of efficiency of rural protocols than it is made present through the nurturing and strengthening of their embedded architectural potentials. The intensified actualization of rural systems, isolated, intertwined, and mutually activated, the Suprarural works as a dynamic assemblage that reduces the responsibility of the comprehensiveness of models in order to articulate and magnify particular iterations of the architectural structures latent within systems. Such intensified actualization is a diagram in itself, fed by new sets of protocols that get continually indexed and integrated in the framework. New frames of evaluation are constructed, investing the rawness of the rural with a progressive directionality. The loop slowly constitutes a complex set, and keeps incorporating determinations as it evolves as a vision. The Suprarural project thus remains an open question and retains its in-between nature as an essential part of the further development of its procedures. Narratives are left open, ideals are made relative, universals are subsumed to their own vacuum, and permanence remains unspoken. The generality of Suprarural models consists of the becoming singular of recurrent games between regulations and emergences. Clearly not a defined product, Suprarural Architecture is one design phase among many. Its visions are both bred in and removed from the statics of the rural, and impelled towards the configuration of artistic territorial actions. Suprarural is, in that sense, the art of territorial activation.

Pocket Manifesto

Anna Font

Of late, specializations within the disciplinary field have been responding directly to problems proposed from outside the discipline, whether from other fields—sociology, economics, engineering, ecology—or based on other logics—developmental, market, technological or environmental. Architecture has been progressively subjected to external frameworks characterized by extreme situations or states of emergency and, in most cases, it has served an instrumental purpose, first ironically, then literally, and finally in a celebratory way. This has configured an acritical, apathetic or fetishistic cultural attitude with regard to how the problems themselves are put forward, limiting both the responsibility and the potential of the work of the architect to immediate actions, that quickly become obsolete and irrelevant. In this context, it is again necessary for the discipline to anticipate the problems that are handed down to us, as opposed to accepting them blindly as a given. Defining the spaces for action from within them does not imply indifference to the tendencies and needs of the present. Rather, it entails framing them in larger and more inclusive contexts. This construct has been strangely set back by the supposedly urgent necessity of making our forms of knowledge indispensable at a time of abrupt changes in the economic model. The internal compartmentalization of the discipline has segregated the discussion at schools and disciplinary debate forums, corporatizing practice and, paradoxically, postponing thought on a more effective disciplinary construction. Without setting aside its instrumental sense, *Suprarural* claims the recovery—or proposes the construction—of a new mediation project, so that a more tempered figure of the architect can serve, at the same time, as both agent and author.

To that effect, *Suprarural* involves working in the still undifferentiated area, largely lacking in operativity and often unorganized, located between the rural and urban territory. This space of investigation is pulled between the reductionism of the traditional peasant—who regards the exceptional qualities of the countryside as an undesirable series of errors that need to be minimized in the process of consolidation or definition of productive spaces—and the indifference of the contemporary metropolitanite who, in his comfortable isolation, enjoys the qualities of the countryside for pleasure, entertainment and other forms of distraction, assuming that they are inherent to the decorative aspect of a passive idea of nature, without any awareness of its actual productivity or of its transformative potential.

This intermediate space lying in-between productivist and consumerist concerns appears today as a segregated sphere, sterilized of its inherent complexity. *Suprarural* is put forward as a construct founded on the hypothesis of creating reciprocities based on tying together new continuities between the existing rural systems, so that this polarization can be absorbed and made operative within wider ranges or spectrums of variability, which participates in the more pervasive gradient of the urban territorial. The construction of these spectrums takes as a reference the way in which these systems currently operate, using their know-how and common sense as a source of rationality—i.e., as engines—and activating them through their description in protocols which, on the one hand, enable their use and, on the other, help strengthen and extend them beyond their initial limitations. The aim is to act on the territory from within, transforming it not by imposing urban orders but by working on the differentiation of its own mechanisms and propensities.

The agenda is built upon the following points:

01_Thinking of architectural design as an open-ended process, whose creative potential emerges from and through the material of study.

02_Generating architectural design from the bottom up, from local organization to structural organization, conscientiously.

03_Investigating rural systems with the aim of defining their components and their variability in order to calibrate and direct their potentialities.

04_Constructing systems to "architecturize" the territory based on the control of precise geometric and performative characteristics.

05_Deducing those characteristics from protocols derived from legal regulations, material traditions and existing organization systems.

06_Proposing that, like any system of rules, these protocols—commonly understood as extra-architectural, extra-urban, extra-landscape and extra-infrastructural—contain an underlying line of thought.

07_Understanding that this system of rules does not constitute an accidental, vague regulation, with limited applicability for the formal texture of the territory and with a dull urban character that is removed from the formal traditions of urban design. Rather, it constitutes the abstract foundation for configuring a means of construction of substrate.

08_Building quantifiable methods of control, patterns and mechanisms of evaluation, based on the differentiation of a primitive according to an intelligent system that generates a loop with specifications of its own, thus constituting an alternative to the conventional way of developing formal urban planning and landscape codes, regulations and rules.

09_Promoting the idea that the architect's work does not consist of imposing conceptual logics a priori, but instead in shaping an organization through these control methods, investigating their formal properties, learning from their inherent logics and forming highly creative and robust generative systems.

10_Proposing that the shape of the territory, understood as superficial pattern and virtual substrate, should be established—prior to the languages of representation and symbolic identification—as a material medium or active datum, onto which successive performative relationships are deployed and integrated.

11_Perceiving the territory as a battlefield—prior to a means of representation—and formulating that it is in the deployment of its dynamics that the metropolis has access to an infrastructure of effective transformation.

12_Strengthening the idea that the actual processes concerning use and construction are determined in the fluctuations of that performative datum, and not based on its stability or its figurativeness.

13_Prompting thought about architectural design with a territorial aura, where the intangibility of the idea of a local quality is not mythologized as an ungraspable essence but is cast as a specific medium.

14_Determining a notion of architectural material based on formal attributes, organizational variables and performative properties that can be manipulated through communicable control systems.

15_Literally designing the territory, understanding it as pre-urban architecture on a large spatial scale and with multiple temporalities.

16_Outlining a new threshold within the expansive idea of architectural practice.

Through the Architectural Atlas of Rural Protocols, the taxonomization of agriculture and livestock technologies and systems in the Argentine Pampa and the American Midwest is laid out as the base material for models of urban territorial development. These models are derived from premises that are shaped into an agenda through their processes, and which consist of the speculative and projective deployment of rural protocols. The test sites are located in Lobos, Buenos Aires Province, in the Argentine Pampa, and in Williston, North Dakota, in the American Midwest. In the past few years, both regions have experienced rapid growth and increasing complexity in the composition of their population, as a reflection of an increasing productivity and of the paradigmatic change that is happening in their relationships with their own urban centers. In this context, *Suprarural* focuses on anticipating potential developments in a territorial culture that is currently under construction, where fields and metropolises work as components in an integrated geographic, economic, cultural, and political dynamic. This assimilation process leads to outrageous but realistic territorial cities: intricate but austere, utopian but efficient, experimental but critical, and teeming with new models for urban life.

The Midwest

Paul Andersen

My dad and I were driving across western Nebraska, talking about numbers or cactus or eating with your fingers. He stopped in the middle of a sentence to look curiously out of the left side of the windshield.

"Yeah, there it is. That's the start of the Midwest."
"The start of the Midwest?"
"I think so. Up to this point the hills roll up and down and they're covered with sage and prairie grasses. Here we drop down a little bit, but never really come back up. And you see crops. There's a little bit more moisture in the soil. It's the first field, going in this direction, and pretty soon we'll be surrounded by fields and feedlots."
Defining something as nebulous as the American Midwest is paradoxical, intriguing and unreasonable. Many have tried to do it in many different ways. People analyze speech, food, geology, industry, voting patterns, immigration history, social habits, music and pretty much every other landscape feature and cultural habit. The U.S. Census Bureau defines the region as 12 states, ranging from Ohio west to Kansas and north to North Dakota, though it considers a handful of those states to be in the Great Plains region for some of its reports. The Gateway Arch in St. Louis is known as the "Gateway to the West" but few would dispute that Kansas, its western neighbor, is a solidly Midwestern state. Historically, distinctions between the two parts of the country have been ambiguous, fluid and contradictory. Yet my dad had pinpointed a precise boundary between them. *There is an almost imperceptible hill on I-80, just west of North Platte, and the top of that hill is where you enter the Midwest.* Why hadn't somebody already discovered this crucial spot?

And even if he was the first to see it, can the transition between two areas of the country really be that abrupt? According to him, the border between the West and the Midwest is a point—not a line or a zone. My dad was a math teacher. He knows geometry pretty well. Wasn't it obvious to him, of all people, that the boundary between two areas, positioned side by side, can't really be a point? But seeing it with my own eyes, it's true. As irrational as it may seem, the West becomes the Midwest at a point on the highway. Even after he'd arrived at this absurd and specific conclusion, he kept testing.

"The funny thing is, I've looked for this spot coming the other direction, going west. And it's much harder to find."

"Hmm. Why?"

"I think it's because going east, you gently drop into the Platte River valley. You see the first field. Going west, you don't really see the prairie on top of that low rise. At least not until you're already in it."

"So you've been working on this for a while."

"Oh yeah. I've even looked for it down by Wray and on I-70. It's not there."

My dad grew up in Iowa and most of that side of our family still lives there. I don't know how many times he has driven there and back from Colorado, but it's a lot. Repetition—and irregularities—are fundamental to the Midwest. In Nebraska, for instance, you drive for hours past nearly identical fields and feedlots. No towns—they're all built a mile north of the interstate. You might notice aberrations in the crop rows, irrigation equipment, distant cottonwoods, or highway overpasses far from any exit. Some of the weeds and native grasses have odd colors. Pretty soon, the Grand Canyon seems more banal than the fencing, planting patterns, irrigation ditches and power lines that rhythmically combine and occasionally fall apart, disappear, or veer from field to field. It took my dad a long time to see the combination of small differences that converge at a single spot on the highway to mark the start of the Midwest. He had driven that route dozens of times—and had taken other roads, too—without knowing when, exactly, he passed from one region to the other. Repeating the same trip across the same territory slowly sensitized him to the changes in the landscape that matter most. Once he knew what to look for, the edge of the Midwest was clear. Or clearly obscure, if he happened to be driving west.

The Midwest is not known for variety. People often dismiss it as tedious and undifferentiated, but against a background of sameness, even subtle idiosyncrasies stand out. It's a fascinating place, not in spite of its monotony but because of it. A profound, Midwestern perception of the most subtle differences can lead to preposterous and novel points of view. We typically create novelty at the edges, and the most interesting edges are often in the middle.

WR80-31
WESTFIELD

Protorural, Suprarural

Francisco Cadau

Man's mission, as a prosecutor of creation, as an intelligence that envisages, as a will that aspires, as an intent that accomplishes, is to develop the forces that are at his command, combining causes, modifying effects, strengthening elements and revealing secrets that nature has seemed to keep swathed in impenetrable mystery. (1)
José Hernández

The Argentine Pampas encompass a huge expanse of plains that define an extremely flat landscape. The characteristic flat horizon for hundreds of kilometers dulls the senses and hides minimal differences from fleeting, unprepared glances, differences which are only sporadically introduced by the soft waves of the topography and certain isolated groups of trees.

The anesthetizing effect of the continuity of the Pampas can be seen as a condition that is inherent to the considerable contrast in scales that exists between its vast territorial extension and the limited range of its variation. As Gregory Bateson wrote: "All perception of difference is limited by threshold. Differences that are too slight or too slowly presented are not perceivable." (2)

On the other hand, this limitation of the perception of difference fuels the cultural construction of a monotonous and naked landscape, which shuts off any kind of objective registration of the nuances in a self-confirming relationship bereft of any quality.

Based on this pseudo-insubstantiality of the landscape, or a deliberate aspiration to autonomy, certain organizational models disengage from the qualities of the territory and equate the predominantly flat and empty condition of the Pampas with a blank slate and the empiricism of John Locke. Like a vacuum, lacking in any inherent qualities, they can only be provided with attributes based on an accumulative process of actions; on the foundation of this logic, the organizational models are defined abstractly with respect to the territory that supports them.

It is the case with the exogenous, gridded and invariable model organized under the Laws of the Indies, which, with an extension and a speed that have never again

been matched, were imposed generically as a pattern for urban development for the purpose of commanding and controlling these regions and all of colonial America.
As a counterweight to the colonial model, the protorural precedents of the original inhabitants of the region, native cultures that are inseparably tied in with the environments where they developed, recognized and systematized a range of subtle variations in the landscape of the Pampas as a way of appropriating and organizing the territory. The in-depth knowledge of the water conditions, the vegetation, the topography and the land allowed those cultures to develop an elaborate network of connections: the *rastrilladas* (3). Deep furrows formed in the earth as a result of the comings and goings of the Indians; they left behind their traces in deep tracks that defined those paths (hence the word *rastrillado*, raked). These scars on the territory scored the Pampas, connecting the Pacific Ocean with the Atlantic, and bringing together the Indians in those regions with others in the north and the south, while determining the boundaries between the different ethnic groups. Consolidated by the passing livestock, these roads lay parallel and in winding paths; they ran closer together and farther from one another; they joined and forked, creating a rhizomic organization that connected reference points and survival structures: watercourses, lakes and elevated areas. Their winding routes, seemingly random, negotiated sandy bogs, swamps or marshes and responded to strategic needs where travel was calculated in stages (a day's journey between wet areas and grazing areas for livestock).

From the largest *rastrilladas*, the main roads in the system, a number of smaller branches led off toward the Indian camps. These initial settlements, generally hidden in the hills or among the sandbanks, often grew into rest points, small hamlets and later villages. The *rastrilladas* constituted a complex network of connections developed by the Indians, which were later used by the conquistadors, the gauchos and even the creole army in their punitive campaigns against the indigenous peoples.

And that was how part of a strategy that was largely opportunistic and circumstantial was consolidated, corresponding with those paths: routes that are now a large part of the traffic infrastructures and urban development we see today.
This accommodating and circumstantial method responding to the pre-existing indigenous conditions that began during the conquest gradually distanced itself from the logics that lay at the origin of these paths, retaining the forms that were emptied of meaning as a witness to those absences.

The system of *rastrilladas*, whose veiled traces still exist on the Pampas like a palimpsest, allows for ways of acting on the territory that are removed from purely abstract or contingent actions, from extreme or selective models which level that contingency or that adopt it acritically in a non-systematic manner.

The protorural models developed by the indigenous cultures, however, suggest the recognition and the classification of differences to create specific systems that are, in turn, combined and connected—taking on meanings that transcend their particular specificities. These original organizations seem to wisely integrate the best of each model as they organize differences into a system that becomes adaptable and open—part of a strategy which, in that sense, exceeds the negative aspects of the polarized models.

The recognition of aspects that could be seen as evolved within those original models revises the concepts that have been assigned to those "backward" cultures; it establishes a paradoxical relationship by recognizing evolved models in what is primitive, which, in this sense, have the potential to be taken into account for the future development of the territory.

(1) Hernández, José, *Instrucción del Estanciero, tratado completo para la plantación de un establecimiento de campo destinado a la cría de hacienda vacuna*, lanar y caballar, Sopena, Buenos Aires, 1882.
(2) Bateson, Gregory, *Mind and Nature: A Necessary Unity*, Dutton, New York, 1979, p. 29.
(3) Mansilla, Lucio Victorio, *Una excursión a los indios ranquelas*, Imprenta litografía y fundición de tipos, Buenos Aires, 1870 (English version: *A Visit to the Ranquel Indians*, University of Nebraska Press, Lincoln, 1997).

Risky Businesses

David Salomon

"Pooh, being a bear of very little brain,
decided to invite the new sound [aka Tigger] in." (1)

Farmers are smart. They are generalists. They understand the weather, the soil, seeds, animals, machines, herbicides, fertilizers and futures trading. They know how things work. They operate and repair mechanical and biological beasts. They know how to plan. They anticipate changes in things as unpredictable as the climate and the commodities market. In other words, the farmer is someone who knows how to make and interpret patterns.

Another jack-of-all-trades, Gregory Bateson, defined patterns as "Any aggregate of events or objects [that] can be divided in any way by a 'slash mark,' such that an observer perceiving only what is on one side of the slash mark can guess, with better than random success, what is on the other side." (2) All patterns contain redundancies and these redundancies produce "information" or "meaning." Importantly, he notes: "All that is not information, not redundancy, not form and not restraints—is noise, the only possible source of new patterns." (3)

There are all kinds of patterns on a farm and all kinds of noises that need to be squelched or amplified for it to succeed. Some of these patterns are abstract, temporal and scientific. Some are physical, spatial and natural. It takes many types of intelligence to decode them with better than random success. The farmer is a master at integrating them into a complex yet consistent whole.

This is not an isolated talent. One could say analogous things about the relationship between architects, buildings, landscapes and cities. Substitute these terms in a few places above and it describes a similar scenario.

The research carried out in the Suprarural project recognizes this overlap. But instead of simply looking at conventional architectural types found in rural settings, or using agriculture as a metaphor, they seek out the architectural patterns embedded in common agricultural elements such as fencing, sprinkler systems, windmills, rototillers, cattle chutes, etc. In other words, the patterns from one arena become productive noise in the other. The new patterns that emerge out of these encounters reaffirm the disciplinary necessity of letting new sounds in.

To talk of patterns and farming and information is to see alluring images. Aerial photographs depicting an irregular patchwork of fields, meandering stripes of green and gold, and rigid grids dotted with homesteads or filled with circles are a few that immediately come to mind. The fascination with these sometimes monotonous, sometimes cacophonous, pictures rests, in part, on their ability to embody the desire for beautiful manmade forms to emerge directly out of functional considerations. Whether taken by well-known photographers like Alex MacLean and Georg Gerster, or found on Google Earth, agricultural patterns are understood as the indexical result of the interactions between specific tools, topographies, soils and species. Horse-drawn tillers produce differently scaled stripes than tractor-pulled ones. The soil has a different color in Colorado than in California. Wheat generates a different texture than peas. Linear irrigation systems produce radically different results than radial ones do. The cultivation of hillsides creates wavy rather than orthogonal stripes.

Of course, these effects cannot be seen from the ground. They are not designed. They are the unintentional consequences of an otherwise utilitarian process. However, these pictures cannot easily be written off as the objectification of nature. Agricultural crops are cultural artifacts long before they are photographed. Nor can they be dismissed as artificial, random or superficial. They are the result of highly logical operations and literally made from natural materials and processes. Such patterns are the epitome of the nature-cultural hybrids that Bruno Latour has rightly recognized as the hallmarks of modernity. These appealing patterns reveal agriculture's combination of organizational and aesthetic efficiency that would make any modernist proud. One wonders, following Bateson, what would happen if one began the design process with such images rather than ended with them?

While the demarking, plowing, planting and harvesting of land has always been geometrical, the patterns generated by industrial agricultural methods have a cleaner, crisper quality. However, it would be a mistake to conclude that less geometric patterns are wasteful. Looser patterns are often the efficient result of having to adapt to the limits, aka noise, of a particular topography or technology. Similarly, it would be wrong to conclude that more fluid patterns are always more visually appealing. An endless array of monochrome curves can be as visually tedious as a grid of identically green dots.

Yet even highly repetitive patterns, when seeded with different crops or planted at different times, can produce variegated effects. At one scale they illustrate the highly repetitive, mechanical, industrial logic, while at the larger scale a more diverse sensibility is present. By drawing our attention to the always present combining of spatial and temporal symmetries and asymmetries they undermine any strict division between the standardized and the unique. Both need to be present to recognize the agency of the other.

What one finds on the other side of the slash from these highly graphic images is the false choice between the predictable, mechanized and quiet on the one hand, and the idiosyncratic, personal and noisy on the other. By closely examining and then manipulating a series of generic rural artifacts, the Suprarural project reveals the multiple choices, and futures, present in this highly standardized context, when one takes the time to understand the complex spatiotemporal-technical patterns already present there.

The practice of agriculture (and architecture) is one of managing the future; of predicting what's on the other side of the slash from today. The goal is to produce desirable results over the short and long term. While we associate such control with modern managerial methods and machines, farmers (and architects) have been making accurate forecasts for millennia. Historically, this was achieved by being conservative. The same methods and materials (and forms) were used over and over and over again. At its best this produced fine-grained, empirical and local knowledge. At its worst it deployed obsolete solutions to new problems and was inflexible in times of rapid change.

During the 20th century a variety of mechanical, material and financial/informational technologies altered the role of the farmer (and the architect). Agribusiness (and the building industry) benefited from industrialization's emphasis on economies of scale and specialization like any other. The function of the farmer (and architect) stayed the same but its form changed. It is now fragmented and disembodied. Agricultural (and architectural) intelligence is as likely to be found in the lab or factory as it is barns or on the farm (or on the building site). The ethos of isolation and optimization has replaced the ideal of a composed whole. The multifunctional farm has long given way to the aggregation of mono-cultural environments. (4) The generalist farmer (and master builder) gave way to a series of agricultural (and architectural) engineers.

Temporally, this condition privileges faster behavioral patterns. It favors short-term goals over long-term ones. Spatially it engenders larger, mono-functional places. The emphasis on speed and size comes with a greater pressure to deliver predictable yields. This requires devices that can inoculate the cultivation (or design) process against damage from random events and agents like bugs or budget cuts. Genetically modified seeds, chemical fertilizers and trading algorithms are all instruments that help agribusinesses predict the future with better than random success. The architectural analogs include building simulations (both physical and aesthetic), sensing devices to monitor environmental performance, and CAD/CAM technologies.

All these techniques rely on negative feedback loops. Their goal is to eliminate any noise that threatens the chances of a predetermined result from occurring. Once a pattern is established on one side of the temporal slash everything is done to prevent any new sounds from coming in and disturbing it. The future will be predictable and without any noise. All is silent.

Despite every effort, as investments of time and treasure, agriculture (and architecture) remain risky businesses. Whether one looks to the past or the future, noise is difficult to eliminate. The future is not so easy to control—though that hasn't prevented people from trying.

Many responses to the limitations of industrialized agriculture fall on either end of a predictable spectrum. One side looks back to slower and smaller ways of farming. The other side looks ahead to a food supply system ever more dependent on information management. Slow food, urban farming, CSAs, farm-to-table programs, etc. represent the former position. Genetically modified species, invasive insecticides and intelligent sensing devices illustrate the latter. A similar divide exists in architecture. Calls for the return of the master builder, of using only local materials and vernacular methods nostalgically look backwards. Attempts to seamlessly integrate design and construction via digital methods look forward to yet another utopian future.

The Suprarural project distinguishes itself by avoiding these two poles. Instead, it focuses on what exists in the here and now. It avoids reifying or ignoring the present. By closely studying and then recombining the internal logics of common elements and patterns found on the American prairie and the Argentine pampas, it learns from and expands their potential to generate a variety of alternative spatial and temporal patterns. It recognizes that one must first understand the existing patterns before recombining or replacing them with other ones.

The prairie and the pampas. Flat, wide and fertile. Organized and productive. It would be difficult to find zones that have been more thoroughly and rigidly subdivided. The precise patterns most often found in these places are clearly demarked by orthogonally arranged roads, the evenly spaced lines of cultivators and plows, the precisely engineered dimensions of livestock pens, the gigantic lateral and radial sprinkler systems, and the regularly spaces homesteads and fences.

It is the rigid nature of these elements that Suprarural surprisingly recognizes as productive. Instead of rejecting the standardized objects and apparatuses that dot and define these landscapes, they use them as the starting point for designing a variety of alternative conditions. The resultant images are messy yet logical, unpredictable yet patterned, irregular but efficient in their capacity to combine unlike but integral elements with one another.

Such research generates rather than validates data. In opposition to many agricultural (or architectural) endeavors, they do not simply criticize the past or try to predict a particular future. The intention is not to constrain future outcomes but to invent as many new ones as possible. It uses positive rather than negative feedback loops that integrate noisy with normative patterns. Doing this with greater than random success requires many types of intelligence. As the Suprarural project attests, architects are smart too.

(1) "The Many Adventures of Winnie the Pooh," Dir. Wolfgang Reitherman and John Lounsbery; Perf. Sebastian Cabot, Walt Disney Productions, 1977; It is based on the book: A.A. Milne, *Winnie-The-Pooh* (London: Methuen & Co., 1926).
(2) Bateson, Gregory, *Steps Towards an Ecology of Mind,* Ballantine Books, New York, 1972.
(3) Ibid.
(4) Pollan, Michael, *The Omnivore's Dilemma: The Search for a Perfect Meal in a Fast-Food World*, Bloomsbury, London, 2006.

Protocols and Ubiquity

Axel Cherniavsky

We don't perceive space in all its purity; the same thing occurs with time. As Saint Augustine pointed out, the question of space is no less perplexing than the question of time. Indeed, we don't perceive time as such, but the feeling that there is not enough of it when we're hurried, or that it drags when we're bored. In the same way, space is not the actual immediate information of consciousness. It is the *plane*, as when our feet don't pick up any variation; or what is *nearby* as opposed to *far away*, as when on the highway we see the fencing go by faster than the cows behind it, which, in turn, seem to pass faster than the trees in the far distance. In each case, it isn't space itself that we perceive, but rather the *dislocation or the superposition of fragments of space*. We could say that a horizontal plane is the overlapping of two spaces in a vertical sense, that the nearby is the dislocation of two locations in the horizontal sense, and that the far away is what corresponds to a larger dislocation in that same sense. In any event, far from presenting itself immediately to perception, space is constructed on the basis of at least two spaces, two portions of space, two places and their respective positions. We can imagine space in general as an elastic material capable of expanding and contracting, which gives rise to all the potential distances between the indivisible point and the infinity of the universe. Between these extremes, we situate north and south, east and west, the depths of the sea and the unreachable heavens, what is close by, what is remote, and vertigo.

Indeed, there is no reason to limit the conception of space to so-called exterior phenomena. Our spiritual life is also organized spatially. Does pride not imply believing oneself superior to others? "I will ascend to heaven; I will raise my throne above the stars of God," Satan says in Dante's *Purgatory* as he makes the proud carry huge stones on their backs, stones which bend them over as far as the ground. We feel crushed, uplifted, belittled or overestimated when we organize our lives according to longitude. We feel lost, found, distant or isolated when we organize our lives according to latitude. In both cases we think about our interior world, and even about its difference from the exterior in spatial terms, and we think about space based on the phenomena of dislocation or superposition.

It is not by chance, then, that Sigmund Freud represents the psychological apparatus in terms of two topologies. And that later Jacques Lacan turns to topology to account for the greatest and smallest dislocations in our emotional lives, from the slip that constitutes a lapsus, to the fracture that is psychosis: the true laying bare of our own tectonic plates. However, if pathology may be understood in terms of dislocation, it follows that we should be able to arrive at a definition of health based on its opposite. What does it mean, otherwise, to "find your place" or to "be on track"? And don't we say that appropriate conduct is "in its place"? No less than their opposites, these phenomena reveal the nature of space, only this time it isn't based on a difference between places, but on a coincidence or a superposition that we will characterize as *ubiquity*. No doubt we will need to distinguish this ubiquity from its etymological and theological meaning as the ability to be present everywhere. We will use ubiquity to mean *the superposition of two spaces*. It is parallel, if you will, to the relationship between *timing* and time. Why don't we simply talk about location? Because, to continue with the parallelism, location is to ubiquity what punctuality is to timing: a special case. Punctuality means arriving on time. Having timing means knowing how to mesh with the rhythm of a situation, no matter what hour of the day it may be. In the same way, location can be understood as position; it is nothing more than the position of a particular space with respect to another space. We also reserve another meaning for ubiquity: namely the superposition of two spaces. In that sense we say that health is always a question of ubiquity, of location if you prefer, but not of position.

Now, is ubiquity what we experience when we have the feeling that we've "found our place"? Is comfort what we actually experience as such? In reality, what we perceive is not just a situation in terms of a state, but a situation in terms of a process, a change: the shift from dislocation to location. Something similar occurs with comfort. We would not feel comfort if it were our eternal and natural state. We experience it occasionally when it comes in the wake of being uncomfortable: when we take a stone out of our shoe, when we adjust our clothes so that they fit just right. As such, we are led to conclude that what we experience is neither space in the abstract sense, nor exactly the dislocation or superposition of two spaces, but rather *the passage from dislocation to superposition or from a lesser dislocation to a greater one*. We would not have the experience of an exterior or an interior without comings and goings, highs and lows, ups and downs. In the same way, we don't experience normal vision until we've put our glasses on, or health until we are recovering from an illness. That is why René Leriche defines health as "life lived in the silence of the organs."

A sign of success on an ethical level, ubiquity also serves the same function on an aesthetic level. A certain musical note is not the right one just because it is played at the right moment, but also with regard to its position in relation to other notes. Its need is not given only by its horizontal position on the pentagram (which represents its place in time), but also by its vertical position (which represents its place with respect to other notes). And if some arts seem to depend more on the use of temporality—a narrative is well put together with regard to its rhythms—other arts, especially the plastic arts, seem to be based on the manipulation of ubiquity. Or have we not come to see proportion as an ideal of beauty? And do we not say that a city is well founded, or that a monument is well located, when *the space they are* enters into a certain relationship with the *space they occupy*?

At any rate, we should be careful of conceiving of ubiquity, understood as the abolition of dislocation, as a sign of success. Health is not the obsessive superposition of our regions, resulting in a numbness of our capacities, but lies instead in knowing how much we need to move and how to do it, how to bring things face to face, how to separate them or join them together. This is the reason for the importance of the adjective that qualifies protocols as *differential*. Protocols are unique in each case. They are unique in themselves—in each application, they are displaced with respect to themselves—and unique in relation to the space that they occupy, since two protocols cannot occupy the same space. As such, protocols are awarded a double ubiquity: extrinsic and intrinsic. Intrinsic ubiquity measures the degree or type of displacement of the application with respect to the rule, whereas extrinsic ubiquity reflects the position of the protocol with respect to the space that houses it (which, in turn, has its own intrinsic ubiquity). A water tank may be installed further to the left or to the right in a field; it is also more or less removed from the protocol as is dictated, abstractly, by the norm. But on the level of either intrinsic or extrinsic ubiquity, the ideal should not be conceived as a perfect superposition or coincidence. In that sense, all kinds of connections can be established between the two ubiquities: the terrain requires us to diverge more or less from the rule; the rule encourages us to seek out a particular terrain, and so forth. What is important is to understand that the protocol is not a set of transcendent rules that ultimately inform a material, like a series of molds. Protocols are immanent guidelines that function, if you will, like secret strings that allow for operating with the material in question; they are the bones and tendons of the earth. They simply tell us where to pull to obtain a certain effect; when to let go, where to cut. Like beauty and health, the essence of a protocol resides in its flexibility.

Enclosure and Return

Ramon Faura

Most dystopias paint a future where nature has disappeared. The environment has been transformed into something absolutely artificial. This rejection of the natural is not framed in terms of a prohibition but of a threat. Control over the inhabitants involves convincing them that contact with nature opens the door to the uncontrollable, and the State cannot protect them. Thus, technology creates an independent world that is superimposed over nature, excluding it. This creates a much more insurmountable boundary than the walls that used to encircle cities. It stands between urban space and the environment.

The extensive compilation of utopias and dystopias put together by Daniele Porretta demonstrates their influence on modern urban planning during the first half of the 20th century. (1) In the same period that Modernism began suffering its own particular collapse, science fiction dystopias intensified their vision of a future where anything unplanned had been abolished. George Lucas's first movie, *THX 1138* (1968), is a good example in that respect. The plot focuses on the story of a man named THX 1138, who escapes from the confines of an urbanized territory. Though his destination is unknown, his goal is to return to nature—beyond the city's control. There is no exterior in THX 1138's world. The disappearance of nature encompasses bodies and feelings, even. Everyone's head is shaved. The main character's problems begin when he and his roommate fall in love. The interference of a natural element (a feeling) threatens the productive order of their surroundings; it is then that the merciless law interferes in their "private" lives.

Nevertheless, the disappearance of natural elements is not always synonymous with an imperfect future. If we think back to other films from the same period, like Franklin J. Schaffner's *The Planet of the Apes* (1968), the omnipresence of nature (and talking apes) is the first sign of a catastrophe: the end of human civilization. The final scene—Charlton Heston despairing and enraged beneath the Statue of Liberty half buried in the sand—is part of the same imagery of terror that we see in George Lucas's film: the State against THX 1138; the threat of nature. The Statue of Liberty covered in sand also reminds us of Giovanni Battista Piranesi's ruins, where weeds split stones and crack moldings, and where nature reclaims what was once its domain. Unexpected natural events make time something that "flows on, never comes back." (2) Obviously, one of the fundamental differences between Man and other species lies in his relationship with nature, influenced by language. Man's opposition to nature is based not so much on his actions "against nature" as in the act of naming it. Even the most radical stances in favor of human extinction so as to liberate the planet, such as VHEMT, (3) are formulated using a language that inevitably operates through "denaturalization." However, exploiting the environment is not an exclusively human attribute. Beyond mineral extraction or agriculture, animals also base their existence on plundering the land—leopards eat antelopes, which in turn eat bushes and grass. The essential difference has to do with the technical capacity for affecting the environment; that is where language—as the mother of all technologies—creates an imbalance. Paradoxically, at the same time language makes human beings the only species concerned with preserving the environment (though that doesn't necessarily imply a *commitment* in that respect).

The natural/artificial antimony is timeless. Every period in history engages in its own particular debate, but in the early 1960s and the late 1970s this discussion took on a particular significance. The oil crisis, the threat of overpopulation (another recurring element in dystopias) and an awareness of the limited nature of natural resources, which was unprecedented up to that point, raised the ecological debate to a new level. From that time onwards environmental preservation has had more to do with a concern for humanity than a reductionist altruism focused on nature. Ecological consciousness, if it is to be effective, can no longer be envisioned in terms of compassion: how can you feel for a pea, for something that isn't a subject with the capacity for suffering? Ecological consciousness cannot be approached from the Romantic penchant for the picturesque. The Romantic sublimation of the landscape transforms nature into an allegory of the non-rational, the incomprehensible and, therefore, the non-exploitable. It becomes the image of a space that we are unable to access—an abyss that is far greater than us. Of course, environmental consciousness after the oil crisis could not succumb to Luddite alarmism in the face of the new—the return to nature incorporates technology. The fight is not against technology but for technology: to take control of technology in order to apply it in a different direction (another potential dystopia). Preserving nature first entails accepting its denaturalization. Since nature is only conservable via its transformation, preservation relies on intervention: rationalizing (and democratizing) the benefits we all obtain from nature. Obviously, in this instance we don't understand intervention in nature as covering the planet's surface with cement. Rational exploitation entails not asphyxiating the planet, but respecting its rhythms; not preventing nature from restoring what we have taken from it.

At the same time as George Lucas was warning us about the threat of a world without nature, in such other spheres as architecture, urban planning and art, proposals like Superstudio or Ant Farm were emerging. Their images problematized our relationship with nature, pointing to a new synthesis: only technological development can reintegrate the artificiality of our lives into the natural environment. It is no coincidence that the inhabitants of the technological images created by Superstudio wore long hippie hairstyles. In contrast to the shaved heads in *THX 1138*, the fascination with technology no longer excludes nature—the very opposite is true.

The issue of hairstyles is not merely anecdotal. The degree of artificiality in a given period is easily discernible when we observe how people wear their hair. The geometric gardens designed by André Le Nôtre and his celebration of geometry over nature coincided with a time when courtesans covered their hair with wigs, a far cry from the long locks of the early Baroque. Bodies were reduced to a secondary role, buried beneath the mask of prostheses. Wigs, makeup and, of course, ultra-ornate costumes that disfigured people's bodies made the passage of time imperceptible. Time may be an artifice, but its effects are more visible on natural elements. Romanticism, as well as the Art Nouveau generation much later, implied a return to beards, moustaches, long hair—an image that contrasts with positivism and hygienist principles (Auguste Comte wore short hair and not even a moustache). The avant-garde and its demand for abstraction led to a return to short hair (look at Le Corbusier's and Piet Mondrian's haircuts). At times when technological artificiality is idealized, shaven heads and clean-shaven faces become the norm once again. This was the case at the end of the 1970s, after the hippie years, when New Wave and post-punk turned the human figure into an artifice in neon colors (Johnny Rotten, Devo or *Blade Runner* imitators).

It is worth pointing out that beards now appear to be in fashion again, proliferating alongside smartphone technologies and tablets. However, no one can assure us that, as opposed to being consumers of technology in search of nature, it is not we who (along with nature) are being devoured by technology. The alarming number of criminal urban developments that the economic crisis has (fortunately) left in ruins constituted an exploitation of nature that included the territory and human beings.

The fiction of a "natural being"—the prevention of any action that could violate the natural order of things—always becomes more intense when a new technology comes onto the scene. Plato warned of the dangers of writing as a denaturalization of knowledge (memory), and the invention of the printing press was also accompanied by all kinds of precautions—tying down language in lead-cast molds implied a denaturalization of writing. It also shed light on a new world that was intervening between Man and nature: the printed text which, in contrast to calligraphy, created a conceptual geography that was founded on a multitude of exact replicas, which were not subject to the unpredictability of the human hand. Words and especially concepts that were fixed and infinitely reproduced became landmarks that were more stable than a mountain peak or a riverbed.

If 19th-century Luddism took shape against the new machines of the Industrial Revolution, today's Neo-Luddism has emerged as a reaction to the digital age. (4) In any event, beyond the potential truth of the arguments, the fear of straying from nature or transforming *what we were given* is a primordial fear formerly embodied in God: Prometheus stole fire; Adam ate the forbidden fruit of the tree of knowledge.

Like science fiction or wearing long hair, mythology is also a context in which our relationship to nature is brought into question. The story of Cain and Abel is a good example. Cain, who killed his brother, is a farmer who transformed the territory using technical means. Abel, the shepherd, the good brother who is not our predecessor, limits himself to directing his flock. It is true that, along with pottery making, raising livestock and farming are all part of the same revolution: the Neolithic. They represent an important step in the denaturalization of humanity. From that point on we are no longer dependent on hunting or fishing, or on proximity to a river when deciding where we want to live. However, in symbolic terms the connotations of farming are very different from the associations with raising livestock. On the one hand, the relationship between agriculture and the sedentary settlement is much more binding. Cultivating the land implies being anchored in one place, putting down roots near what you have planted, occupying the natural sphere and creating a place. On the other hand, whereas livestock breeding happens above ground, farmers dig into the heart of the earth. Both Abel and David, who killed Goliath with a shepherd's sling, are good because they do not interfere or alter the natural cycle of the territory to the same degree that Cain does. Farmers accept the meanness of those who dare to claw at Mother Earth and profit from that interference. Farming implies a technical knowledge that modifies nature; it implies taking possession, fencing in and transforming what we have been given.

It is interesting to observe how the moral relationship between Cain the farmer and Abel the shepherd is turned on its head by one of the great myths of the 20th century: the Western. It is no coincidence that the quintessential industrial art, cinema, detected Cain's inefficiency and Abel's productivity. There are also other factors converging here. The propagandist effectiveness of Westerns is channeled in the service of a culture founded on the figure of the pioneer. Cain, the hard worker, who is productive and takes possession of the ground, embodies the values of progress. In both *Shane* (George Stevens, 1953) and *Unforgiven* (Clint Eastwood, 1992)—to cite two excellent examples from different periods—Cain is transformed into an honest farmer. As a homesteader, his purpose is to put down roots in the New World, to fence in nature, to give it a name and make it into a place by working beneath the surface. His action is intended as a civilizing force. In contrast, Abel is transformed into a rough rancher—a rowdy cowboy who tries to intimidate the farmers so he can take their land. In *Shane* this conflict assumes an epic dimension. We experience events through the eye of a young boy, Joey Starrett; he is the son of a farmer who is being harassed by the ranchers in the area, the Rykers. The Ryker family is destroying the homesteaders' crops with their livestock until Shane, a drifter, decides to help the Starretts. Shane takes over the conflict with the ranchers and saves the homesteaders from harm. Years later, in *Unforgiven*, Abel the shepherd is also put into the role of an underhanded cowboy. The characters Dave Bunting and Quick Mike embody the tyranny of savagery; they disfigure a prostitute who then puts a price on their heads. The gunfighter who comes to the rescue is a farmer named Will Munny, who has been a bandit in the past. A real-life Cain, after killing his brothers, he had worked to cleanse himself of his sins by tilling the land.

Setting Cain and Abel aside, today we know that the savage colonization of the West wasn't driven by the pioneers but by machines like the locomotive, a very visible element in Western movies. Neil Smith has referred to the myth of the frontier and the figure of the pioneer as an ideological construct invented in the city. (5) In cities on the East Coast like New York the myth of the frontier (colonizing the wild, fighting against the Indians) constructed an exterior enemy for the rich and poor alike. The aim was to defuse the social struggles which stood as the last resistance against the ferocious capitalism of the 19th century. As in the George Lucas movie *THX 1138*, urban space segregates rural areas and creates boundaries; in the end, the myth of the frontier isn't just a capitalist strategy. The need for an exterior to escape to—from Paul Gauguin in Polynesia to the Beatles in Rishikish—has existed in every generation, but information has finally done away with any possibility of an exterior. In the end, the leading role in the true colonization of the wide open expanses of the Old West was played by language. Before the pioneers wiped out the natives and farmed the land, expanses of cables, hung from high poles, transformed the landscape. The telegraph brought the East and West Coasts together much faster than the railroads did. The flow of information put New York at ten minutes from Kansas City, Denver or San Francisco, and it brought the New World and the Old World together. The development of the telegraph in Europe was much less spectacular, since the distances it covered were smaller and more fragmented. In Europe the telegraph was not a colonizing force; it merely passed over the ruins. In 1858, three years before the beginning of the American Civil War, Queen Victoria shared a joke via telegraph with the President of the United States, James Buchanan, (6) crossing thousands of miles of underwater cable. Language, the mother of all technologies, occupies the rural sphere and encloses untouched territories; it crosses over them and alters their scale using electrical impulses and binary code. Samuel F. Morse's dashes and dots were only the beginning.

(1) Porretta, Daniele, *L'immagine della città del futuro nella letteratura distopica della prima metà del '900*. Doctoral dissertation defended at the Universitat Politècnica de Catalunya (UPC), July 2014. Unpublished.
(2) "Life, Thermodynamics, and Cybernetics" [1949], in Left, Harvey S. and Rex, Andrew F. (eds.), *Maxwell's Demon 2: Entropy, Classical and Quantum Information, Computing*, Institute of Physics, Bristol, 2003.
(3) Initials of the Voluntary Human Extinction Movement (www.vhemt.org).
(4) Jones, Steven, *Against Technology (from the Luddites to Neo-Luddism)*, Taylor & Francis, New York, 2006.
(5) Smith, Neil, *The New Urban Frontier: Gentrification and the Revanchist City*, Routledge, London/New York, 1996.
(6) Gleick, James, *The Information: A History, a Theory, a Flood*, Pantheon Books, New York, 2011.

Eight Concepts

Teresa Galí-Izard

1. Pragmatism
A fence that divides a field, a storage silo, a perpendicular intersection between two roads, a tractor or a windmill are basic elements, implements that give us clues to the actions that occur in a given territory. Their selection determines the essential aspects for the industrialization of the place, for the implementation of a new ecosystem. They are signs that help us understand in an environment we are not familiar with and signs for a different future: how it is activated, how it is transformed and how it is prepared. Their combination is just the opposite: a sophistication and a complex design that relates them to one another. "From the unit to the entity" is the expression of the meaning of architecture that, in a complex way, explores the multiple relationships that can be derived from the combination of independent pieces. It is an exploration founded on a rule-based system of unexpected relationships that lead to apparently impossible formalizations, which will be integrated and absorbed as normal in a not-so-distant future.

2. Abstraction
Abstraction almost as a sickness bent on reaching perfection. Simplification. The search for relationships, repetition and contrast. The absence of units. An exercise in the definition of form. The importance of formalization in attaining the desired information. Its consequences for the imagery of a new ecology. The opposite path is not so evident: when abstraction is no longer abstract and biophysical materiality appears, alive and changing; when a system conceived as perfect comes to life in a pre-existing culture at a moment of economic instability, with a need for production, the limitations of place, the dynamics of the market, traditions. What is the result of the confrontation of the system with the passage of time, its interaction with living elements and with decadence?

3. Infrastructure as place
Its scarcity. The absolute transformation of the environment generated by the infrastructure that is embraced by another ecosystem. The negation of geology resulting from this new entity. The establishment of new opportunities that break with the past forever. The intuition that the infrastructure is the place that irreversibly defines and determines the system. The different degrees of

transformation and the visualization of the new process that is being activated. The discovery of the place's potential through testing the limits of the infrastructure, of the new machinery that will make it work. Gathering energy using simple mechanisms. Maximums, minimums. Measuring.

4. Time

The time it takes to fill a silo, the time left before field capacity is reached. The time for watering, for evapotranspiration, absorption, the brief intervention in maintenance. The fauna and the flora that connect us to far-off and short-lived natural systems, which act in spite of us. The geological time that makes us responsible for irreversible processes, the formation of the ground and its movement as a result of meteorological phenomena: wind on the great plains, gravity in the mountains. Rotations. Distributing crops across time and the alternatives: distributing crops across space. The annual and biannual crop cycles. The generation of plant structures, which transform into seeds that the wind scatters, or waste matter that accumulates, decomposes and mineralizes at imperceptible speeds. Fire that devours material and transforms its properties in an instant.

5. Invisibility, imperfection

A gaze that has to be trained to see what has not been drawn. What is the medium that allows for architecture, and how does the medium inform its configuration? Imperfection, the meeting place for irregularity, for error, or for everything else that has no place, despite its existence. That which does not follow the rules. The unknown. The directions of crops versus the patterns of crop management, which never coincide. The direction of the harvest in relation to the direction of how the crops were sowed. The moment of turning the harvester back along a parallel path, which is when the driver can take a pause. The only personalized path on the field that gains strength year after year, until it becomes a motive of interest, a place in and of itself. The discovery of the system's language. What its limits are, where it changes and where the outlines blur. The wind affects the water from the sprinkler and creates a wavy topography of corn, because evapotranspiration and the imperfect water distribution don't allow for adhering to the provisions of homogeneity in the distribution. The new system as a process that is inevitably shared with unpredictable natural processes.

6. System metabolism

Its physiology. We can intuit the artificial relationships among designed elements that are derived from a position, from measurements. The maintenance of fences, access points, the circulation of water. The trails of other animals across this network: snails, rabbits, lizards, etc. And a physiology of survival too, of simple microbiological systems that occupy this nondescript homogeneity. The exposure and the changing conditions for the micro-organisms in the earth, the disappearance of sensitive organisms and the disproportionate proliferation of the most resistant ones. Survival in these extreme conditions.

7. Dimensions
The endpoint of the process that begins with geology and weather. Vegetation as a biological indicator of the combination of both factors, and production as an expression of optimal growth based on the selection of species, genetics, infrastructures to support the process, and the management and overseeing of the cultivation. All factors participate throughout the production process, resulting in the final dimension of the storage warehouse, the silos, the size of the plots of land. The dimensions of the fenced lots can be determined, based on the length of the fencing, which determines the pressure and the rotations of livestock. It would be possible to follow this path in the other direction, beginning with dimensions and arriving at different combinations of geology, weather and surface area. An exercise in combining parameters for each crop would undoubtedly lead us to all of the climates and geologies on the planet, simply by modifying the extension of the production. The units of measurement.

8. Drawing
Drawing allows for envisioning the organization of our thoughts, our priorities. The systematization in drawing lets us discover relationships between elements that we could never describe through language. The exercise of drawing associated with systematization intended to order and classify, but also to discover. The windmill, the enclosure or the legs of the grain silos drawn using the same language; the same dimensions, forms and materials make them combinable. Drawing is a powerful tool for the discovery of possible relationships, which only occurs by putting it into practice. A calm and systematic drawing leads to reflection; a drawing with no other goal than discovery helps us avoid hurrying. Our ego can rest, and the subconscious begins to speak in a translation of knowledge that we don't quite understand ourselves. Drawing other logics using the same language is left for another day. The ground (not just physical ground) that conceals life and micro-organisms. The agents of weather: wind, temperature, dust and rain, act powerfully on the system, effecting changes. How the outline of a powerful pattern is blurred and how the next step is drawn; decadence, decomposition.

Weeds

Lluís Viu Rebés

In the last few years there has been an evident increase in architecture that is endowed with "environmental sensitivity." This has occurred at the same time as the discipline submitted to a process of reformulation on another front, as technique was entirely absorbed by digitalization: architects today do not draw, they program. Contemporary form and space are generated using numerical values, parameters that feed into and structure the algorithms used as the foundation for their designs.

Concept and technique, "environmental sensitivity" and "object-oriented programming" seem to be the new paradigms for architecture at the beginning of the third millennium. We might draw sustenance from the fact that we are participating in the articulation of a new aesthetics of the digital, if only we could willfully forget that we will soon be living in a world plagued by overpopulation, the exhaustion of most of our natural resources, and an adverse and dangerous disruption of climate patterns. In such a world the UN predicts that there will be large-scale climate-induced migrations of the population by 2050, which will lead to geopolitical tensions. By that time Arctic summers will be entirely ice-free, and climate change will have resulted in massive losses of food crops.

By then our only option may be to hope once again that technological development will be able to guarantee our future. We will depend on the industrial capacity of a techno-agriculture based on desertifying monoculture crops that have been dosed with toxins; and we will depend on a biotechnology capable of designing programmed hybridizations to detach living things, whether grown or raised, from their natural genetic tendencies. It is precisely at this moment, when irreversible intersections between the natural and the artificial are taking place, that nature is in need of just the opposite. Using its own language—plagues and extreme climate conditions—it evinces its delicate situation and its state of stress.

We can imagine an exhausted and medicated planet where only weeds—a spontaneous, unregulated plant life which continuously negates human control over a systematized nature—will continue to slowly reduce all built material to rubble. A planet where weeds are the last expression of the free will of nature.

In this global emergency situation the efforts of architectural practice are centered on the urban milieu and on how to reduce the CO_2 emissions of the city and the individual energy demands of its buildings. Even the most skeptical of architects recognize buildings as artifacts that fundamentally act as environmental regulators. It even seems that the discipline might recover the standing it has lost due to the anesthetized predominance of a hollow architecture of profit during the last quarter of a century. Ironically, it is the facet to which little attention has been paid by architects—the air we breathe, which fills a space that has hitherto been thought of as being empty—is taking center stage and demanding a leading role. Laden with a hefty dose of moralism, thermo-architecture has been born and only time will tell if it is doomed from the start.

Soon, the two extremes of the Earth's three main habitats will be regulated. On the one hand, we will find natural habitats confined to biosphere reserves scattered across the planet and protected (what arrogance!) by the laws of human beings. On the other, the ever-growing urban habitat, absorbed by its own constant reconstruction, in which most architects, armed with the new moral sensibility that has brought meaning back to the discipline, are unleashing their entire technical-conceptual arsenal to repair what they themselves have destroyed. And in the middle, like the air between the walls, lies the rural habitat: a space in which it is difficult to distinguish between natural and non-natural elements. A residual territory between urban areas and nature, where nature alone appears to dwell, albeit without escaping the cultural cloak of the city, which systematizes and cultivates it. This is where the raw materials needed to feed the urban population are produced. This territory not only feeds them; it also serves as their preferred setting for leisure activities. This intermediate space, the rural sphere, is the only continuous space at the global scale, in which pristine natural spaces and impure urban spaces appear as disconnected islands.

Almost subliminally, since those who dote on it do not live there, the rural habitat has been subjected to the most radical changes, in addition to demonstrating the utmost complexity and richness in its progression from natural to artificial. To give an example: in the Pyrenees traditional farmland is being abandoned and reabsorbed by homogenizing woodland, whereas in other areas old-growth forests are being cut down to make way for toxic techno-agriculture. The cynicism operating in the rural sphere is a particular variation of the new environmental moralizing born in the city. Initially, aggressiveness is tolerated; then, once the resources have been used up and the original inhabitants have been contaminated, mistreated and dispossessed, a solution is attempted or the land is simply abandoned and left to the weeds.

Cities on the Prairie?

Julián Varas

This book proposes a specific move forward in our conception of the relationship between the city, the countryside and the suburbs. Urban planning theory has warned us about the environmental and social unviability of the suburbs, but in doing so, instead of expanding on our categories and narratives about urban space, it has surreptitiously reintroduced a dichotomy, which seemed far behind us, between the country and the city. The city returns as the typical place for production and cultural consumption, and the countryside takes on a technical dimension and an association with material production. The Suprarural project gives an intelligent spin to this framework, reclaiming the discursive space that has been left behind (by architecture) in the countryside as an available space for operation and research. At the same time, it provokes a crisis in the anthropocentric conception of urban space, suggesting that form precedes content. If, as research shows, agriculture, ranching and other activities that take place in the rural sphere are disciplined to increase their productivity in the service of human production, there is no reason why we cannot imagine that this research has brought forth the concepts, the tools and the images necessary to move that relationship toward becoming more ambiguous, less unidirectional. The initial merit consists in having opened a crack in the conceptual framework of our discipline, outlining a promise for expanding and renewing its horizons.

Although the strategic cultural action of the Suprarural project focused on the present, its mechanism is heir to different movements and traditions which overlap, lending it a formal richness that is expressed through its multiple layers, facets and reliefs. Suprarural's operations do not just play out on the conceptual plane; they also imply the exploration of a style. Whereas both the fields of information—and the protocols through which formal production is controlled—are physically and thematically local, it is evident that the project is intended to be constituted as a contribution that goes beyond the semantic and pragmatic levels of architecture. It does not only deal with the structure of meaning we touched on earlier, nor is it content to hint at radical material transformations in the farming and ranching territories of the American Midwest and the Argentinean Pampa. It incorporates a problem that is based on a logical, expressive and organizational order, which would have been described some decades ago as *syntactical*, but which it now makes sense to call *stylistic.* (1) Suprarural builds up its stylistic design arsenal in a space that stretches between two theories which have been brought into play, and not by chance. At one end, the city is present figuratively as the disciplinary regimen that scores the territory, subdividing it according to economic (efficientist) and institutional (legibility) criteria. At the other end we have the countryside—not in a functional, social or environmental sense, but rather as the possibility of a smooth space where difference can be represented as a system of vectors that are sensitive to local conditions and relationships. The formal systems presented in this book simultaneously consider both contingent and universal conditions. Their formal relationships are measured computationally (composition has been eliminated or is carefully hidden) and, as a result, the hierarchies are hazy or difficult to discern. They exist, but instead of being organized in a pyramid, they are organized in feedback circuits. However, the results of these actions do not lead to the same results that the concept of "countryside" incited in architecture in the wake of its appearance in the 1990s. There is a multiplication of symmetries, formal regularities and ideal figures, revealing a desire to work with geometric orders that are external to the site in a way that would have seemed anachronistic a decade earlier. Without giving up on a materialist conception of architecture or the actual continuity of the material environment, *Suprarural* discretely criticizes the exhaustion of a research program based on the exploration of the continuity and spatial fluidity which, focused on the surface as an articulating element, constituted the principal trope of globalized space as it emerged after 1989. Its style recovers the aesthetic and operational value of certain typological solutions with a reduced formal definition, whose brusqueness is complemented by the use of techniques based on the mediated overlapping of multiple layers of information. It is worth highlighting the fact that typological tools work within the operative spectrum of the style, and not outside of it. Typology is imprinted as a generic form with more complexity than what, until recently, could have been offered by a primitive geometric function.

In short, the Suprarural style implies a turn that filters complexity or localizes it within predominantly regular systems. The consequence of, or the instrument for, this combination of a conceptual operation with the development of a new style for the prairie—whether it is conscious or not—is a series of proto-cities which, as we suggested at the beginning, take on a mysteriously inhuman appearance. By combining forms and uses belonging to systems that architecture has always understood to be incompatible, these proto-cities take on a status of uncertainty and improbability which makes them intensely desirable. What time do they belong to, these buildings crossed with watering systems, highways, sheds, silos, forests, hills, windbreaks, slaughterhouses, prairies, etcetera?

(1) This distinction looks to avoid a return to the structuralist linguistic paradigm as a theoretical framework for architecture, and with it a definitive release from the moral precepts installed by a certain branch of modern architecture which, in rejecting eclecticism and historicism, threw out the baby with the bathwater. See the argument put forward by Patrik Schumacher in *The Autopoiesis of Architecture* (vol. I), Wiley, Chichester, 2011, pp. 241-300.

ATLAS OF RURAL PROTOCOLS

This Atlas is organized according to a series of rural systems, distinguishable from each other by their overall functionality, their material evenness, their technological specificity, and their formal and spatial congruence: transport infrastructure, land subdivision, agricultural production, water management, irrigation and fumigation, inhabitation, cattle management, socialization, storage. Each of these systems, often codependent and spatially coincident, have been segregated for the purpose of understanding internal logics and mutual interactions, which this Atlas regards as consistent protocols of systemic relationships and claims as organizational techniques. However consistent, these techniques are not considered as fixed and isolated constituents of a rigid apparatus. Rather, their consistency is constituted by their systematic variability, their adaptability to contingency, and their responsiveness to stimuli.

The techniques of this Atlas have been thus described through the recognition and definition of a series of subsystems at work within rural systems, formulated through parts and components, attributes or variables, ranges of variation and thresholds, internal relationships and modes of interaction, collective performances and, finally, complex behaviors and dynamics. The segregation of information through abstract characteristics is assumed to be multiple but is reduced to discrete sets for the making of definitions of protocols that ground processes of abstraction on restrictions coming from material regimes, technological capabilities, normative limits and freedoms, and a manifold of determinations that are embedded in a number of traditions, rituals, routines, empirical knowledge, and other forms of rural expertise. The Atlas is, in this sense, a manual of disaggregated techniques of territorial determination.

The process of discretizing such behavioral complexity in specific and tangible protocols suggests neither cohesiveness nor exhaustiveness as such, but rather attempts to build up forms of consistency and intensiveness that enable their operative appropriation by a project of the territory, which can be developed as if it were a conventional form of architecture. The sources of information are often diverse and to a certain extent contradictory, as they bring together disparate realms and mediums, ranging from regular documentation and technical specifications to empiric forms of observation, comments, quotes and reviews, into single definitions of protocols. The drive of the Atlas is, therefore, not to portray an objective taxonomy but to provide the devices for an open-ended script of suprarural visions, yet to come. These visions, presented in the next chapter, obviously remain nascent.

After a brief introduction to each rural system, six registers are claimed for as the structure through which their determinations are incorporated in the Atlas: models, operations, systems, dynamics, performances, and effects. These registers make explicit the various aspects through which protocols are able to become common and eventually familiar architectural instruments.

_ Models: lists sets of relationships that are embedded in the systems and their general form.
_ Operations: lists the instructions and actions that regulate the behavior of the system.
_ Systems: lists the subsystems and components that structure the models.
_ Dynamics: lists the behaviors of the model, normally involving feedback loops.
_ Performances: lists the actual uses of the systems.
_ Effects: lists latent architectural organizations generated by the systems and their properties.

It must be noted that the definitions of protocols provided are simultaneously open sources for design and open-ended systemic constructions. The graphic documentation registers trends, habits, norms and conventions in a conscious process of denaturalization and demystification of the rural. And more broadly, it prepares this newly secularized form of information to be re-articulated by expanding, intensifying, diverting or saturating its inherent architectural qualities. Protocols are preliminary machines that open up systems to new spectrums of performance. They do not operate metaphorically but literally. Reassembled for the creation of unfamiliar effects, they take rural systems into an in-between condition, which enables the architect to play seriously, rather than merely idealize. Here, discretization does not merely reduce systems to prefigured linguistic components or closed grammatical rules, as much as it builds up an open source to be endlessly redefined and recomposed.

TRANSPORT INFRASTRUCTURE

AMERICAN MIDWEST / ARGENTINE PAMPAS

Linear organizations that enable various forms of circulation and access from point to point through or bypassing property subdivision, helping configure social, economic and cultural collectives through connectivity, and guaranteeing the fluent distribution of goods and people across the territory.

Model / Networks, grids, branchings, loops, systems of territorial activation and hierarchy, characterized by coexisting levels of regional to continental connectivity and various forms of continental to regional to local accessibility, introducing local disconnectedness between discrete patches of land.

Operations / Looping, turning, knotting, bifurcating, trifurcating, same-level crossing, multi-level crossing, roundabout crossing, cloverleaf interchanging, windmill interchanging, bundling, curving, sloping, dead-ending, U-turning, detouring, stacking, ninety-degree parking, forty-five-degree parking.

Systems / Highways, parkways, primary roads, secondary roads, rubble roads, streets, lanes, paths, tracks, walks, rights of way, traces, bridges, ramps, sidewalks, banks, terraces, mounds, retaining walls, ramparts, guardrails, handrails, parking lots, train stations, bus terminals, traffic signals, control devices.

Dynamics / Several processes of territorial, regional and urban planning, changes of normative and of conventions, material renewal, stabilization, and maintenance, weathering, informal connections, internal access routes, routines of rural machinery, vehicles and pedestrians, animal movement, strolls.

Performances / Increase or reduction of territorial connectivity, variegation of exchanges and intensification of flows, enabling and disabling accessibility, establishing and resetting frontage conditions, consolidating or eradicating hierarchies, and integrating or segregating speeds and reach.

Effects / Multi-scalar networks, parallel linear striations, turning-radius-controlled curves, detours and linear bifurcations, convolutions, twists, layering, stacking, bridging, artificial mounds, slopes, and valleys, left-over lands, chopped properties, broken continuities, territorial barriers, dried-out lands.

Region: American Midwest
System: Transport Infrastructure
Diagram: Variation of lanes
Type: Informal road
Drawing: Plan
Author: Travis Kalina

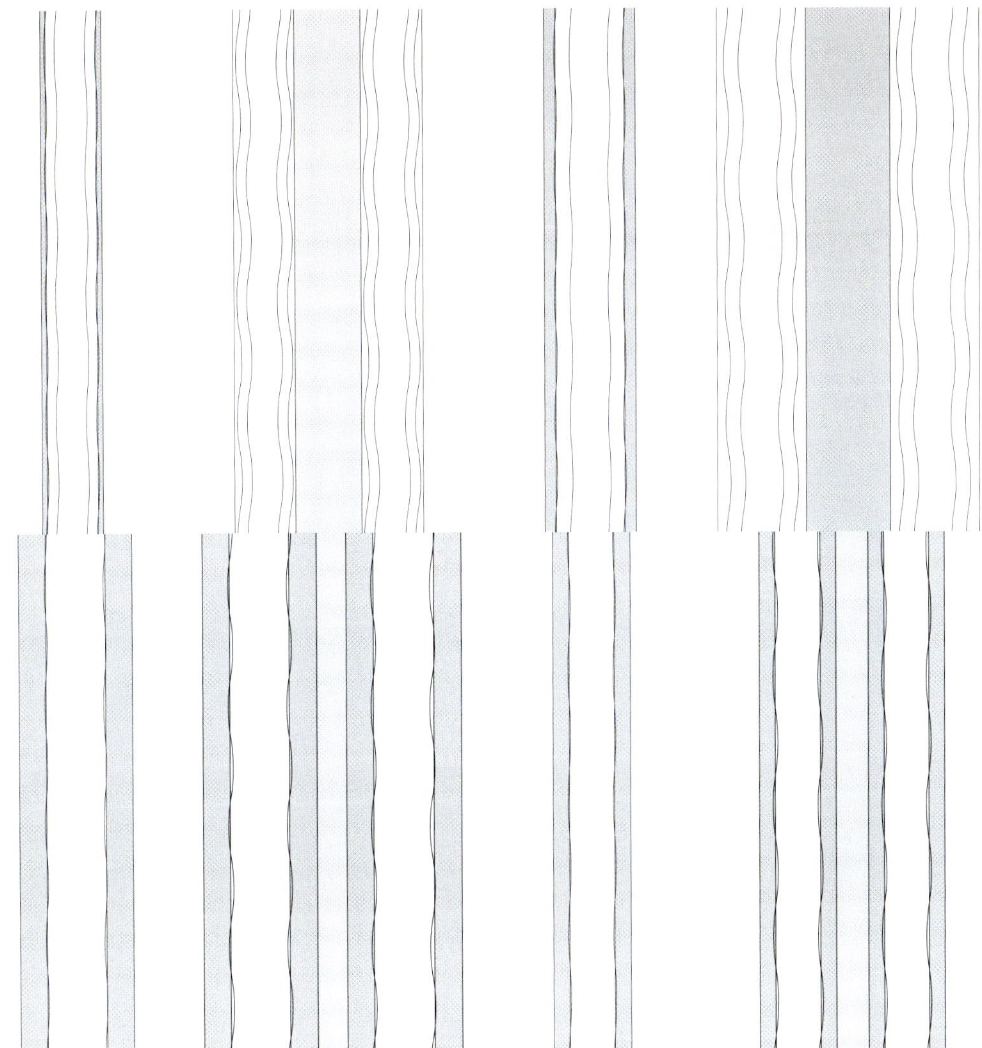

Region: American Midwest
System: Transport Infrastructure
Diagram: Variation of shoulders
Type: Informal road
Drawing: Plan
Author: Travis Kalina

Region: American Midwest
System: Transport Infrastructure
Diagram: Variation of lanes
Type: Rural road
Drawing: Plan
Author: Travis Kalina

Region: American Midwest
System: Transport Infrastructure
Diagram: Variation of shoulders
Type: Rural road
Drawing: Plan
Author: Travis Kalina

Region: American Midwest
System: Transport Infrastructure
Diagram: Variation of lanes
Type: Highway
Drawing: Plan
Author: Travis Kalina

Region: American Midwest
System: Transport Infrastructure
Diagram: Variation of shoulders
Type: Highway
Drawing: Plan
Author: Travis Kalina

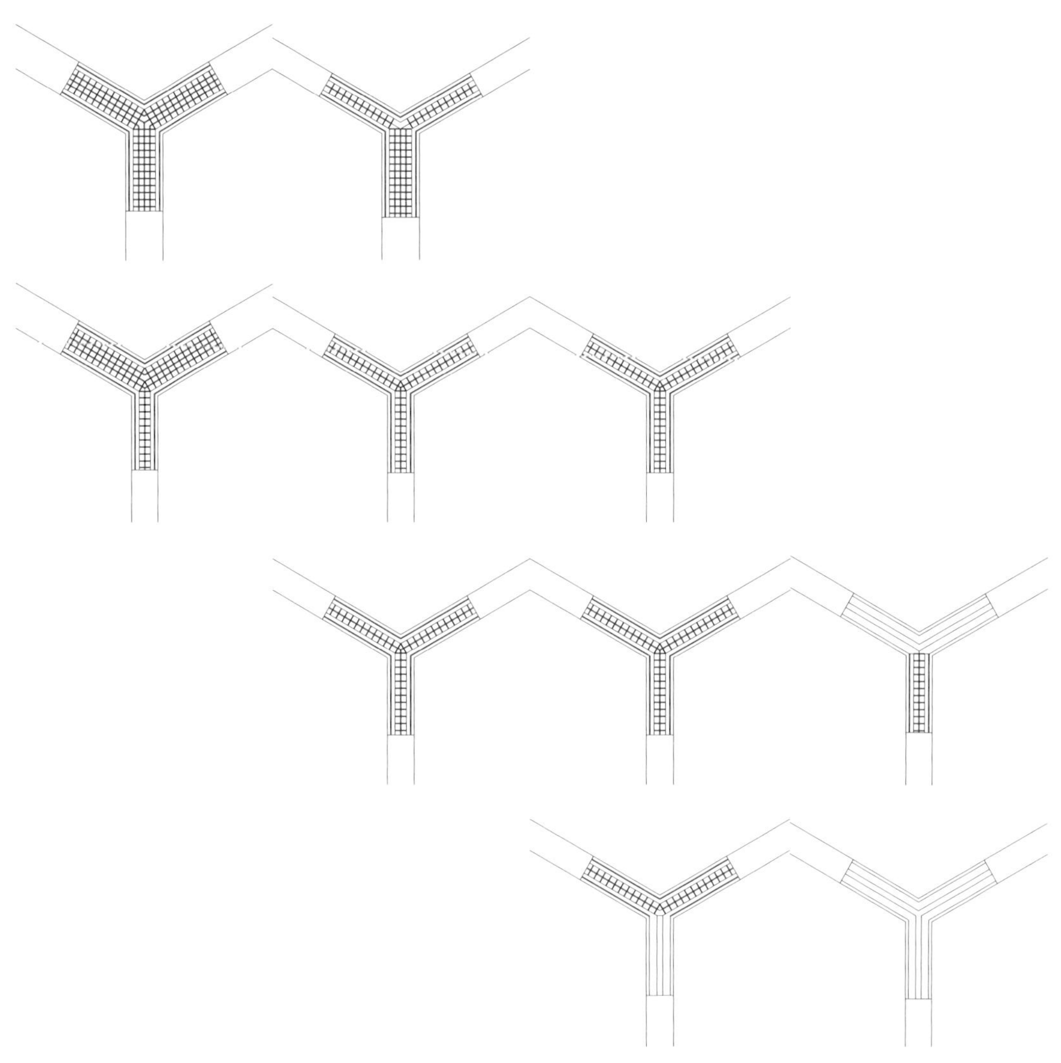

Region: Argentine Pampas
System: Transport Infrastructure
Diagram: Y intersection
Type: Highway, national road, provincial road, path
Drawing: Plan
Author: Josefina Nano

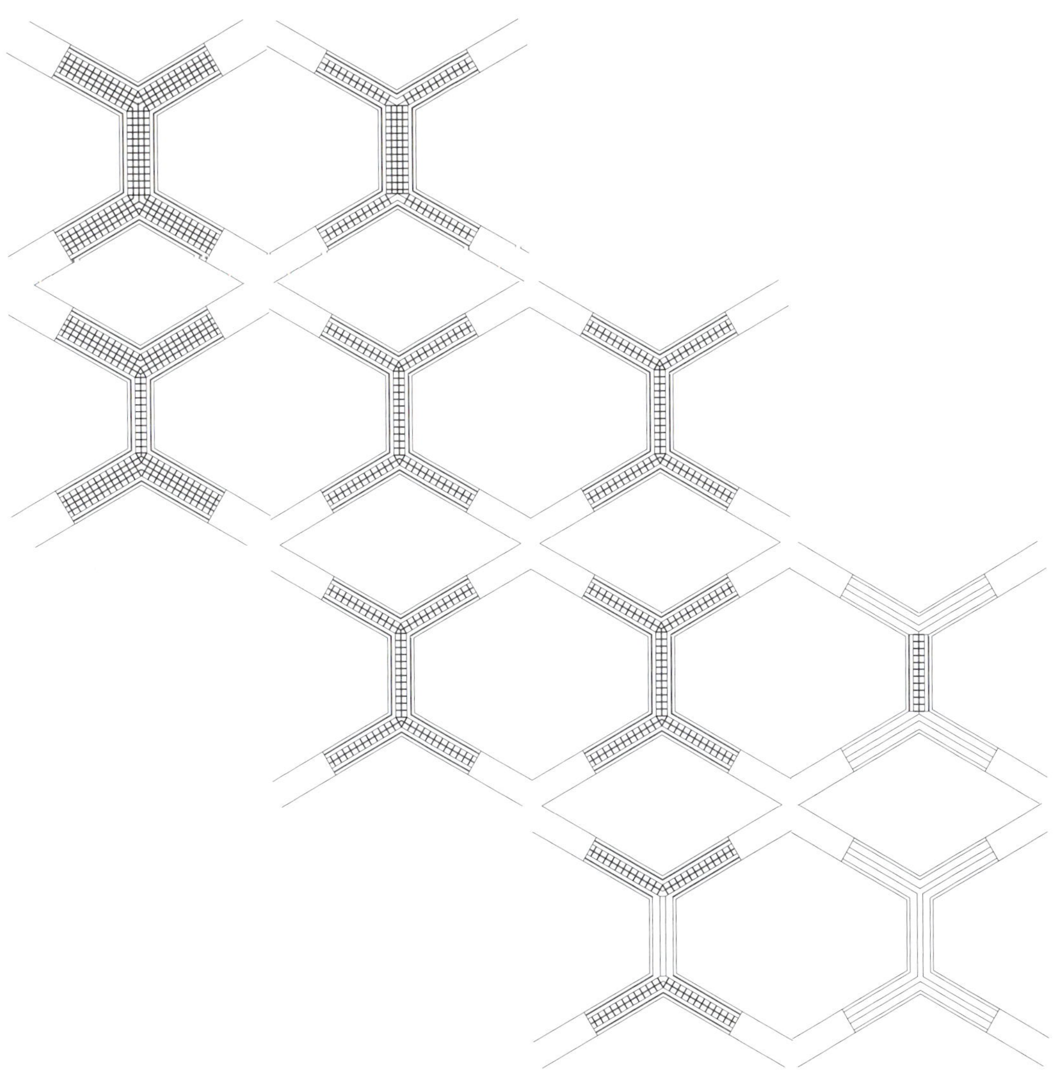

Region: Argentine Pampas
System: Transport Infrastructure
Diagram: X intersection
Type: Highway, national road, provincial road, path
Drawing: Plan
Author: Josefina Nano

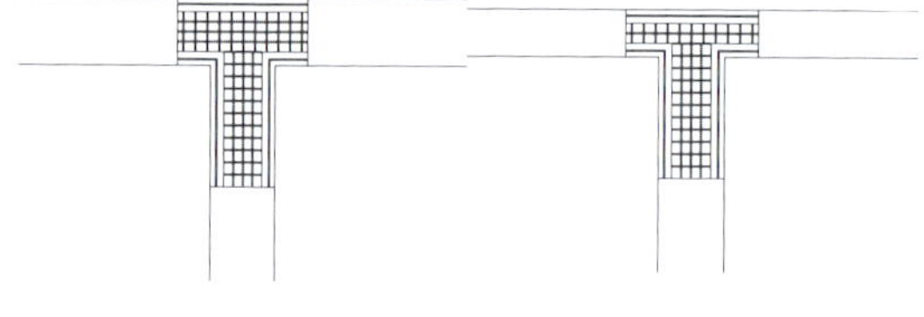

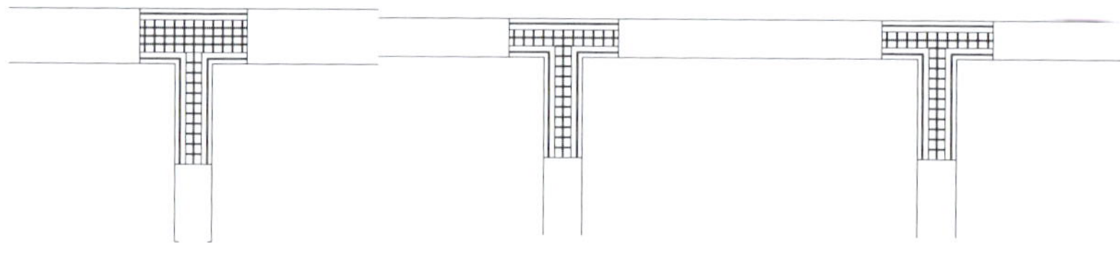

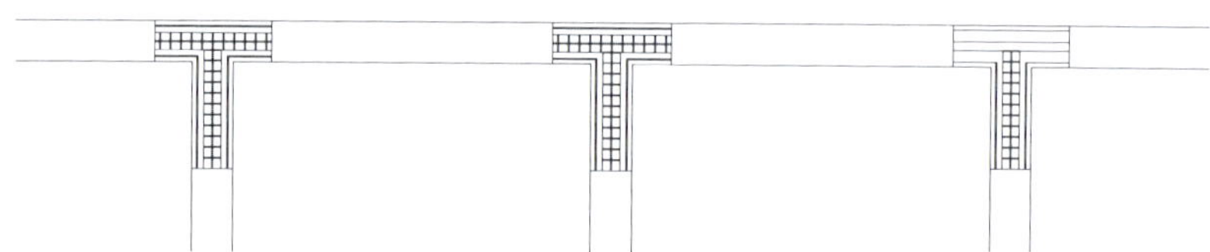

Region: Argentine Pampas
System: Transport Infrastructure
Diagram: T intersection
Type: Highway, national road, provincial road, path
Drawing: Plan
Author: Josefina Nano

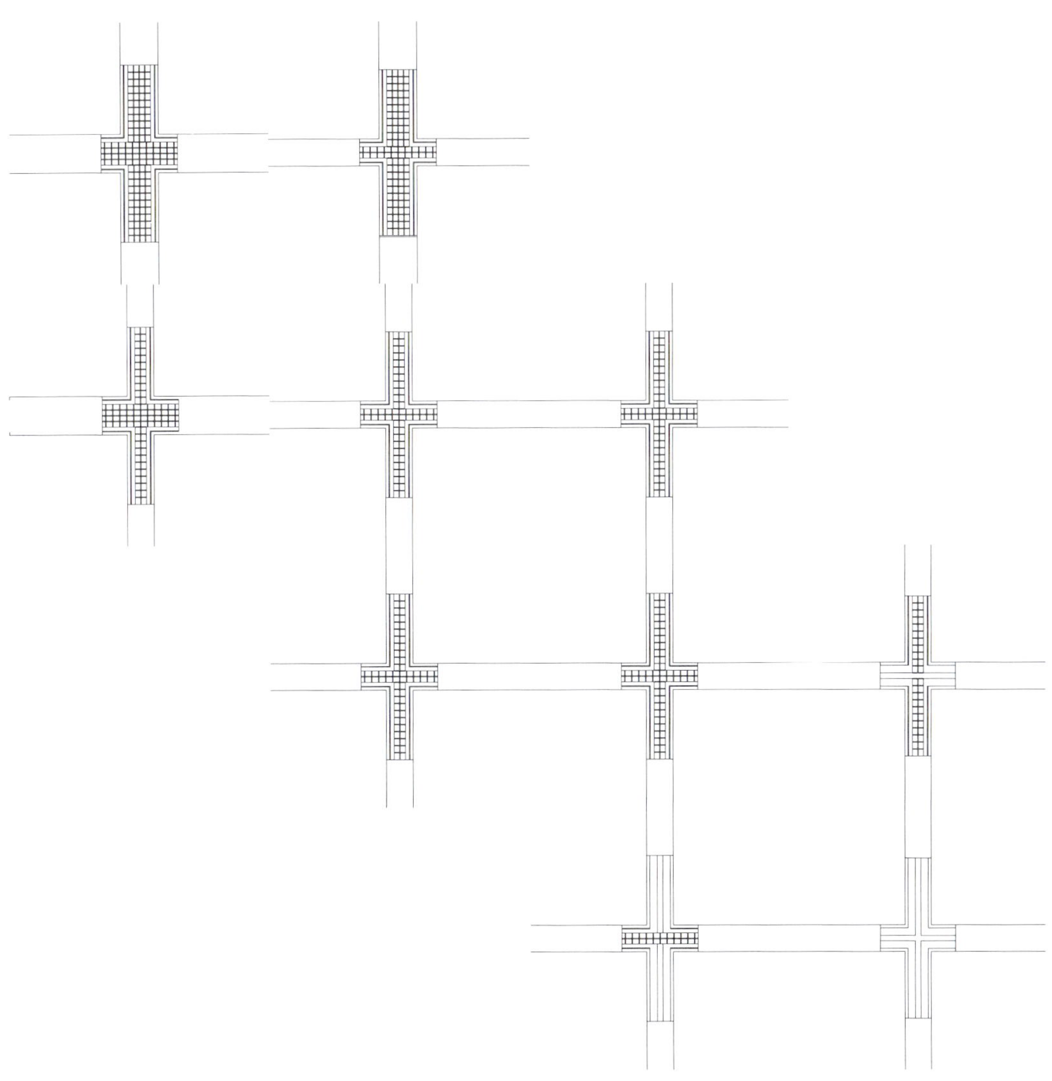

Region: Argentine Pampas
System: Transport Infrastructure
Diagram: Cross intersection
Type: Highway, national road, provincial road, path
Drawing: Plan
Author: Josefina Nano

Region: Argentine Pampas
System: Transport Infrastructure
Diagram: Star intersection
Type: Highway, national road, provincial road, path
Drawing: Plan
Author: Josefina Nano

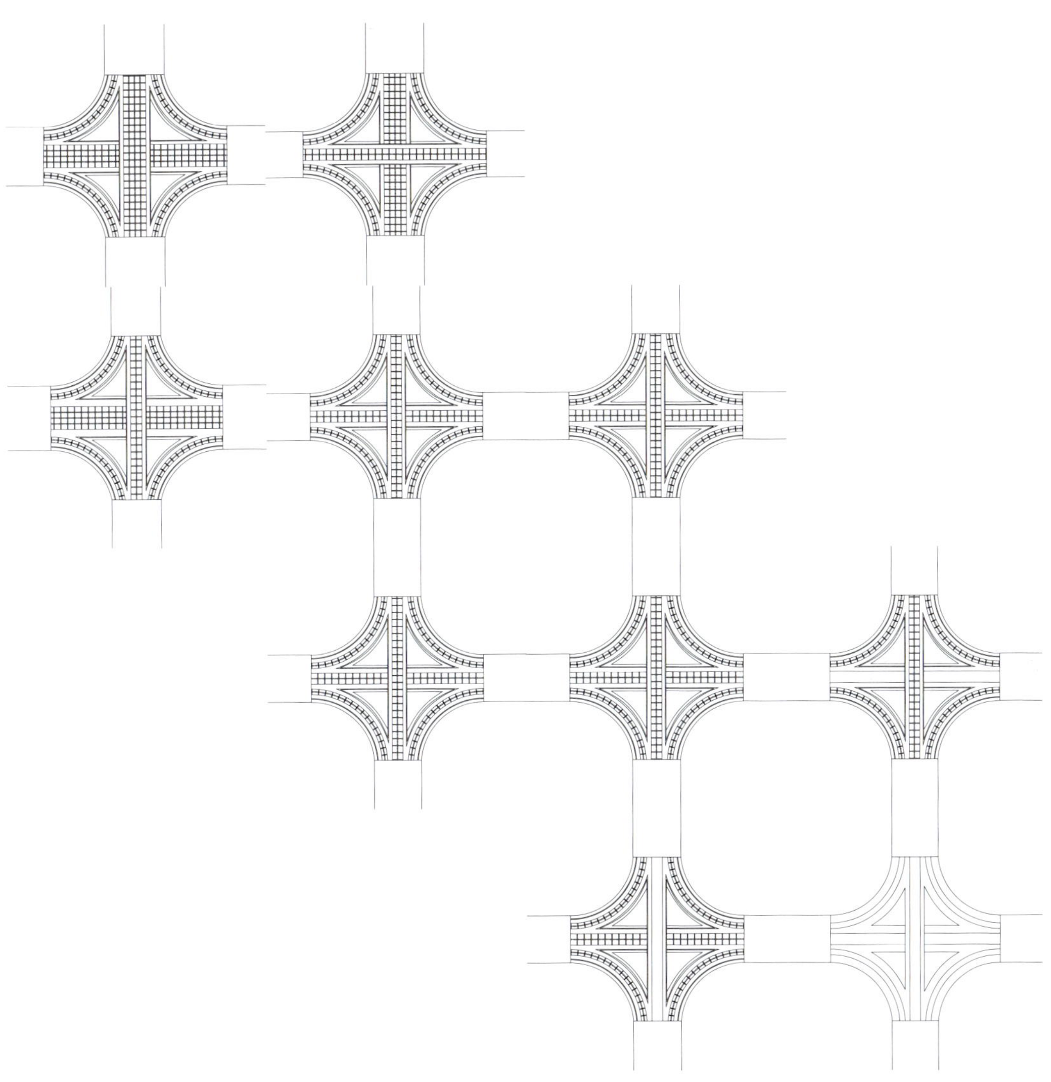

Region: Argentine Pampas
System: Transport Infrastructure
Diagram: Multilevel crossing
Type: Highway, national road, provincial road, path
Drawing: Plan
Author: Josefina Nano

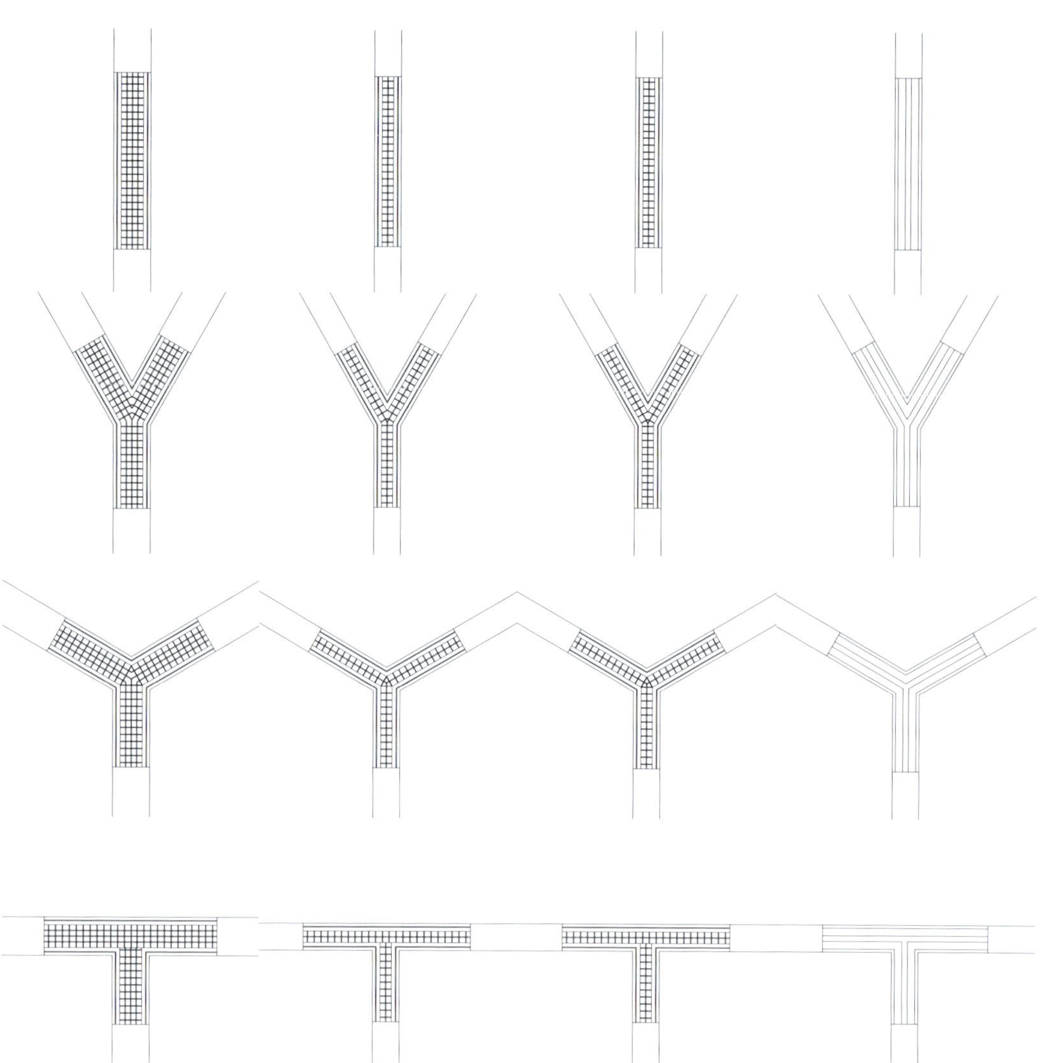

Region: Argentine Pampas
System: Transport Infrastructure
Diagram: Y and T intersections with angle variations
Type: Highway, national road, provincial road, path
Drawing: Plan
Author: Josefina Nano

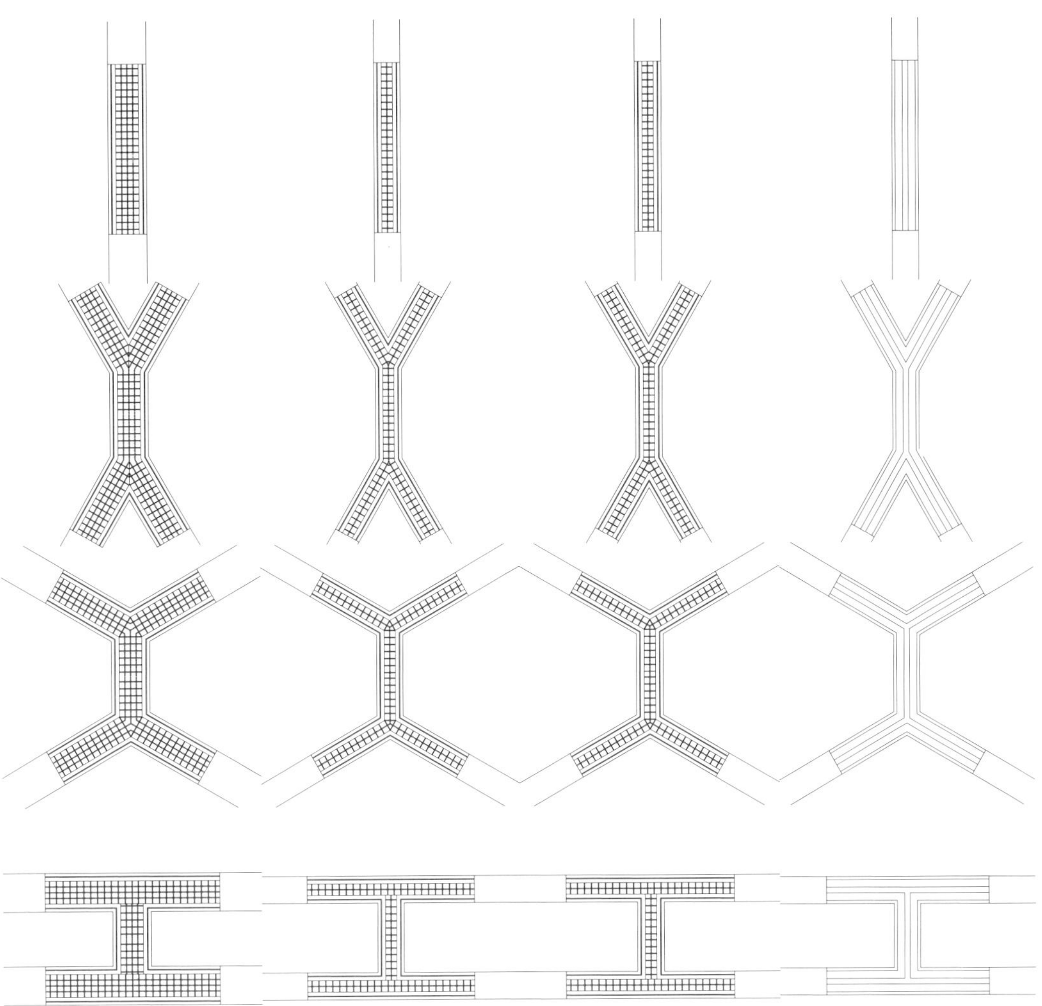

Region: Argentine Pampas
System: Transport Infrastructure
Diagram: Cross and X intersections with angle variations
Type: Highway, national road, provincial road, path
Drawing: Plan
Author: Josefina Nano

LAND SUBDIVISION

AMERICAN MIDWEST / ARGENTINE PAMPAS

Linear organizations that enable various forms of demarcation and subdivision of the land by means of lots, tracts, parcels, patches, regulating the segregation of ownership and the specialization, distribution, coordination and diversification of productivity across or despite the logics of property.

Model / Fixed and mobile orthogonal grids, polar and irregular network grids, and branching systems of territorial division, differentiation and hierarchy, characterized as much by their high inertia as an organizational matrix as by a relatively short time span before getting reconfigured as a pattern.

Operations / Fencing, gating, cornering, bracing, aligning, orthogonal branching, radial branching, non-regular branching, cordon wiring, guide wiring, electric wiring, barbed wiring, chicken wiring, razor wiring, alternating, chain-link fencing, anchoring, wire wrapping, springing, buckling, tightening.

Systems / Vinyl rails, wood rails, worm wood rails, wire rails, barbed rails, woven rails, high tensile electric rails, wood posts, steel posts, fiberglass posts, pikes, gates, cattle gates, fences, sticks, hinges, locks, chains, turnstiles, turnbuckles, reins, tubes on earth, slabs, anchors.

Dynamics / Several processes of territorial, regional and urban planning, production planning, delimitation of production areas, segregation of production processes, crop protection, crop rotation, paddock and corral design, drainage control, circulation of people, vehicles, machinery, animals,

Performances / Increase or reduction of property differentiation, functional specialization in the arrangement of phases of production, material resolution, optimization of productivity, reduction of redundancy, consolidation of organizational hierarchies, human orientation, segregation of domains.

Effects / Multi-scalar grids, multi-scalar networks, patched patterns, pixelated patterns, local matrices, self-similar subdivision patterns, sharp edges, interrupted lands, infrastructural disruptions, territorial scale pockets and dead ends, diagonal trajectories between gates, infrastructural straightening.

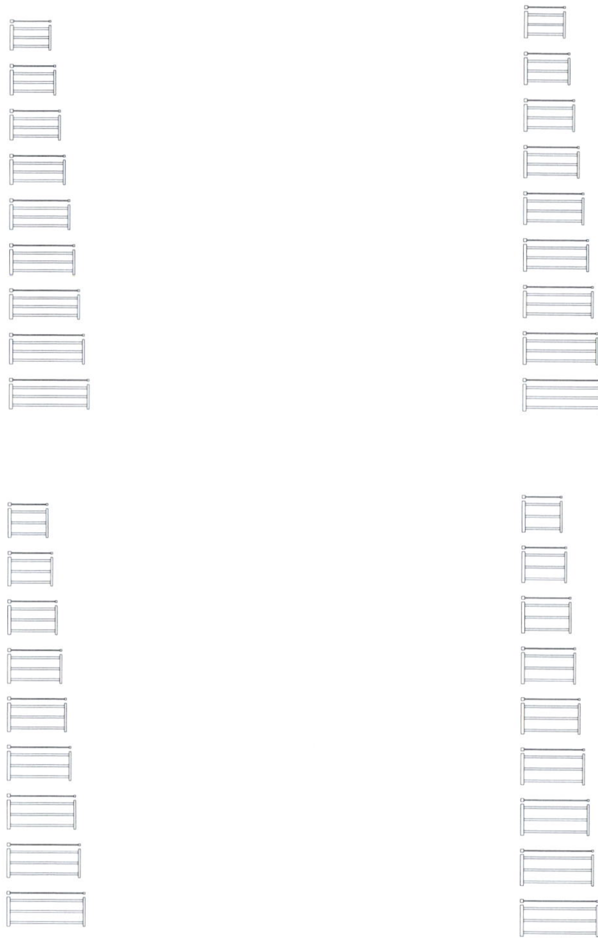

Region: American Midwest
System: Land Subdivision
Diagram: Variations of vertical rhythms and aggregation of sections
Type: Standard wood split rail
Drawing: Elevation
Author: Kim Hibben

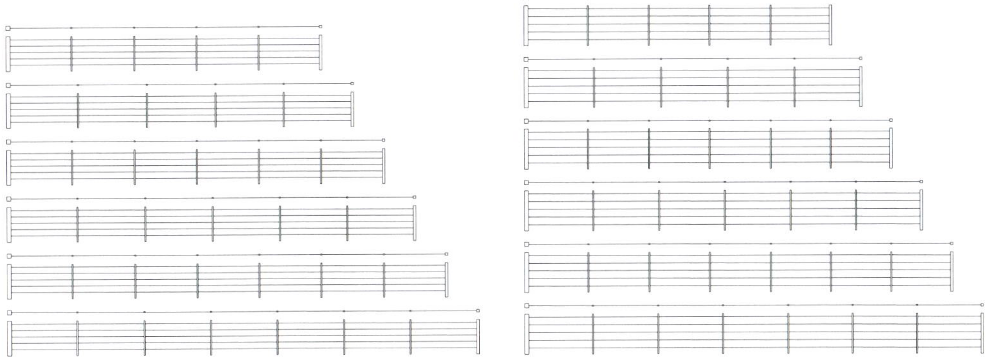

Region: American Midwest
System: Land Subdivision
Diagram: Variations of vertical rhythms and aggregation of sections
Type: Standard barbed wire
Drawing: Elevation
Author: Kim Hibben

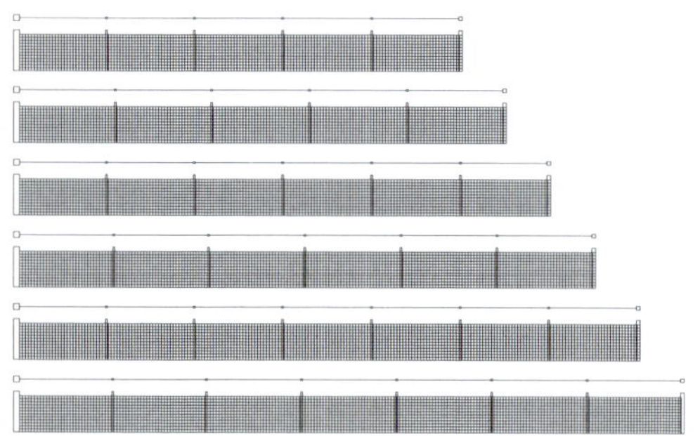

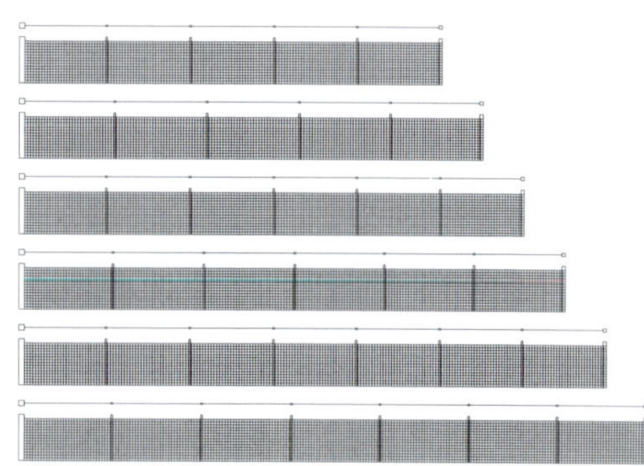

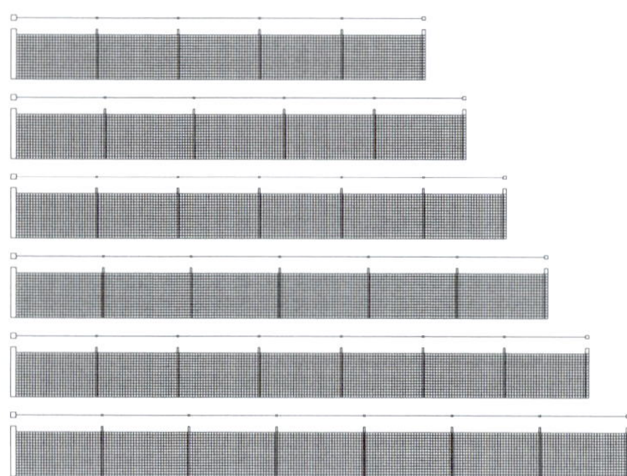

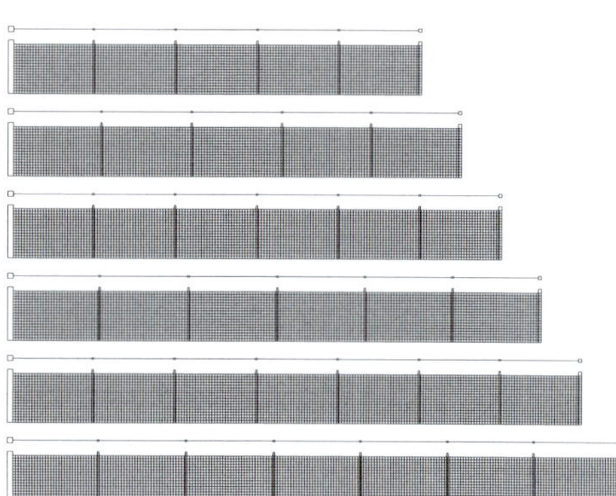

Region: American Midwest
System: Land Subdivision
Diagram: Variations of vertical rhythms and aggregation of sections
Type: Standard woven wire
Drawing: Elevation
Author: Kim Hibben

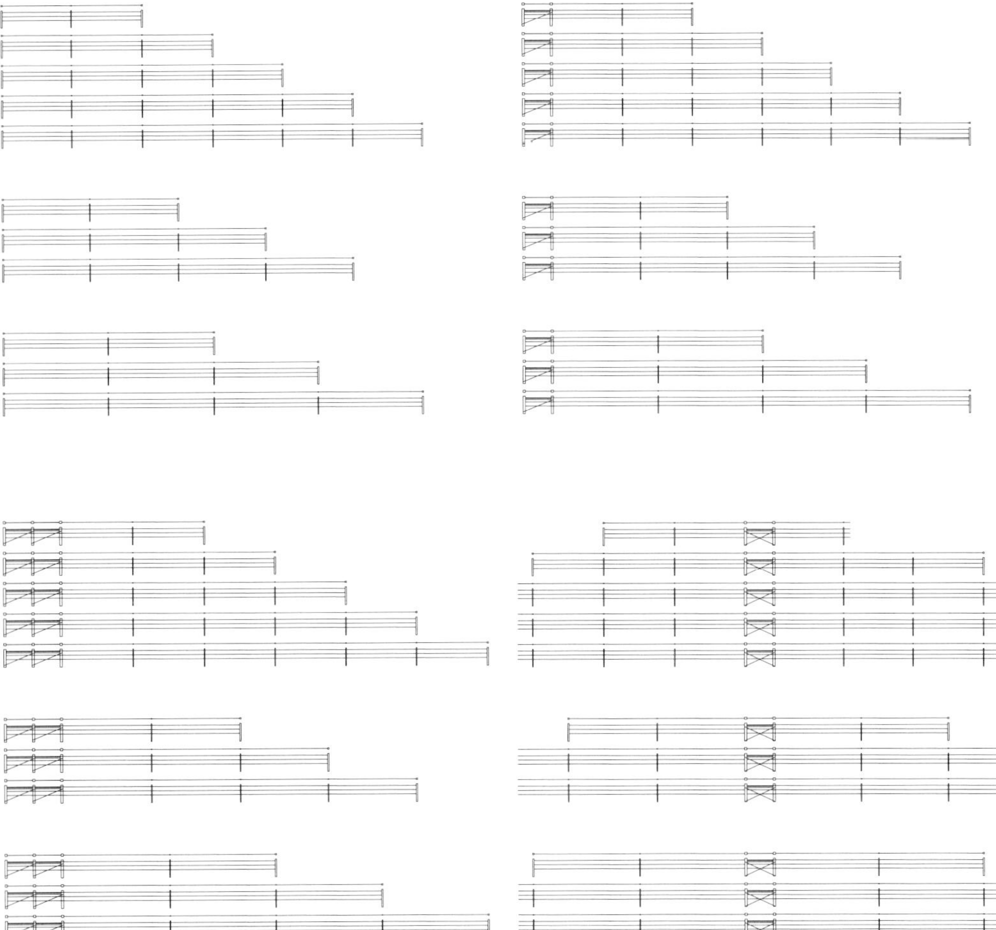

Region: American Midwest
System: Land Subdivision
Diagram: Variations of vertical rhythms and aggregation of sections
Type: Electric wire fence
Drawing: Elevation
Author: Kim Hibben

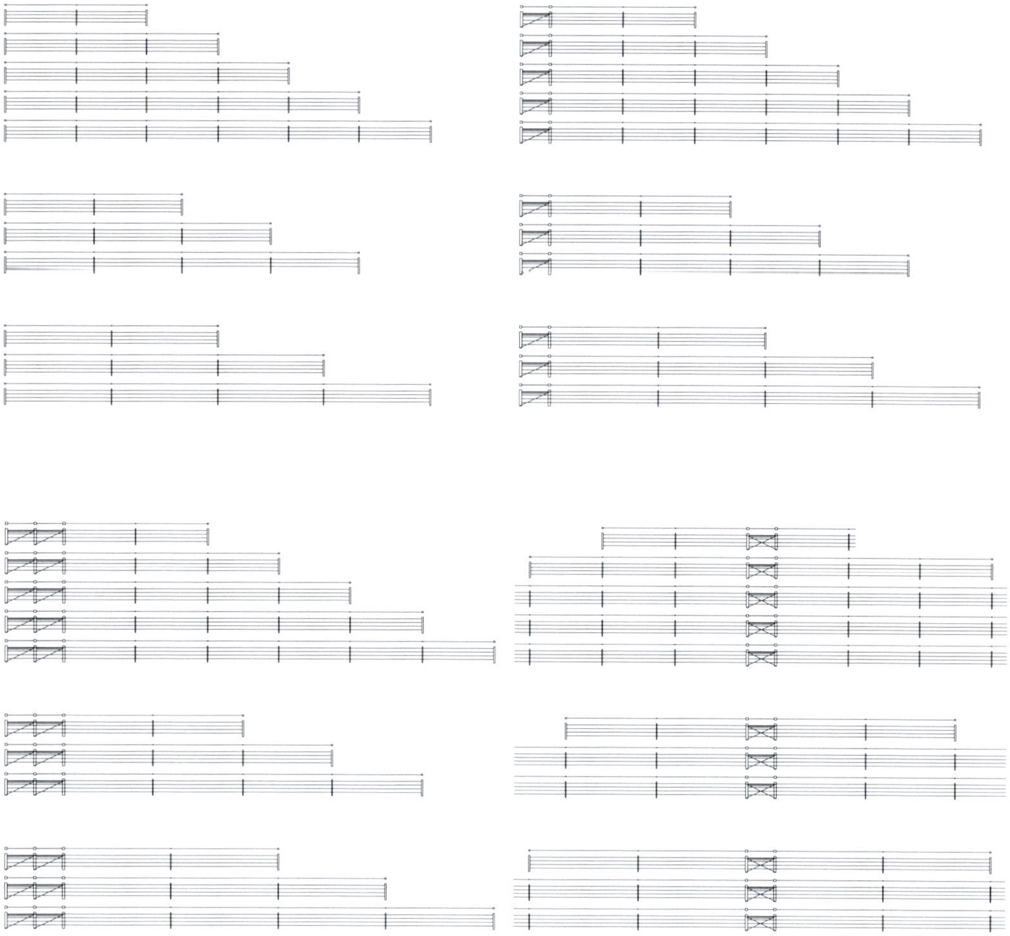

Region: American Midwest
System: Land Subdivision
Diagram: Variations of vertical rhythms and aggregation of sections
Type: Adult horse fence
Drawing: Elevation
Author: Kim Hibben

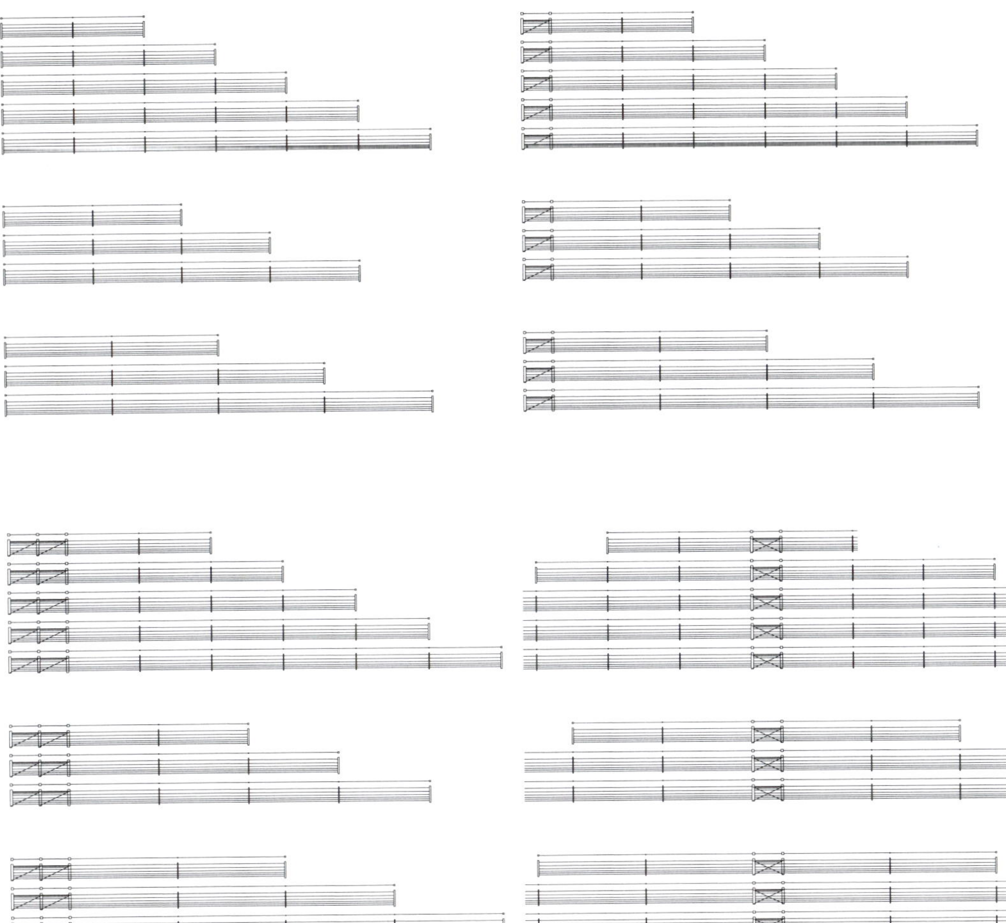

Region: American Midwest
System: Land Subdivision
Diagram: Variations of vertical rhythms
and aggregation of sections
Type: Hog, sheep, goat and predator control fence
Drawing: Elevation
Author: Kim Hibben

Region: Argentine Pampas
System: Land Subdivision
Diagram: Variation of vertical rhythms and variability by superimposition of variations
Type: Traditional wiring
Drawing: Elevation
Author: Santiago Mussi

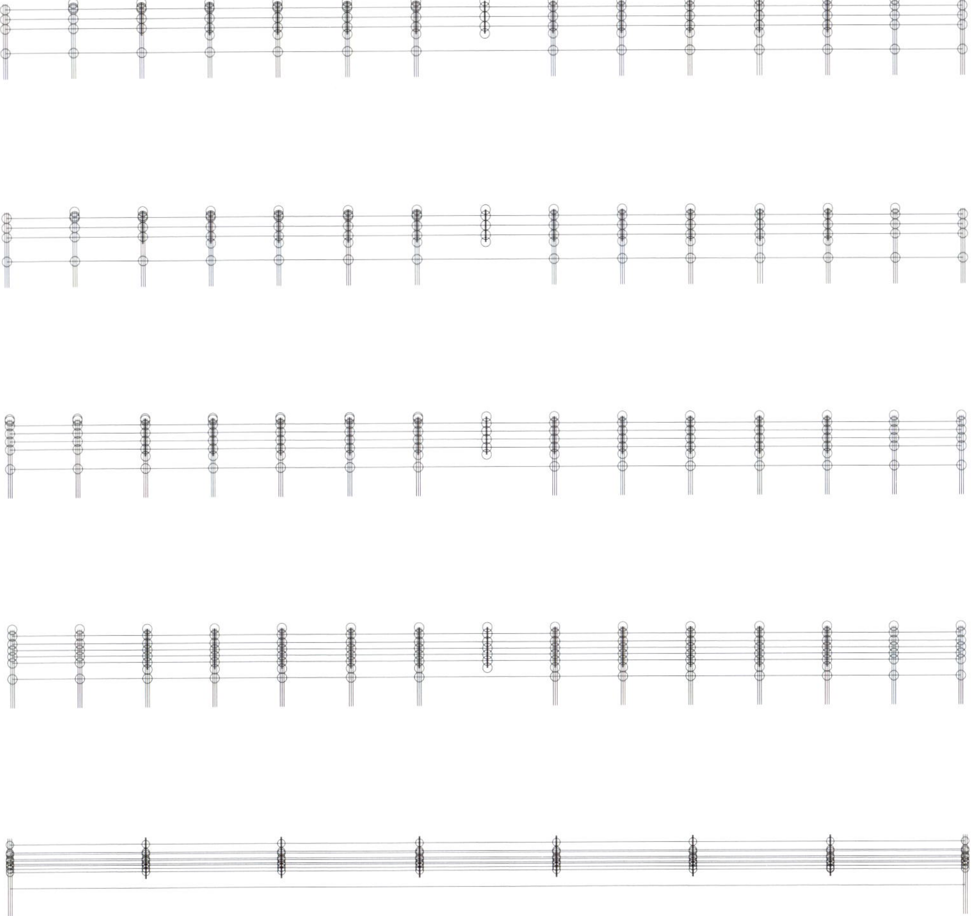

Region: Argentine Pampas
System: Land Subdivision
Diagram: Variation of vertical rhythms and variability by superimposition of variations
Type: Suspended wiring
Drawing: Elevation
Author: Santiago Mussi

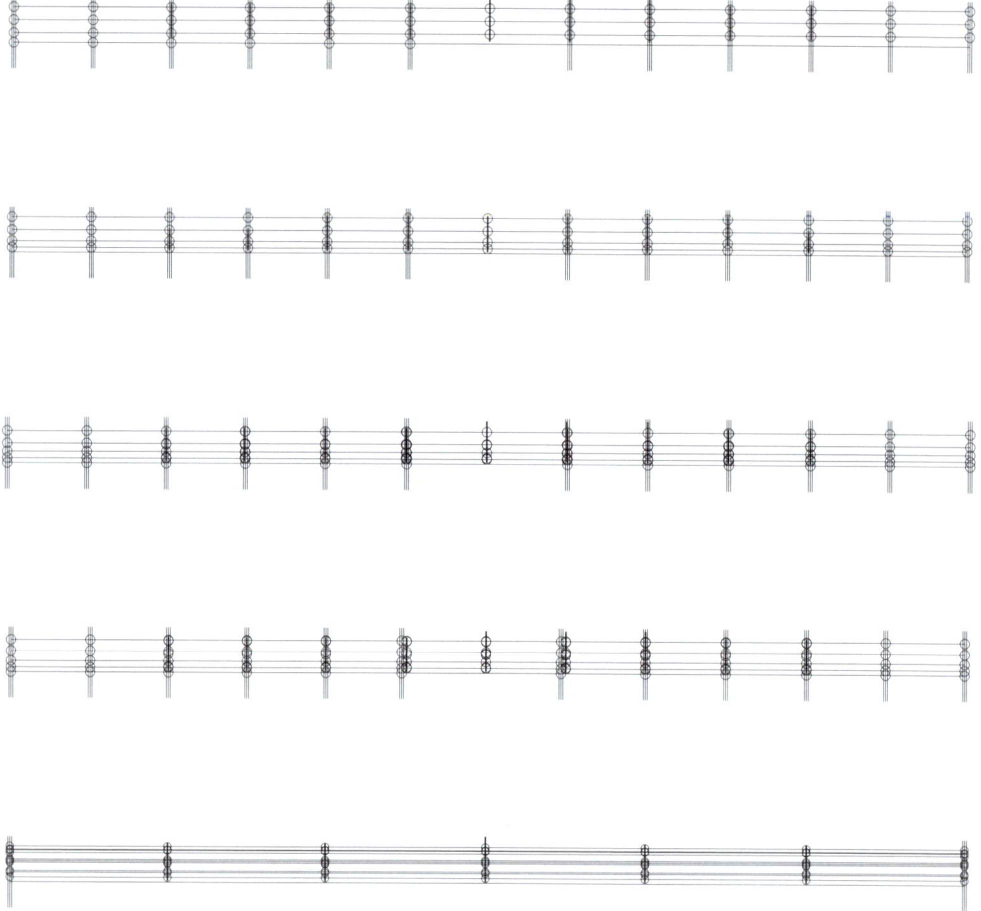

Region: Argentine Pampas
System: Land Subdivision
Diagram: Variation of vertical rhythms and variability by superimposition of variations
Type: Electric wiring
Drawing: Elevation
Author: Santiago Mussi

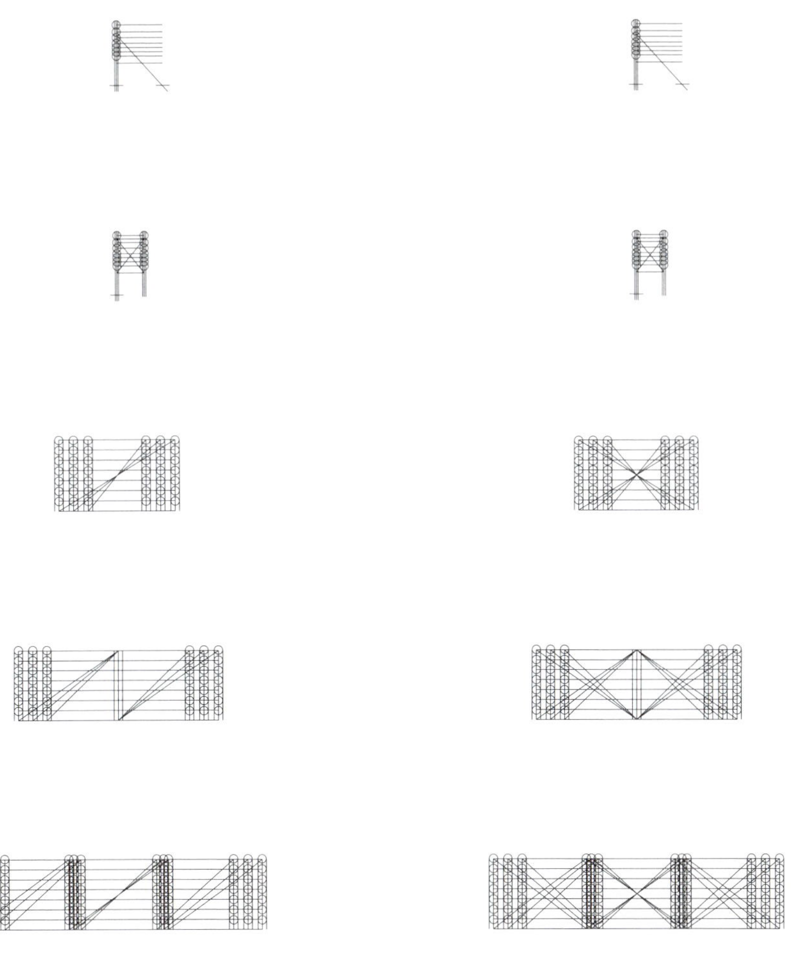

Region: Argentine Pampas
System: Land Subdivision
Diagram: Variation of secondary elements
Type: Simple and double corners, gates of one, two and three structural modules
Drawing: Elevation
Author: Santiago Mussi

Region: Argentine Pampas
System: Land Subdivision
Diagram: Combination of various types of fences and secondary elements
Type: Traditional-traditional, suspended-suspended, electric-electric, traditional-suspended, traditional-electric, electric-suspended wires, at T fence intersections and L corners
Drawing: Axonometric
Author: Santiago Mussi

Region: Argentine Pampas
System: Land Subdivision
Diagram: Combination of various
types of fences and secondary elements
Type: Traditional-traditional, suspended-suspended, electric-electric, traditional-suspended, traditional-electric, electric-suspended wires, at T fence intersections and L corners
Drawing: Axonometric
Author: Santiago Mussi

AGRICULTURAL PRODUCTION

AMERICAN MIDWEST / ARGENTINE PAMPAS

Linear striated organizations that enable various forms of corrugation of the ground for protecting the soil, preventing its tillage and compaction, increasing its diversity, enhancing its performance, adding organic matter, and avoiding pests, for the sowing and harvesting of agricultural production.

Model / Patchworks, matrices, mosaics, overlapped patterns of corrugation, ruled surfaces of two edges rasterized by a prototypical planting section, rectilinear and curvilinear swipes restricted by turning radius of machines and vehicles, curve-to-straight patches and residual areas, traces of cross-circulation.

Operations / Plowing, orthogonal patching, curvilinear patching, linear striating, turning, edge activating, edge deactivating, isolating, corrugating, iterative corrugating, counter-corrugating, repetitive punctuating, accumulating, bundling, piling, rolling, folding, hay baling, layering, flattening.

Systems / Sweeps, blades, tillers, tires, injectors, buckets, scoops, pumps, containers, wheels, trenches, drills, pinwheels, grinders, wires, tractors, tilling, planting, enhancing, and harvesting machinery, harvesting carts, tubes, structures, parking and maneuvering areas, short-term storing and maintaining.

Dynamics / Several processes of territorial measurement, survey, evaluation, diagnosis, occupation and activation, various modes of delimitation of zones of diverse efficiency of productivity, intensity of maintenance and periodicity of renewal, definition of physical and non-physical boundaries.

Performances / Increase or reduction of land productivity, soil erosion, insularity and connectivity, regularity of changes through crop rotation and seasonal productivity, orientation through corrugation and patchwork, activation and deactivation of exchanges of goods, activation of time-based production.

Effects / Multi-scalar patchworks, corrugated surfaces, temporary left-over islands, combed patterns, multi-directional surfaces, color variegations, topographic disruptions, vegetation disturbances, high and low productivity patterns, variegation of shines and rough areas, linear traces and trajectories.

Region: American Midwest
System: Agricultural Production
Diagram: Tiller pattern
Type: Soy, tomato, wheat, corn
Drawing: Axonometric
Author: Jason Mould

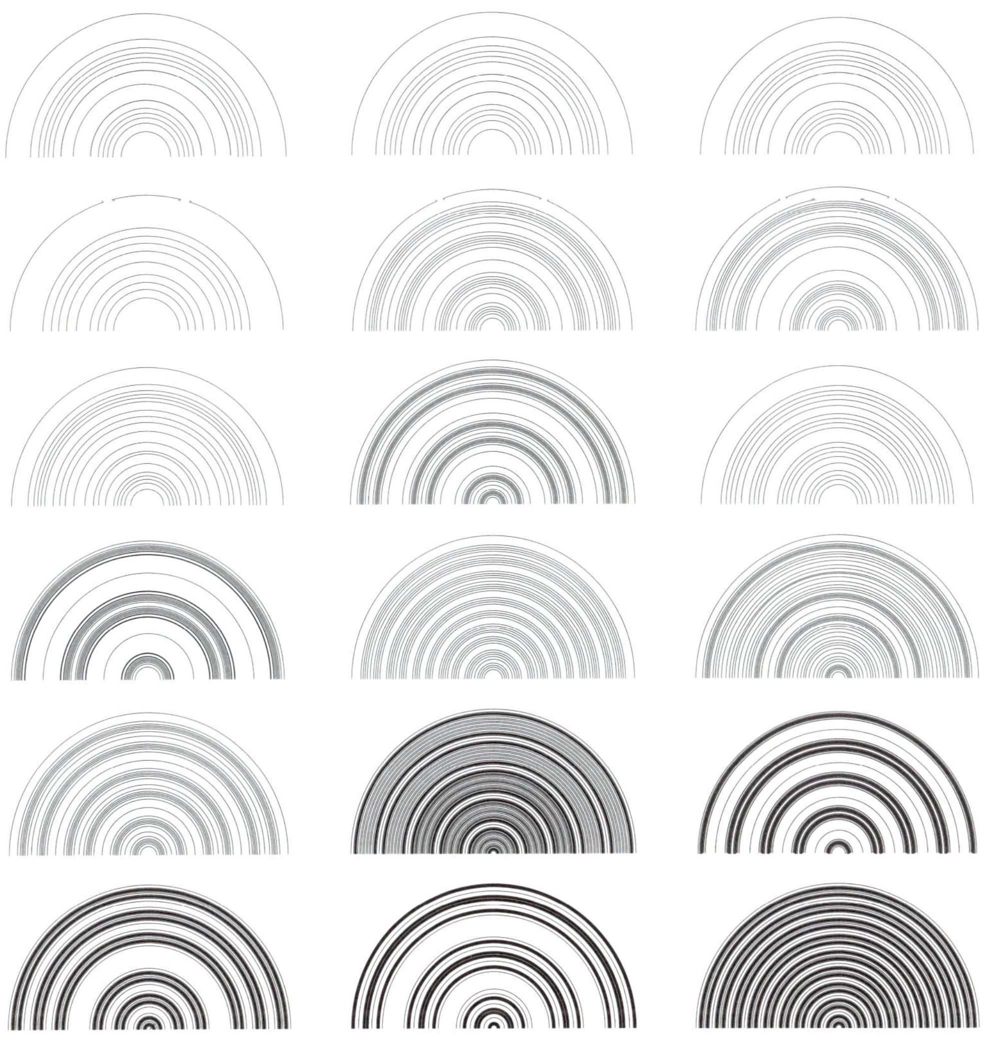

Region: American Midwest
System: Agricultural Production
Diagram: Tiller pattern
Type: Soy, tomato, wheat, corn
Drawing: Plan
Author: Jason Mould

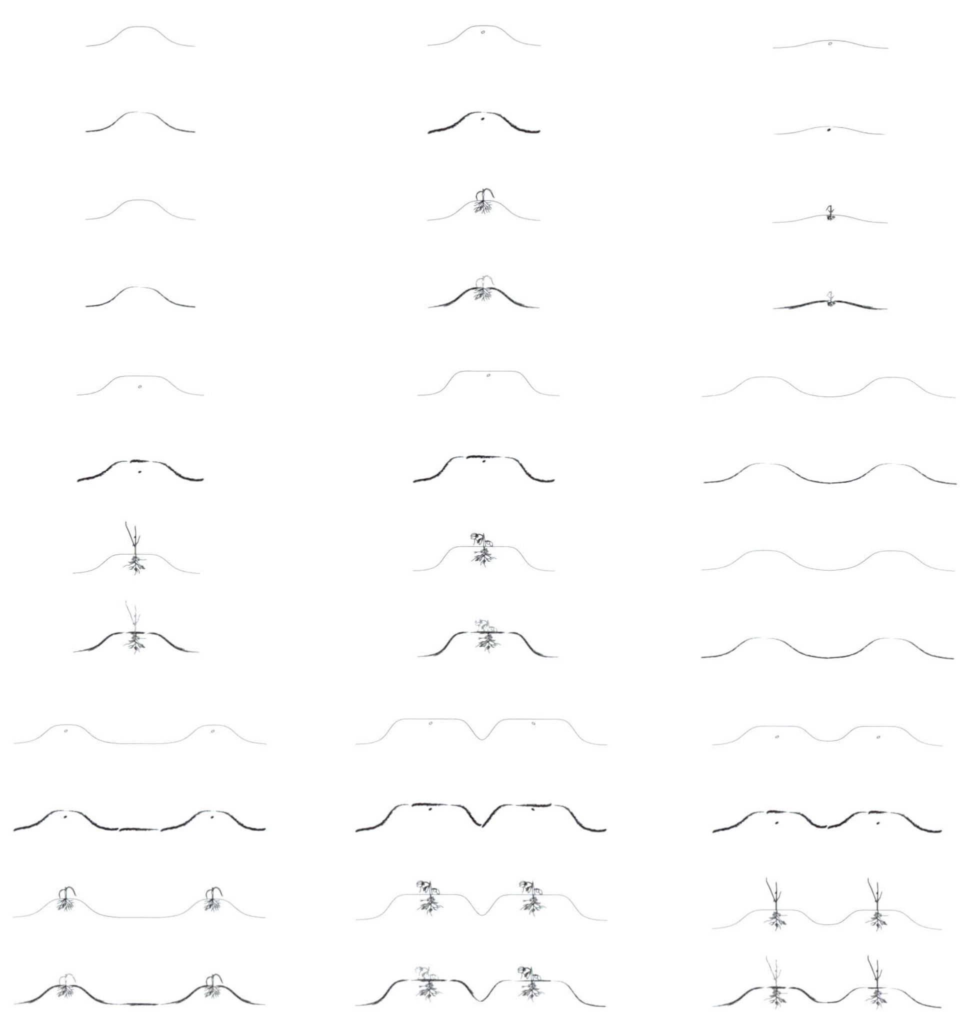

Region: American Midwest
System: Agricultural Production
Diagram: Ground profiles
Type: Soy, tomato, wheat, corn
Drawing: Section cut
Author: Jason Mould

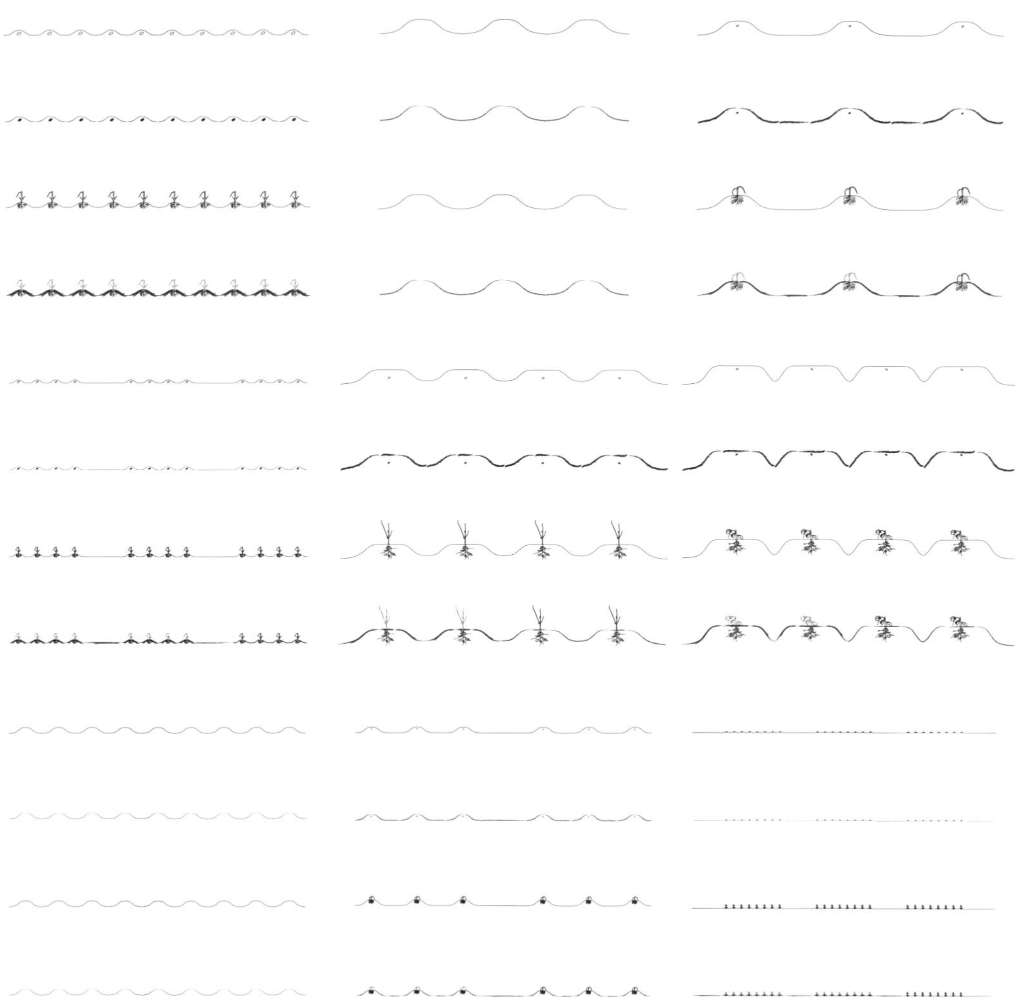

Region: American Midwest
System: Agricultural Production
Diagram: Ground profiles
Type: Soy, tomato, wheat, corn
Drawing: Section cut
Author: Jason Mould

Region: American Midwest
System: Agricultural Production
Diagram: Crop rotation, profile patterns
Type: Soy, tomato, wheat, corn
Drawing: Plan
Author: Jason Mould

Region: American Midwest
System: Agricultural Production
Diagram: Crop rotation, tiller pattern
Type: Soy, tomato, wheat, corn
Drawing: Plan
Author: Jason Mould

Region: Argentine Pampas
System: Agricultural Production
Diagram: Annual crop growth cycle
Type: Soybean, corn, wheat, sunflower
Drawing: Plan
Author: Máximo Sánchez-Granel

Region: Argentine Pampas
System: Agricultural Production
Diagram: Crop rotation with alternating variations
Type: Wheat, soybean, corn, soybean
Drawing: Plan
Author: Máximo Sánchez-Granel

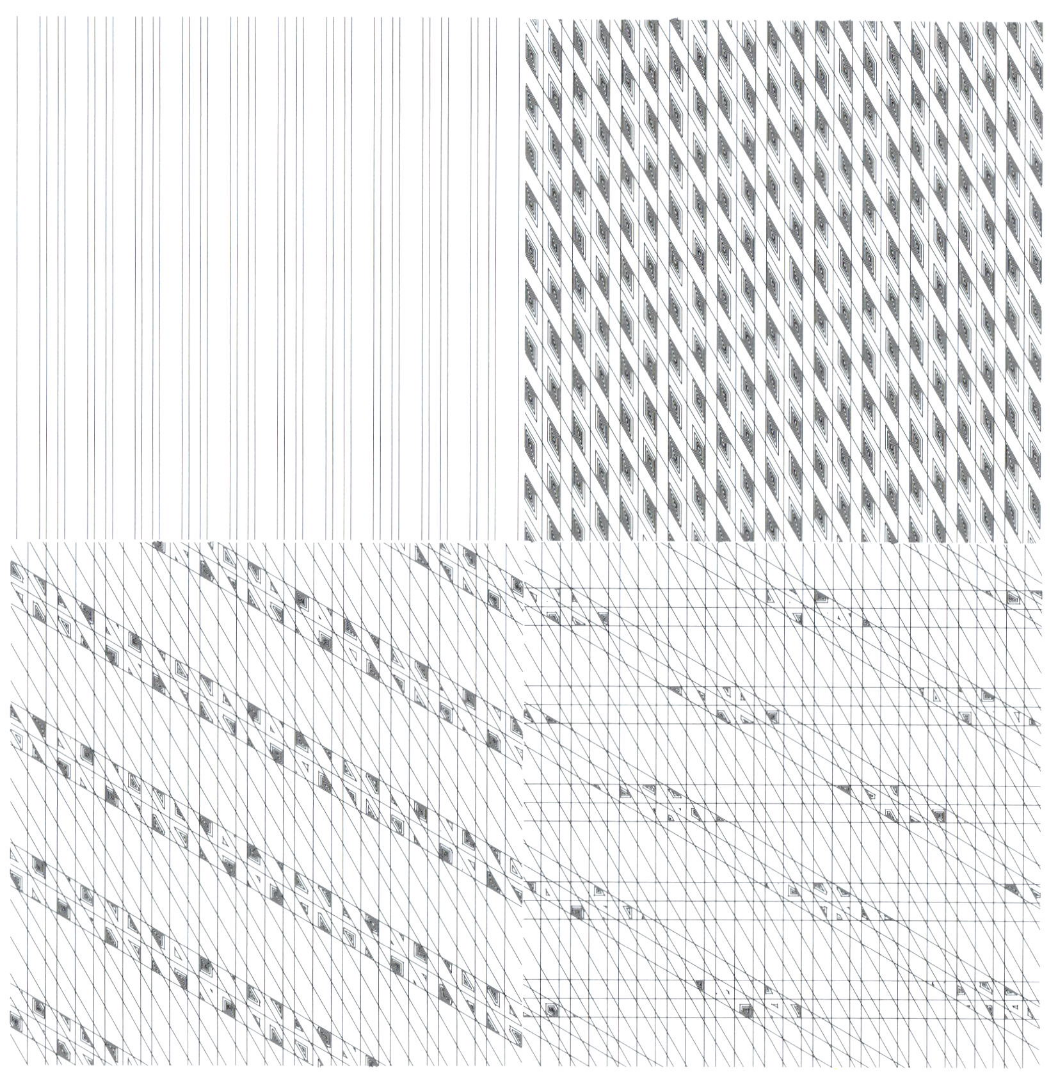

Region: Argentine Pampas
System: Agricultural Production
Diagram: Crop rotation, superimposition of contours
Type: Wheat, soybean, corn, soybean
Drawing: Plan
Author: Máximo Sánchez-Granel

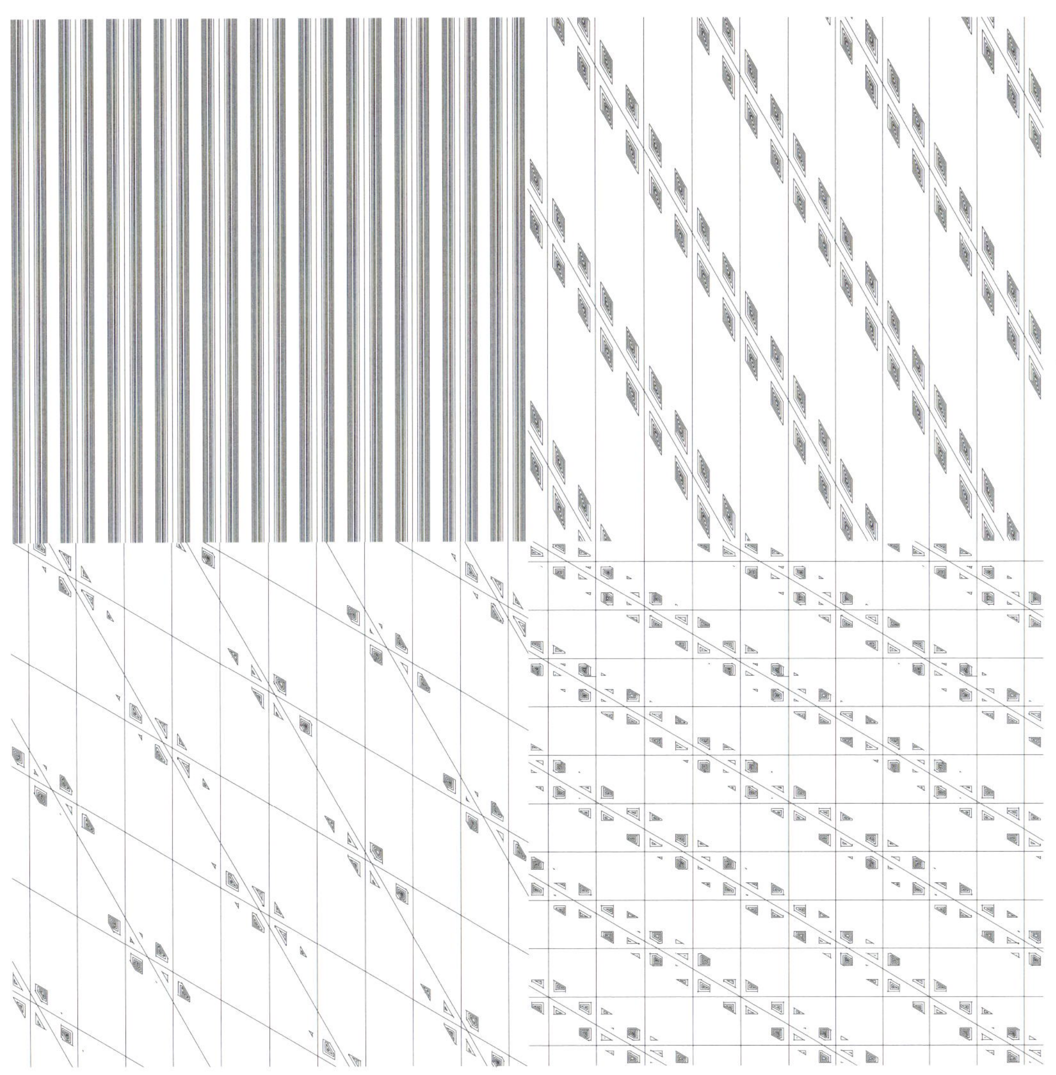

Region: Argentine Pampas
System: Agricultural Production
Diagram: Crop rotation, superimposition of contours
Type: Soybean, corn, soybean, wheat
Drawing: Plan
Author: Máximo Sánchez-Granel

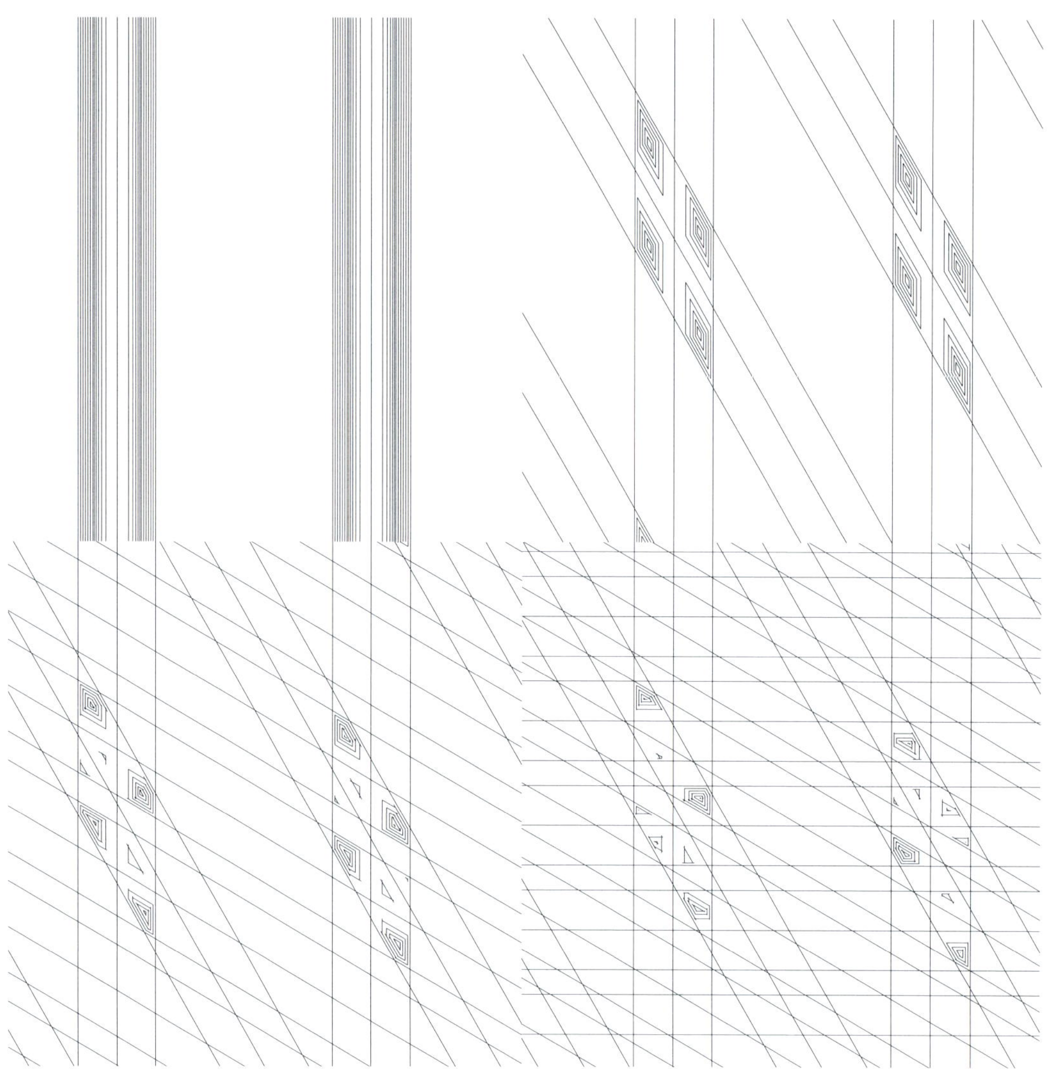

Region: Argentine Pampas
System: Agricultural Production
Diagram: Crop rotation, superimposition of contours
Type: Corn, soybean, wheat, soybean
Drawing: Plan
Author: Máximo Sánchez-Granel

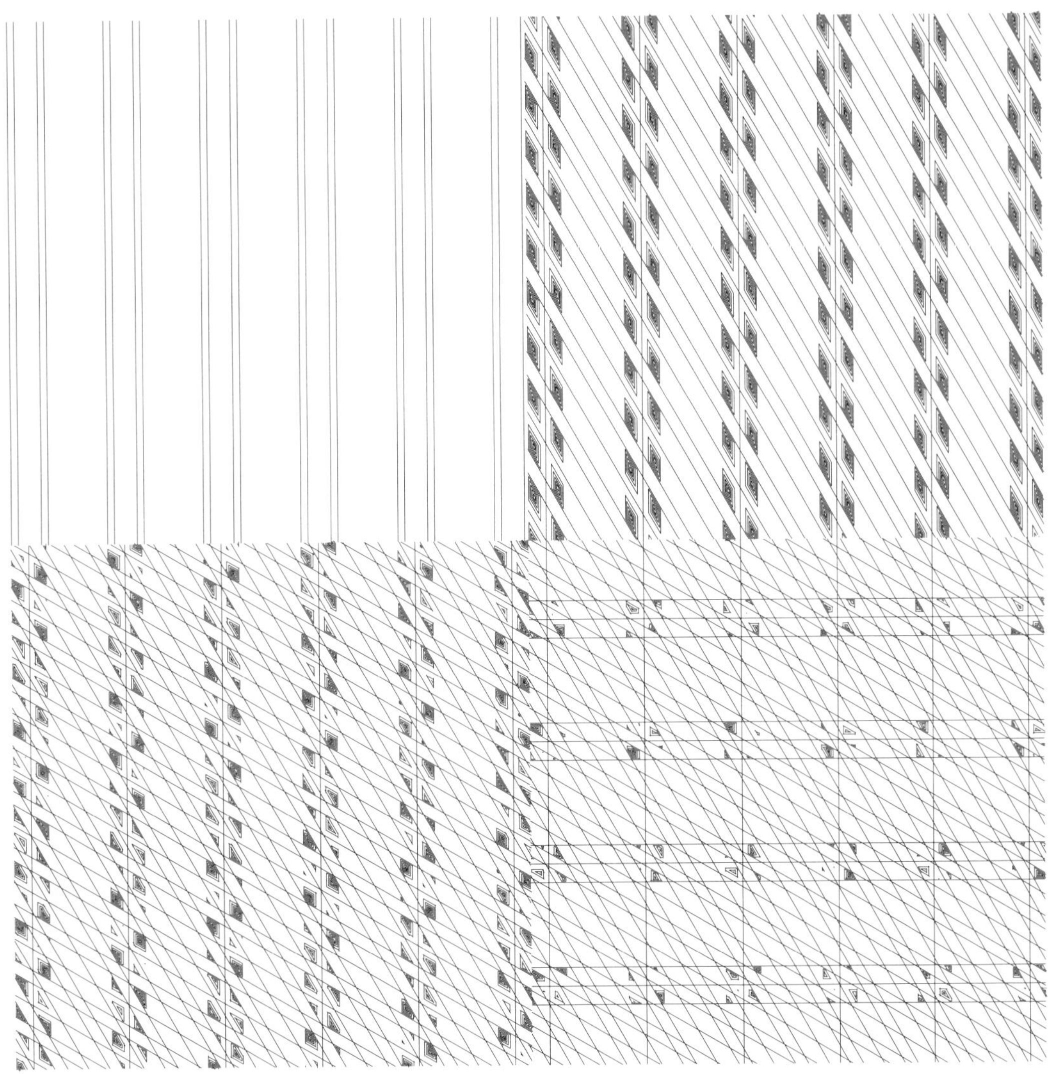

Region: Argentine Pampas
System: Agricultural Production
Diagram: Crop rotation, superimposition of contours
Type: Soybean, wheat, soybean, corn
Drawing: Plan
Author: Máximo Sánchez-Granel

WATER MANAGEMENT

AMERICAN MIDWEST / ARGENTINE PAMPAS

Linear channeling organizations that enable various forms of water extraction, provision, circulation, distribution, management, filtering, accumulation, collection, sewage and drainage, satisfying human, cattle, farming and industrial demands, and compensating for lack of immediate water resources.

Model / Networks, grids, parallel and branching patterns of water provision and drainage, characterized by cascading levels, going from the continental to the regional and to the local, and articulated through the construction of channels, the management of slopes and edges, and the channeling of topography.

Operations / Excavating, plowing, cutting, various forms of earth moving and depositing, natural eroding and accreting, curving, rectifying, turning, knotting, bifurcating, trifurcating, channeling, mounding, consolidating, terracing, sloping, by-passing, blocking, cascading, collecting.

Systems / Prefabricated concrete pieces, pillars, ducts, pipes, pumps, drills, canals, bridges, tunnels, banks, dams, dikes, docks, floating platforms, pressure control devices, valves, weirs, flumes, notches, tanks, basins, furrows, ditches, collectors, mills, gutters, wells, troughs.

Dynamics / Several processes of distribution, collection, storage, drainage and provision of water, commonly attached to the performance of other systems, such as irrigation and soil management, and secondarily contributing to the maintenance and the transportation of goods, people and animals.

Performances / Increase or reduction of land productivity, cattle management, human settlement, human, animal, materials, or goods transport, control of the aridity and fertility of the soil, territorial water flows and drainage, activation of time-based production, land subdivision and connectivity.

Effects / Multi-scalar networks and grids, linear striations, branching structures, wounded surfaces, meandering and straightening, flood patterns, canals, ponds, lagoons, lakes, eroded patches, muddy patches, flood patterns, pond patterns, local depressions and valleys, linearly repetitive mounds.

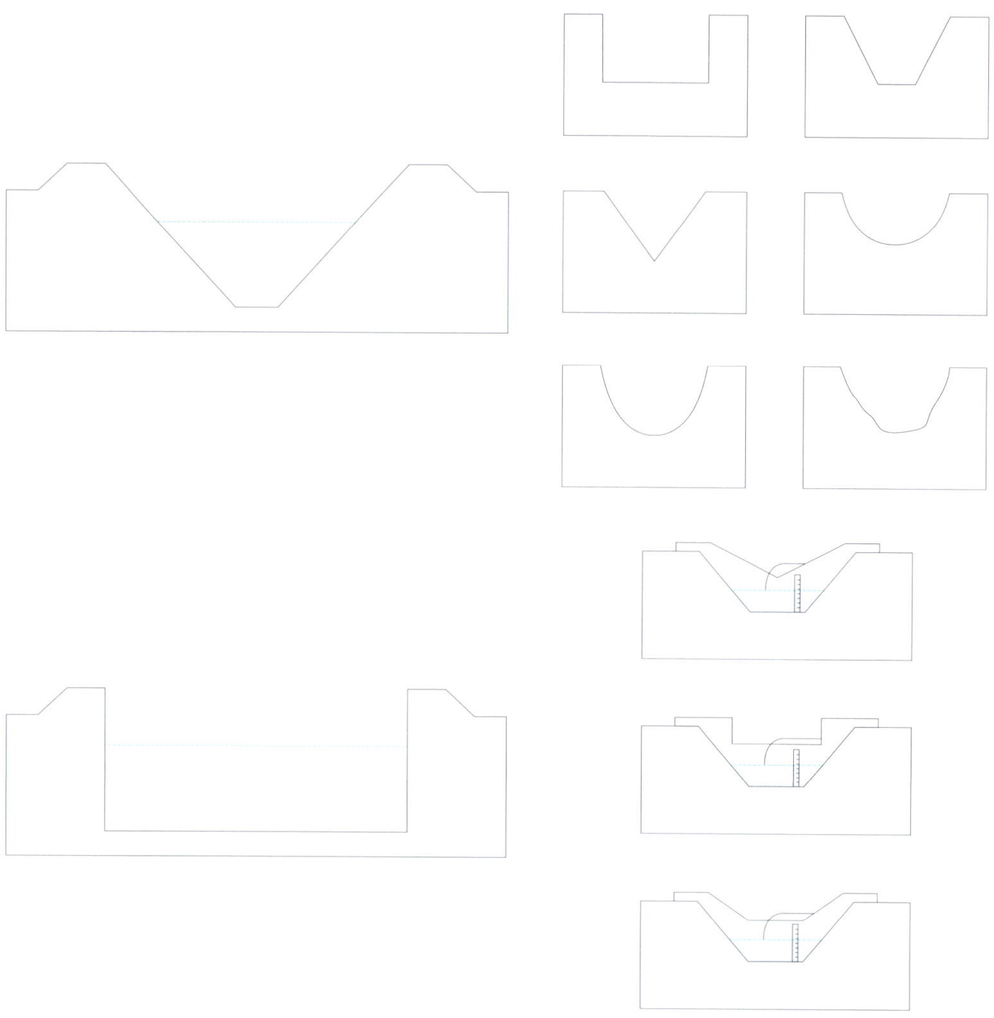

Region: American Midwest
System: Water Management
Diagram: Technical constraints
Type: Canal
Drawing: Section
Author: Paola Gómez-Piñeiro

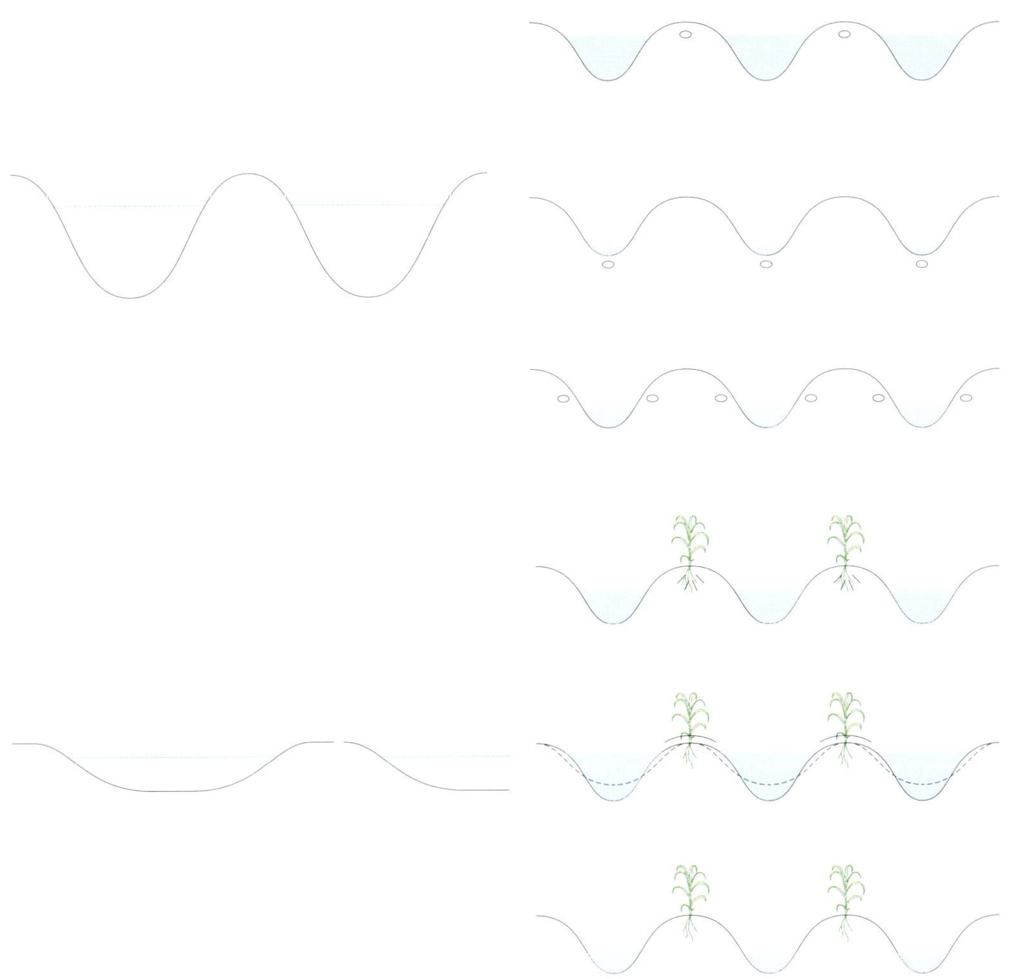

Region: American Midwest
System: Water Management
Diagram: Technical constraints
Type: Furrow
Drawing: Section
Author: Paola Gómez-Piñeiro

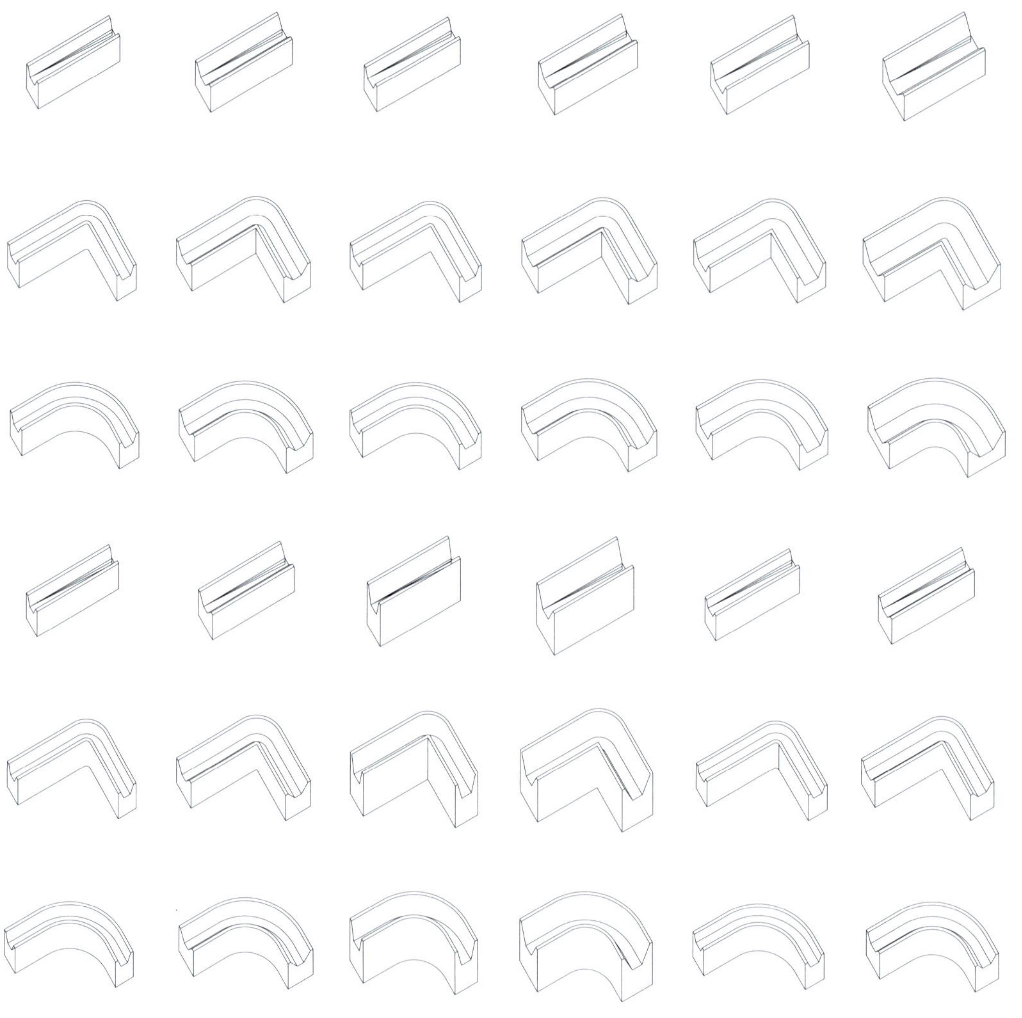

Region: American Midwest
System: Water Management
Diagram: Variety of pieces according to variations of width and turning angle
Type: Canal
Drawing: Axonometric
Author: Paola Gómez-Piñeiro

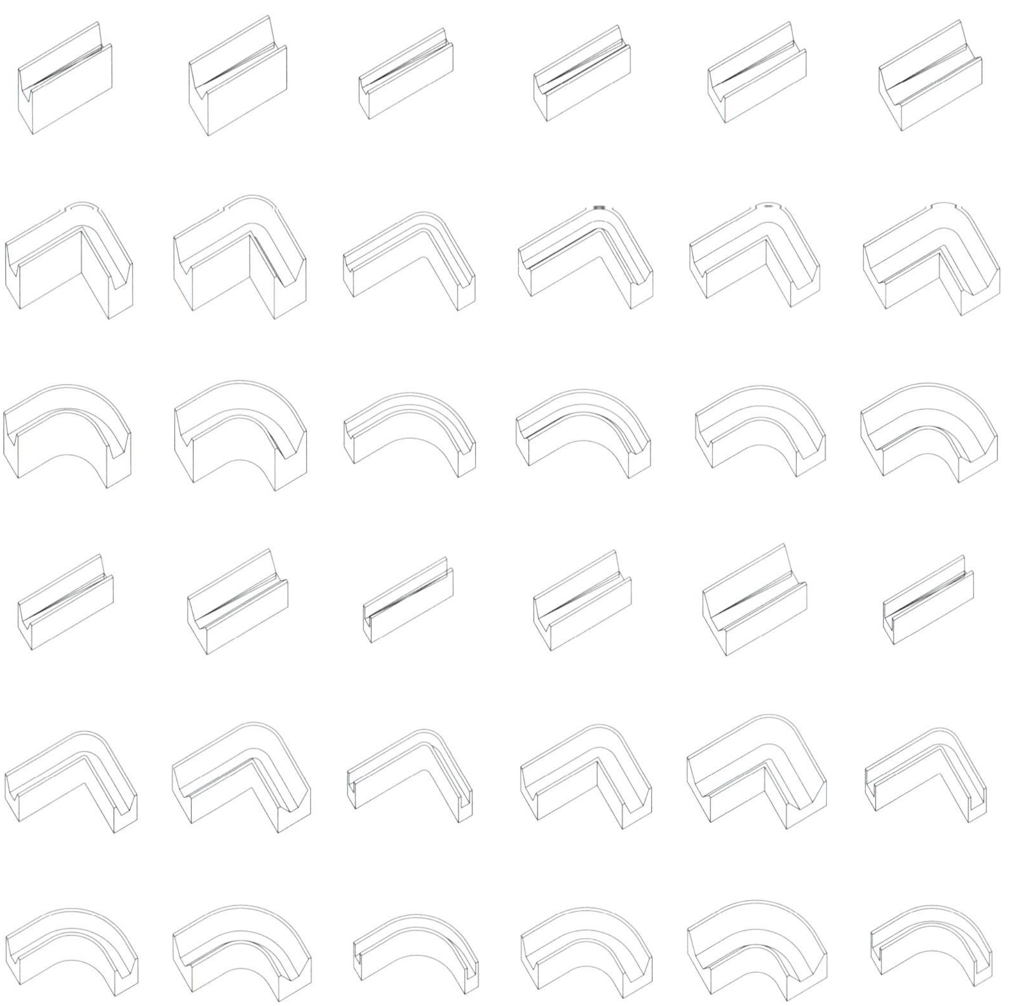

Region: American Midwest
System: Water Management
Diagram: Variety of pieces according to variations of width and turning angle
Type: Canal
Drawing: Axonometric
Author: Paola Gómez-Piñeiro

Region: American Midwest
System: Water Management
Diagram: Variety of pieces according to variations of width and turning angle
Type: Canal
Drawing: Axonometric
Author: Paola Gómez-Piñeiro

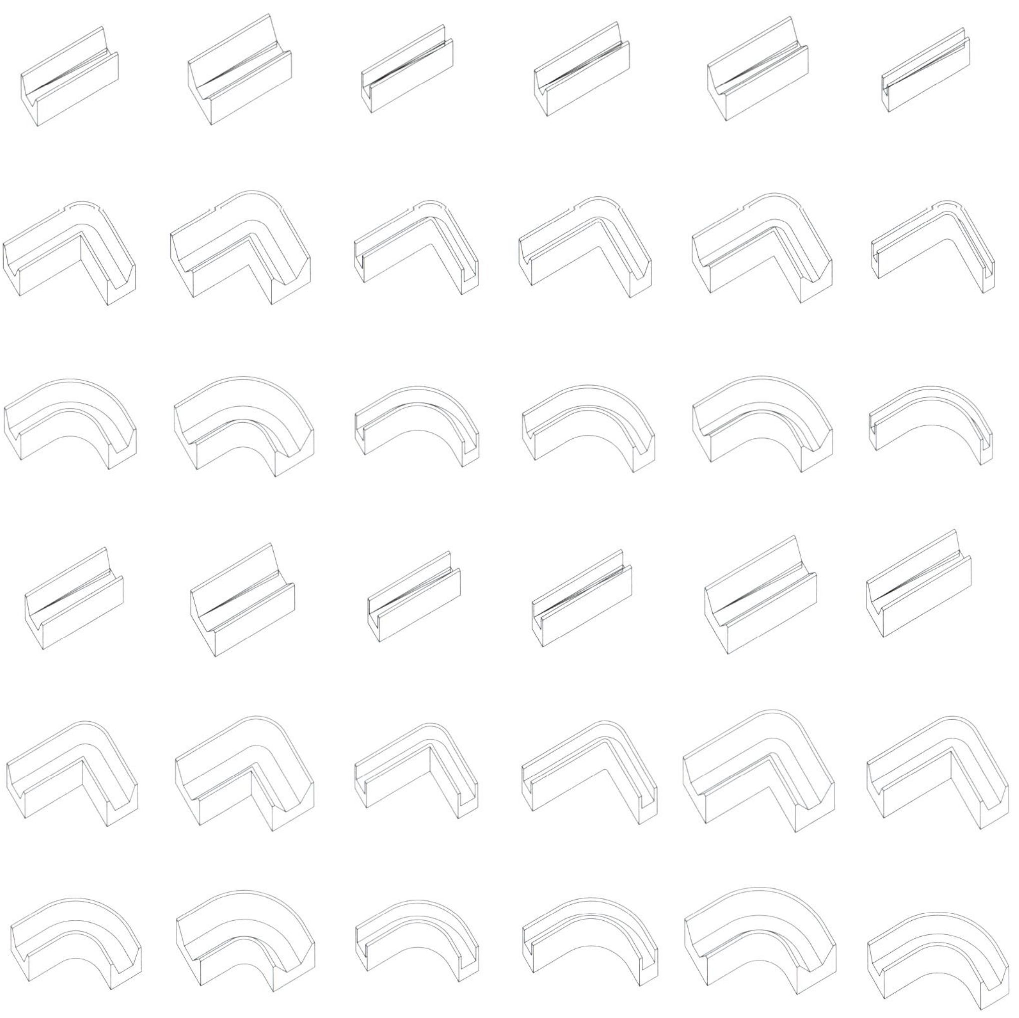

Region: American Midwest
System: Water Management
Diagram: Variety of pieces according to variations of width and turning angle
Type: Canal
Drawing: Axonometric
Author: Paola Gómez-Piñeiro

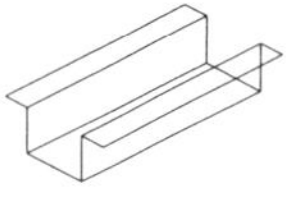

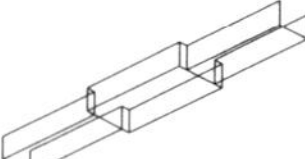
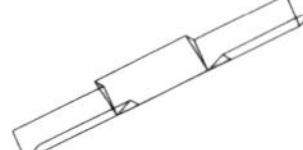
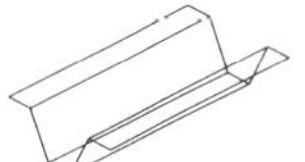

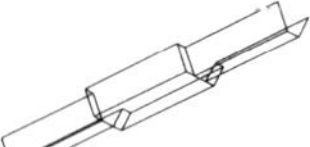
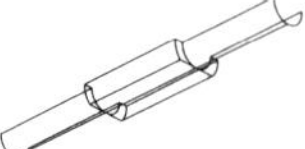
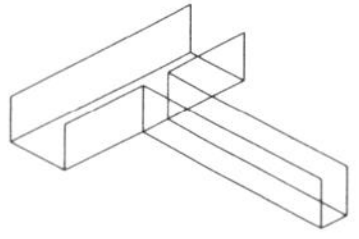
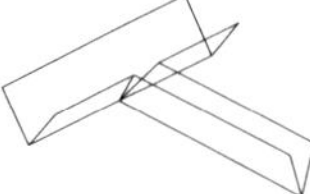
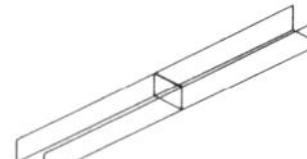
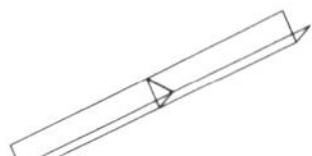
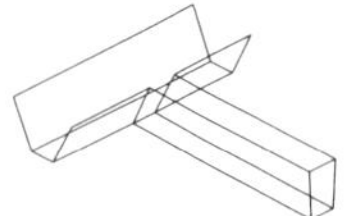
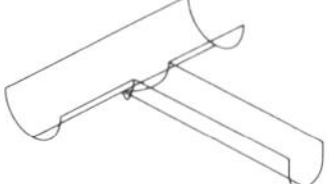

Region: Argentine Pampas
System: Water Management
Diagram: Sectional varieties, distribution boxes, turns, controls
Type: Furrows, rectangular section, in V, trapezoidal, in U
Drawing: Axonometric
Author: Fernanda Raimondi

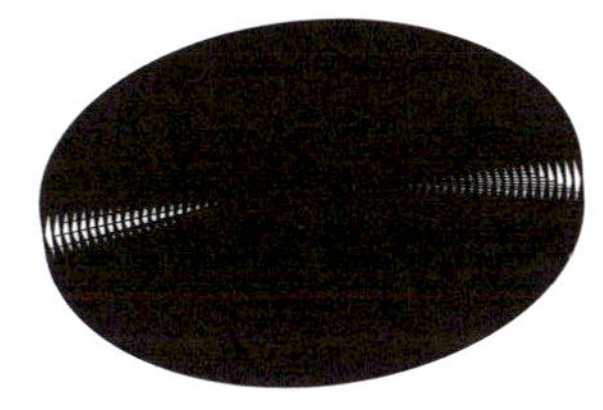
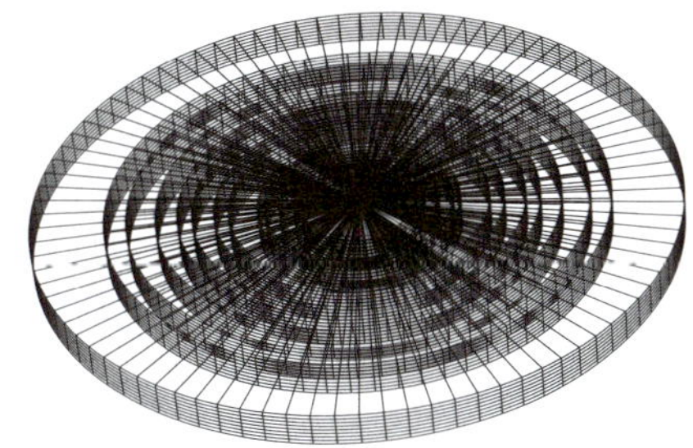
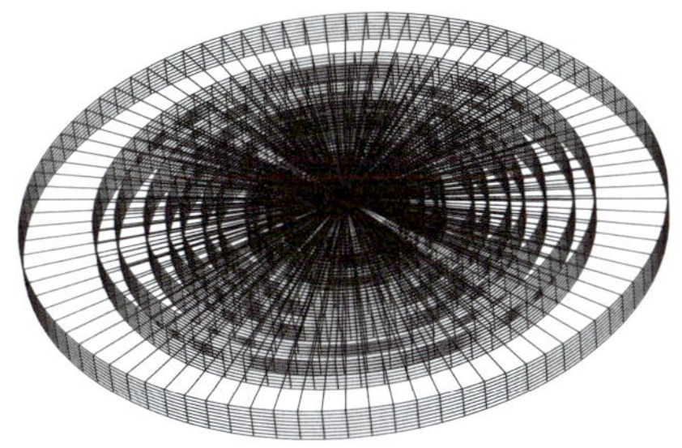
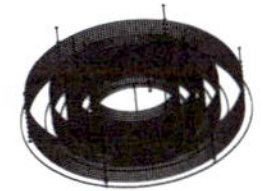
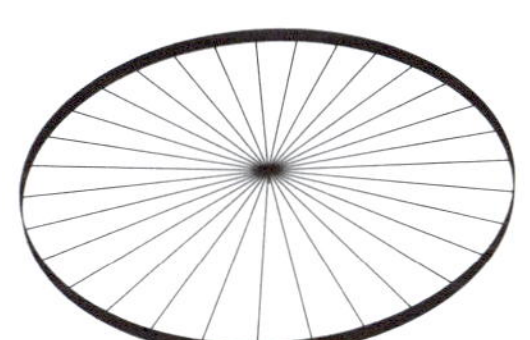
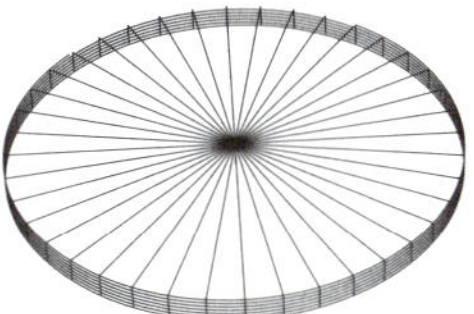

Region: Argentine Pampas
System: Water Management
Diagram: Variation of diameter, thickness, height, transversal and longitudinal structural rhythms
Type: Australian tank
Drawing: Axonometric
Author: Fernanda Raimondi

Region: Argentine Pampas
System: Water Management
Diagram: Variation of height and diameter
Type: Wind turbines, windmills and wheel mills
Drawing: Plan
Author: Fernanda Raimondi

Region: Argentine Pampas
System: Water Management
Diagram: Variation of height and diameter
Type: Wind turbines, windmills and wheel mills
Drawing: Axonometric
Author: Fernanda Raimondi

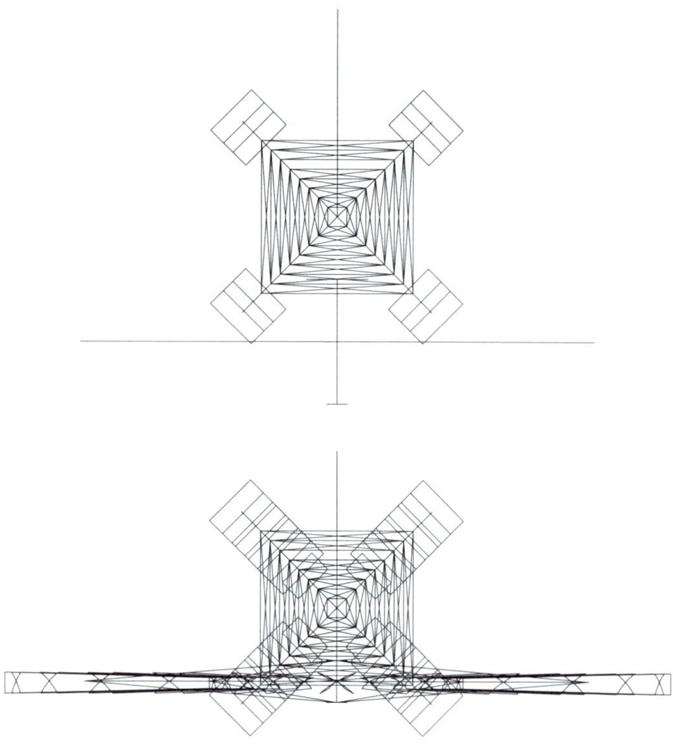

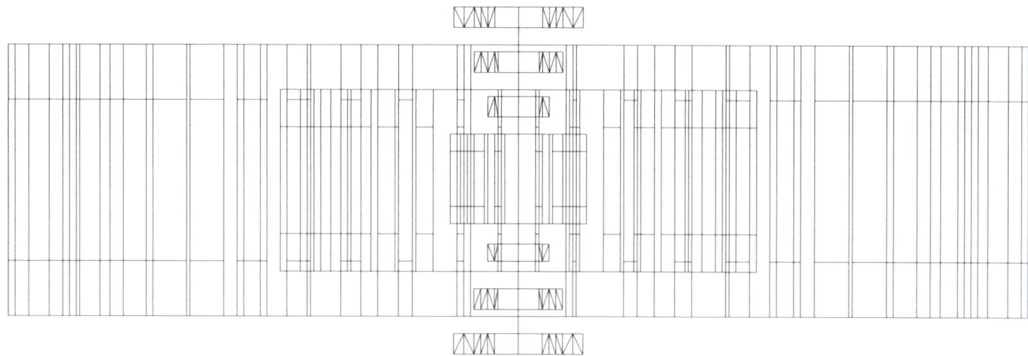

Region: Argentine Pampas
System: Water Management
Diagram: Variability by superimposition of variations
Type: Wind turbines, windmills and wheel mills
Drawing: Plan
Author: Fernanda Raimondi

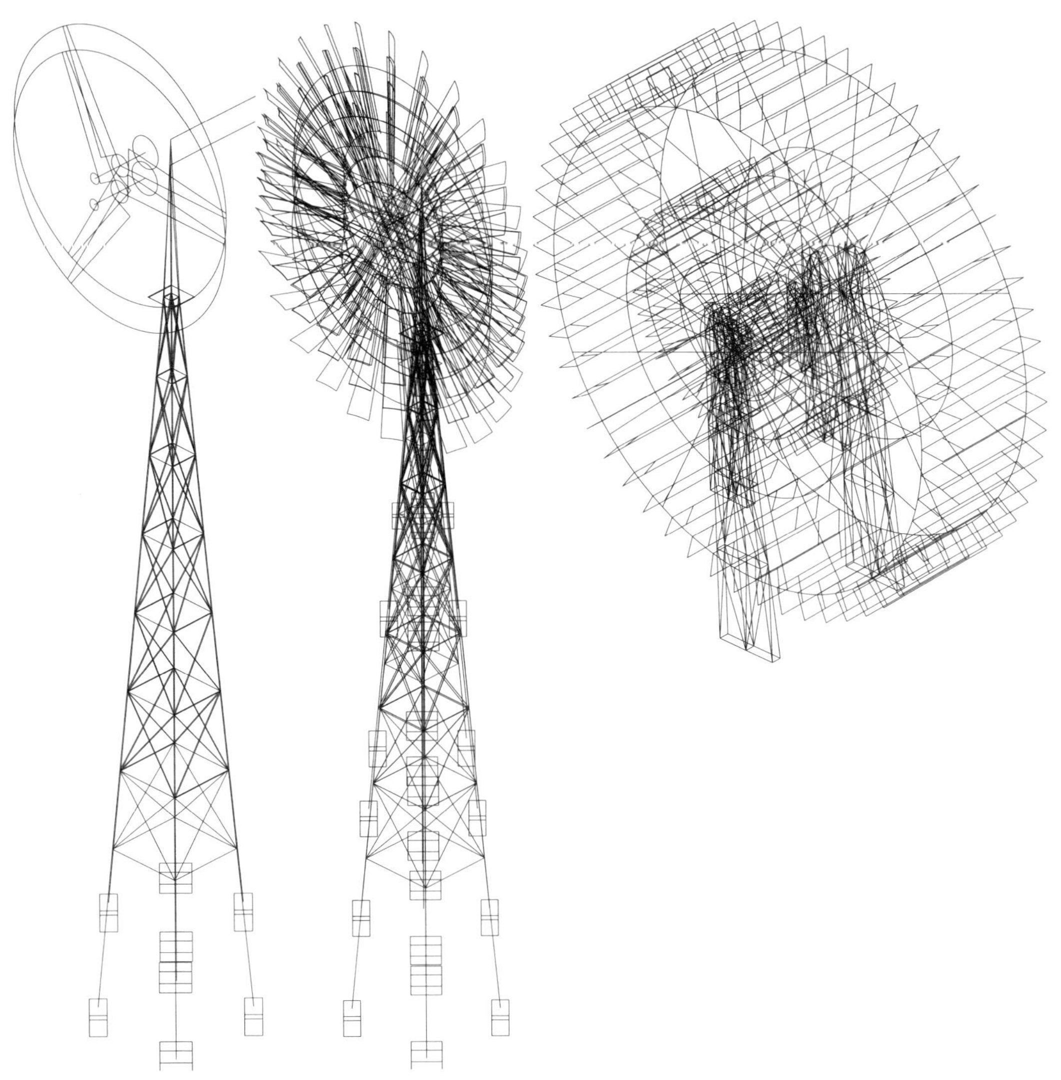

Region: Argentine Pampas
System: Water Management
Diagram: Variability by superimposition of variations
Type: Wind turbines, windmills and wheel mills
Drawing: Axonometric
Author: Fernanda Raimondi

IRRIGATION AND FUMIGATION

AMERICAN MIDWEST / ARGENTINE PAMPAS

Linear repetitive parallel or revolving organizations that enable the even irrigation of water to the soil or supply of chemicals to the crops, promoting the balanced growth of cultivated species, evading pests, plagues and malaises, precluding frost, and avoiding soil consolidation in agricultural production.

Model / Networks of concentric circles and swipes of polar and rectangular arrays of parallel traces populating triangular grids, orthogonal grids and diagonal grids, sprinkling cones of various heights, angles of aperture, and distances that project a diversity of floral patterns overlapped to one another.

Operations / Networking, segmenting, overlapping, linear displacing, changing number of supports, varying beam spans, increasing number of sprinklers, changing distances between sprinklers, raising sprinklers, opening sprinkler cones, modifying quantity of water, regulating frequency of turns.

Systems / Drips, sprinklers, center-pivots, guns, nozzles, sprays, booms, injectors, flow-meters, tubes, gaskets, pivots, flaps, pipes, pumps, agitators, valves, spinners, spreaders, filters, connections, bends, main and secondary structural bars, tensors, joints, vertical triangulated legs, ladders, wheels.

Dynamics / Several processes of activation of productive fields, enhancement of productivity, and preservation and strengthening of products, involving time management, control of simultaneity, spatial rotation and coverage, consolidation and balancing of water flows, increase and equalizing of nutrients.

Performances / Increase or reduction of land productivity, soil erosion, preservation and renewal, soil fertility, persistence of harmful insects and endurance of plagues, activation of time-based production, assurance of water balances, acceleration, consolidation, and intensification of quality of growth.

Effects / Network patterns, patchwork patterns, circular patterns, combed patterns, mosaics, temporary left-over islands, multi-layered directional surfaces, color variegations, water redundancies and lacks, high and low productivity patterns, variegation of shines and rough areas, linear traces and trajectories.

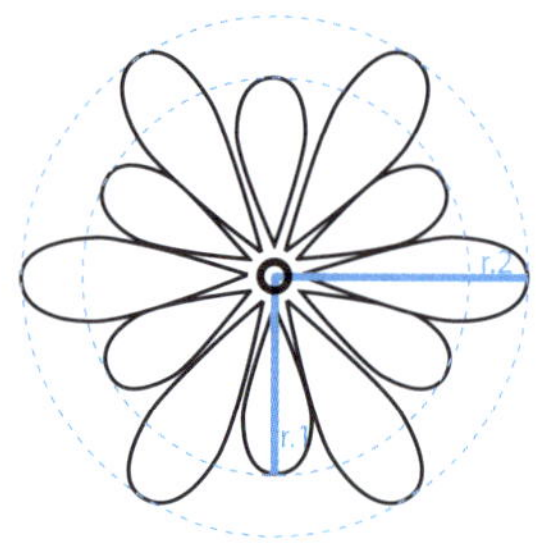

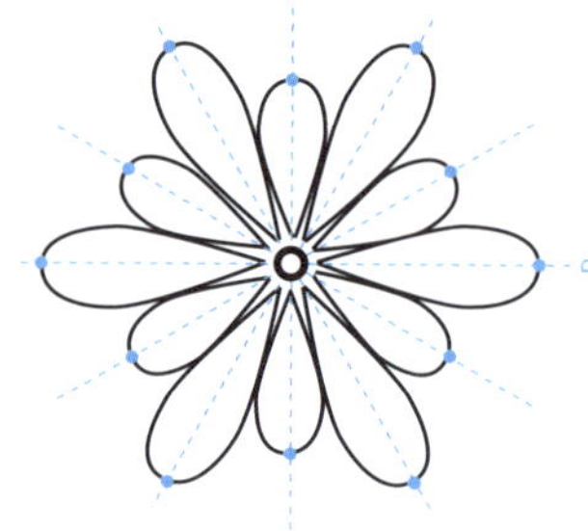

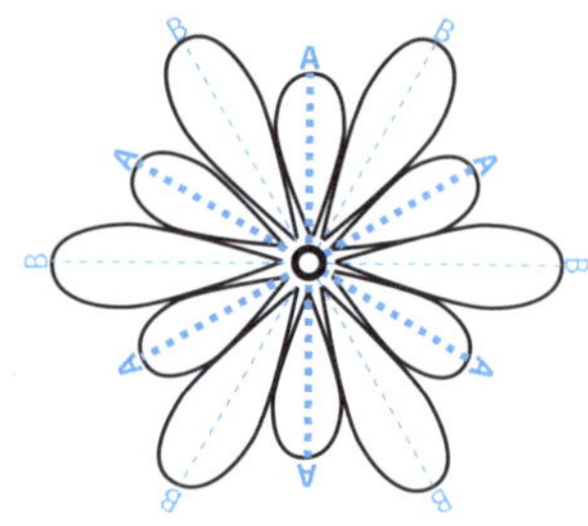

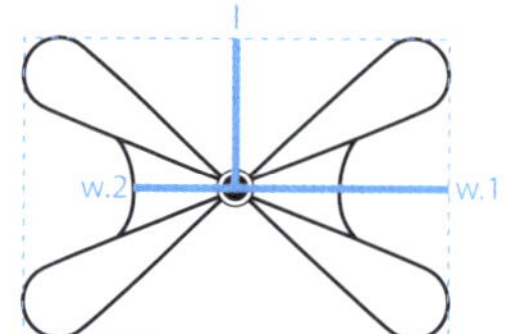

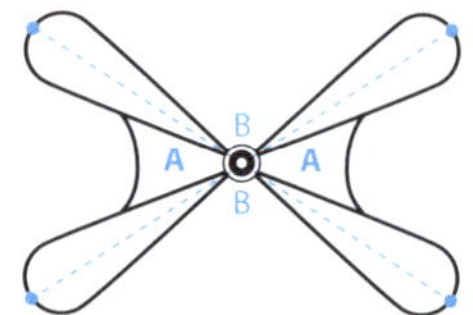

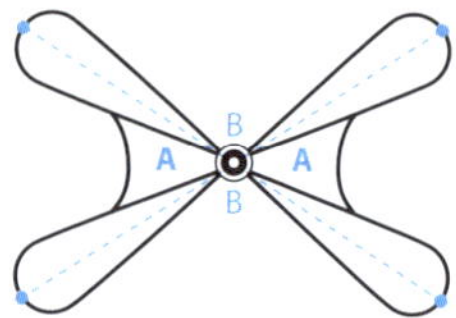

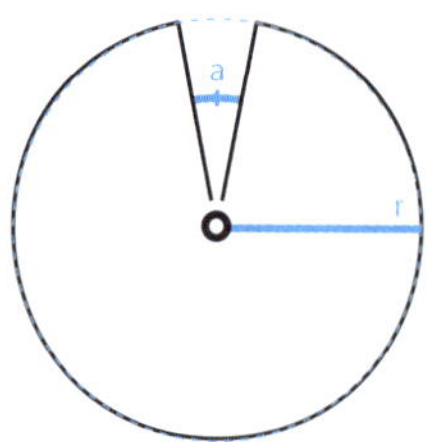

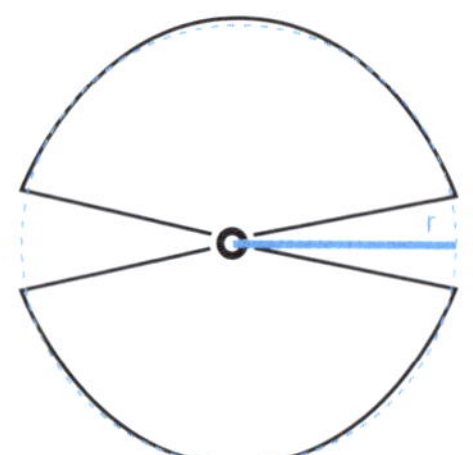

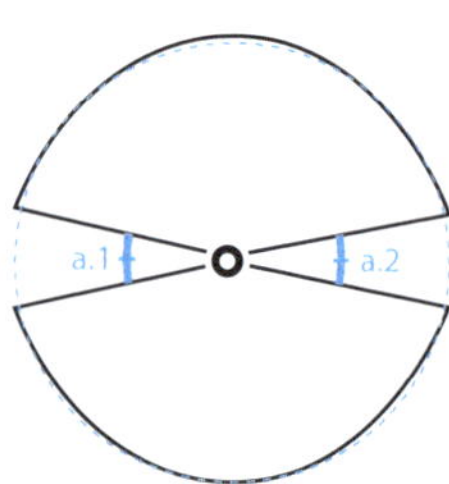

Region: American Midwest
System: Irrigation and Fumigation
Diagram: Sprinkler patterns
Type: Sprinklers
Drawing: Plan
Author: John Sohn

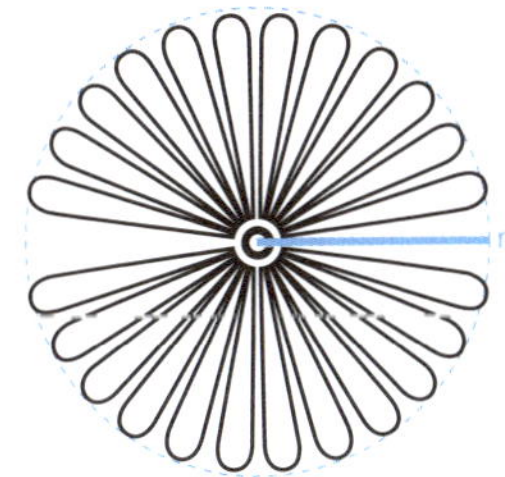

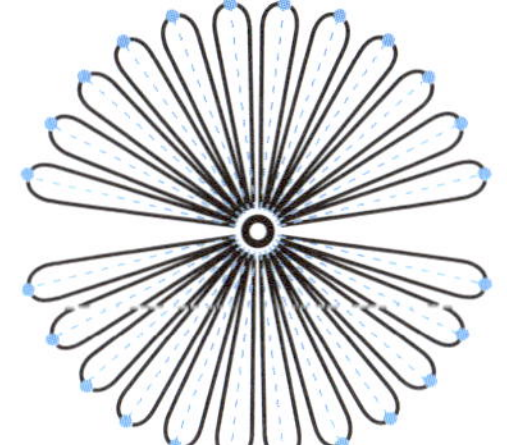
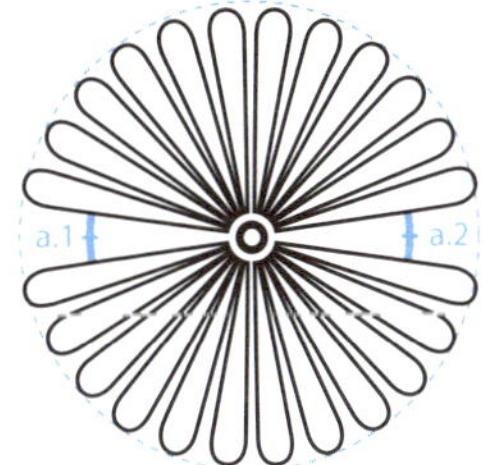

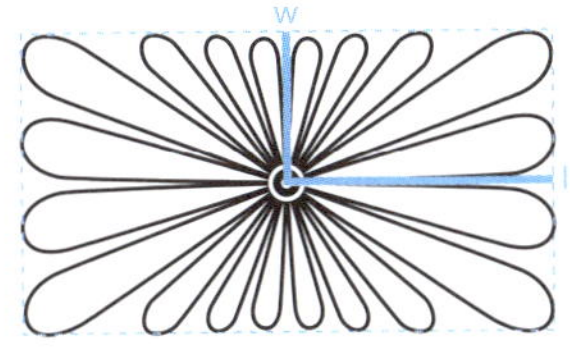

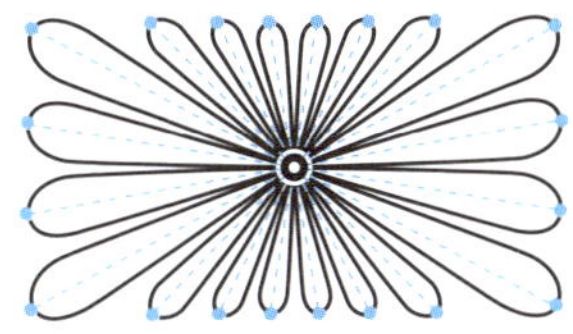
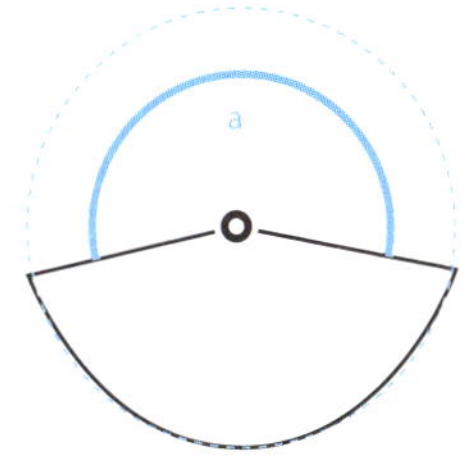

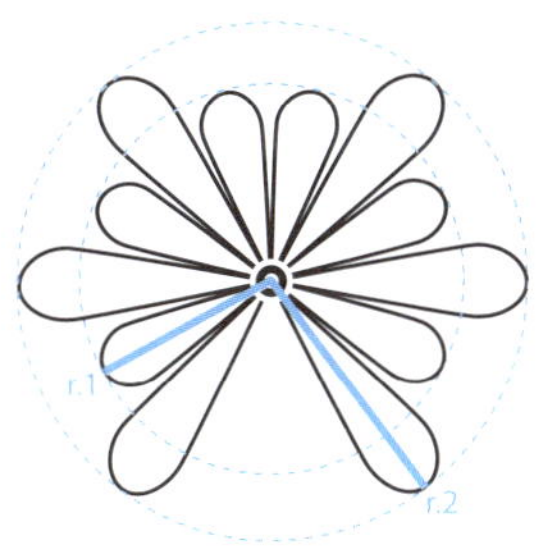

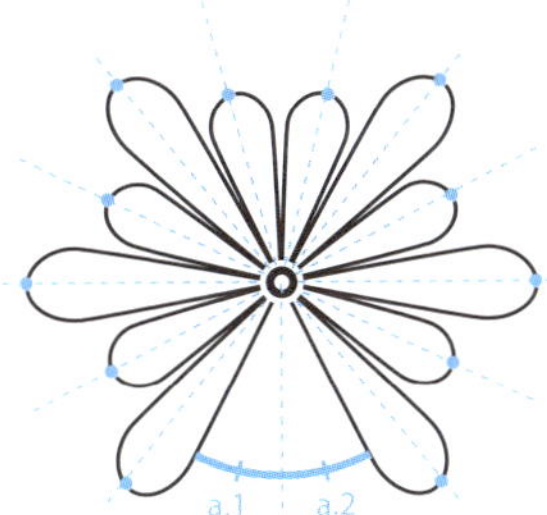

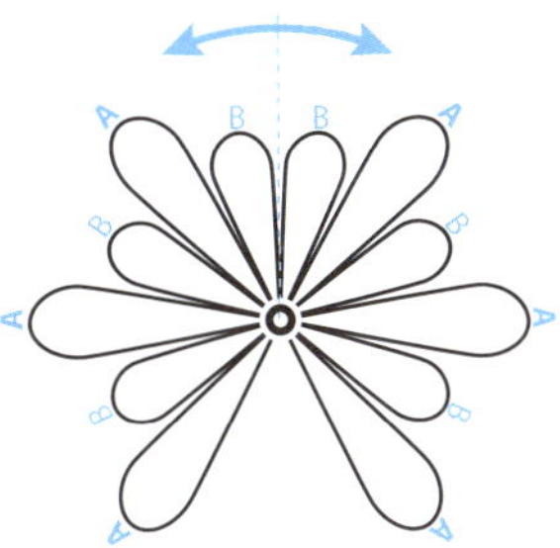

Region: American Midwest
System: Irrigation and Fumigation
Diagram: Sprinkler patterns
Type: Sprinklers
Drawing: Plan
Author: John Sohn

Region: American Midwest
System: Irrigation and Fumigation
Diagram: Irrigation overlap
Type: Sprinklers
Drawing: Plan
Author: John Sohn

Region: American Midwest
System: Irrigation and Fumigation
Diagram: Irrigation overlap
Type: Sprinklers
Drawing: Plan
Author: John Sohn

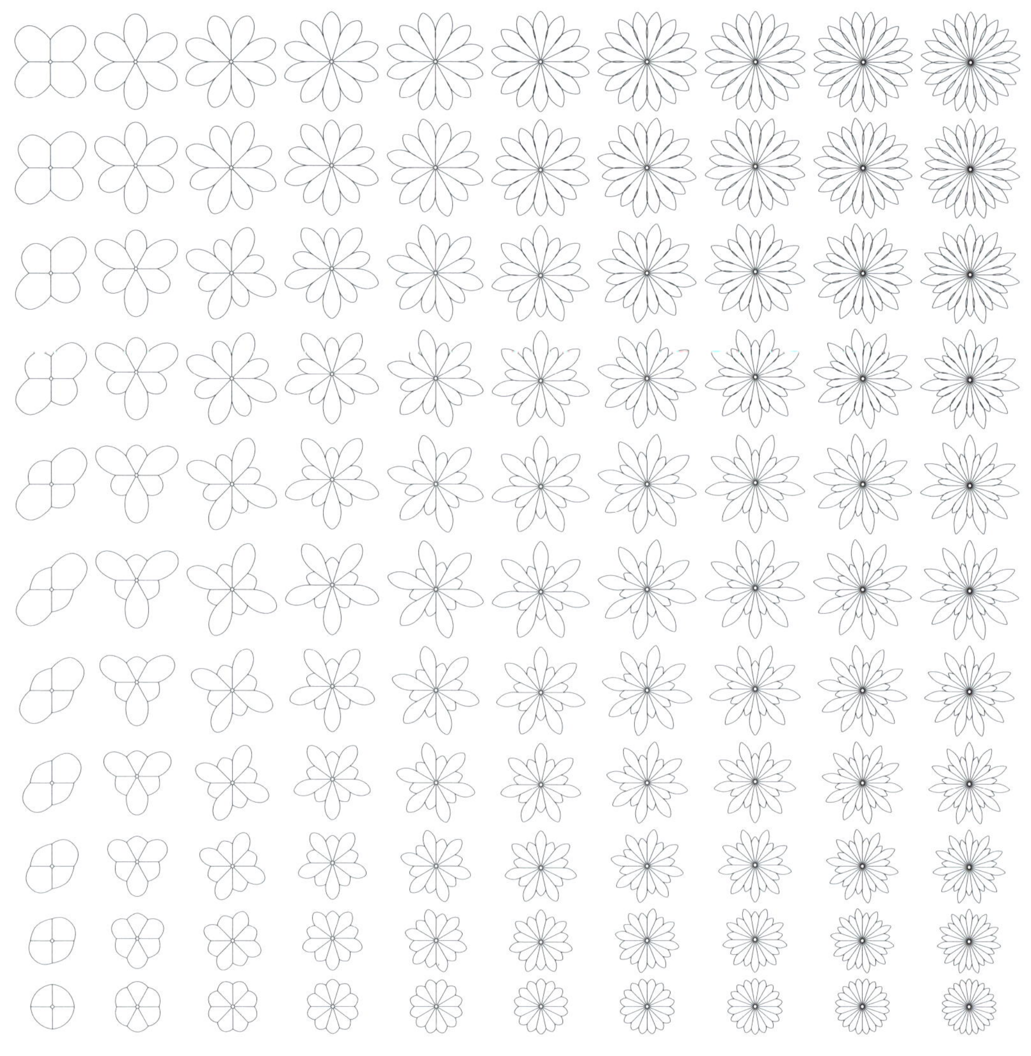

Region: American Midwest
System: Irrigation and Fumigation
Diagram: Spray patterns
Type: Sprays
Drawing: Plan
Author: John Sohn

Region: American Midwest
System: Irrigation and Fumigation
Diagram: Spray patterns
Type: Sprays
Drawing: Plan
Author: John Sohn

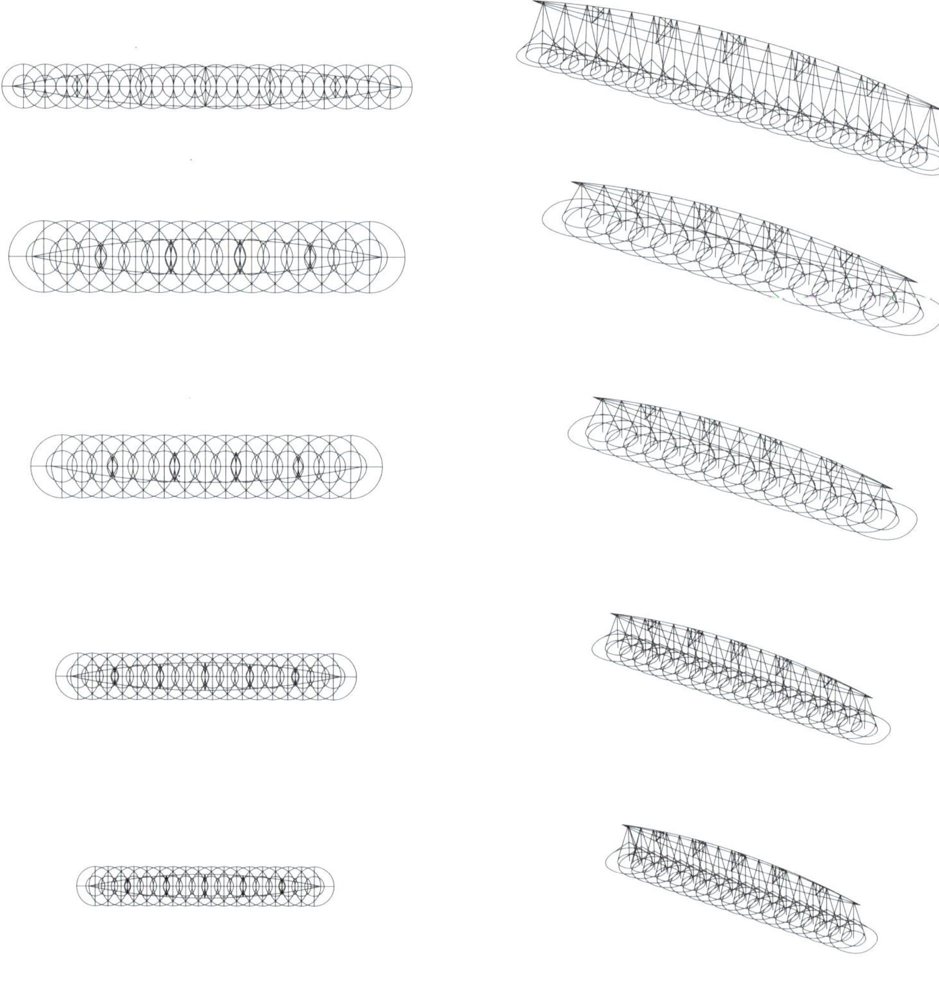

Region: Argentine Pampas
System: Irrigation and Fumigation
Diagram: Variation of irrigation cones
Type: Linear arm and central pivot of irrigation with superimposition of sprinkle patterns of pipeline and gooseneck water provision
Drawing: Plan and axonometric
Author: Julia D'Alotto

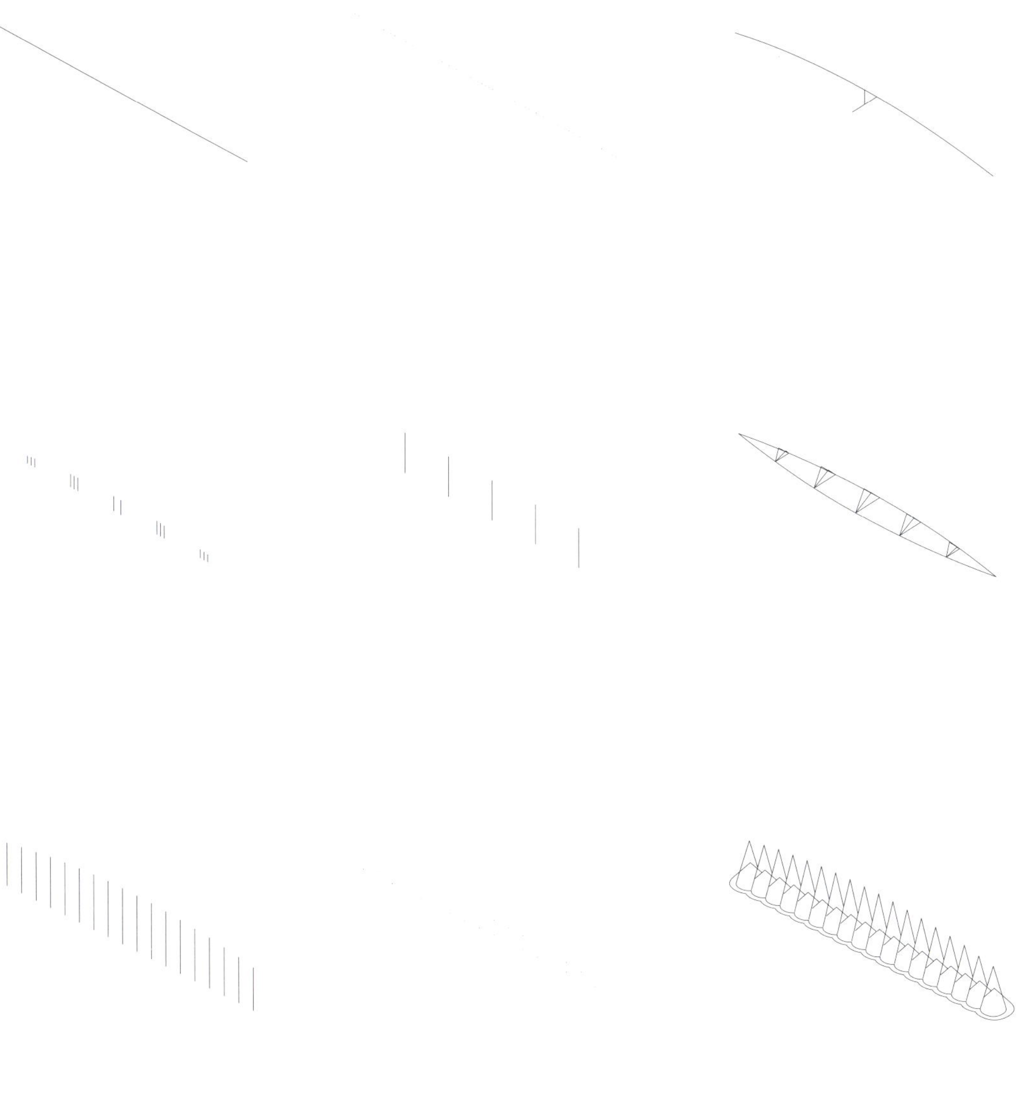

Region: Argentine Pampas
System: Irrigation and Fumigation
Diagram: Irrigation subsystems
Type: Horizontal bars, joints, truss, vertical bars, structural members, goosenecks, spray and sprinkler cones
Drawing: Axonometric
Author: Julia D'Alotto

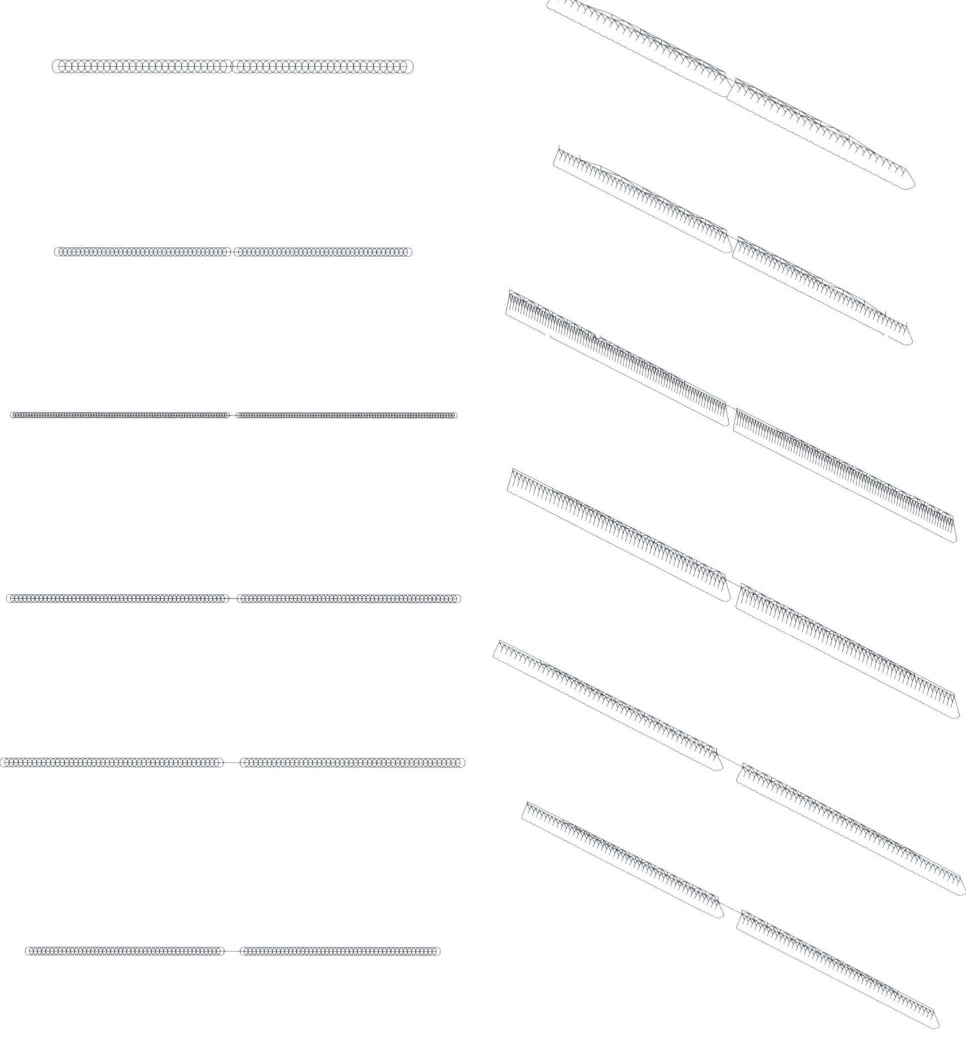

Region: Argentine Pampas
System: Irrigation and Fumigation
Diagram: Variation of irrigation cones
Type: Linear arm of fumigation with superimposition of spray patterns of pipeline and gooseneck water provision
Drawing: Plan and axonometric
Author: Julia D'Alotto

Region: Argentine Pampas
System: Irrigation and Fumigation
Diagram: Fumigation subsystems
Type: Horizontal bars, joints, truss, vertical bars, structural members, goosenecks, spray and sprinkler cones
Drawing: Axonometric
Author: Julia D'Alotto

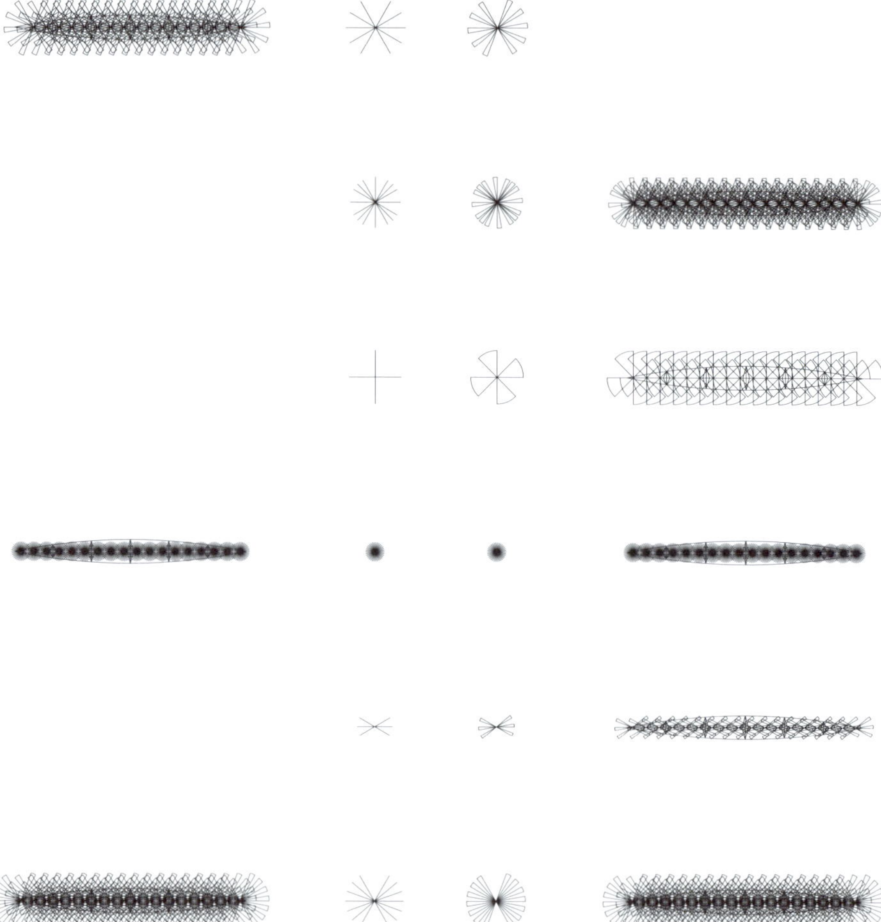

Region: Argentine Pampas
System: Irrigation and Fumigation
Diagram: Variation of sprinkler cones and irrigation patterns
Type: R3000, S3000, N3000, D3000, A3000, T3000 sprays, sprinkle patterns of pipeline and gooseneck water provision
Drawing: Plan and axonometric
Author: Julia D'Alotto

Region: Argentine Pampas
System: Irrigation and Fumigation
Diagram: Variation of sprinkler cones and irrigation patterns
Type: R3000, S3000, N3000, D3000, A3000, T3000 sprays, sprinkle patterns of pipeline and gooseneck water provision
Drawing: Plan and axonometric
Author: Julia D'Alotto

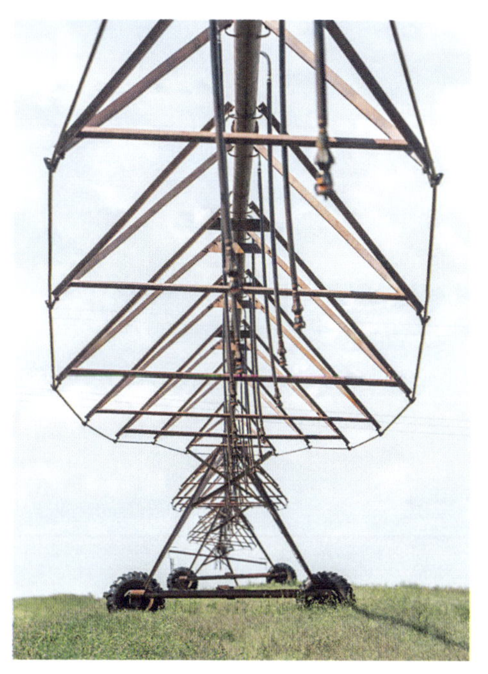

INHABITATION

AMERICAN MIDWEST / ARGENTINE PAMPAS

Clusters of linear and vertical repetitive organizations of units of inhabitation for accommodating people and their immediate goods, everyday supplies, ordinary vehicles, and domesticated animals living and working in the rural world, including housing, vegetation, storage, depots and other facilities.

Model / Polycentric, multilayered, disaggregated clusters of linear repetitions of architectural and natural elements, orthogonal grids of various scales, building singularities, circulations, traces, material accumulations, farms, corrals, provisional enclosures, migrating objects and small constructions.

Operations / Networking, branching, creating nodes, arraying, repeating, aggregating, connecting, splitting, internal networking, changing tree densities, building densities, creating contiguities, delimitating, centralizing, distributing services, defining levels of inhabitation.

Systems / Halls, parlors, porches, hallways, rooms, living rooms, service rooms, corridors, galleries, patios, gardens, roofs, barbecue areas, swimming pools, sport fields, domestic farms, storages, locker rooms, granaries, paths, gates, trees, bushes, pavements, barns, workshops, garages, water mills.

Dynamics / Several processes of activation of local nodes within regional networks, through the provision of infrastructure and access, and the development of equipment and architectural facilities for human settlements, usually directed to the control and management of vast extensions of land.

Performances / Social balance or acceleration, activation or deactivation of production, integration and organization of exchanges between systems, coordination of modes and stages of production, accountability of production, development of new and consolidation of existing lifestyle standards.

Effects / Multi-scalar networks and grids, linear striations, branching structures, clusters, aggregations, overlaps of activities, mosaics of eroded and muddy patches, territorial articulations, local and regional hierarchies, dried-out soils, small-grain patterns of terraces, pools, pitches and service infrastructures.

Region: American Midwest
System: Inhabitation
Diagram: Cases organized according to distances from roads to housing units
Type: Urbanized and non-urbanized areas
Drawing: Plan
Author: Tao Tao

Region: American Midwest
System: Inhabitation
Diagram: Cases organized according to ratios of fenced areas to urbanized areas
Type: Urbanized and non-urbanized areas
Drawing: Plan
Author: Tao Tao

Region: American Midwest
System: Inhabitation
Diagram: Cases organized according to surface areas of non-urbanized areas
Type: Urbanized and non-urbanized areas
Drawing: Plan
Author: Tao Tao

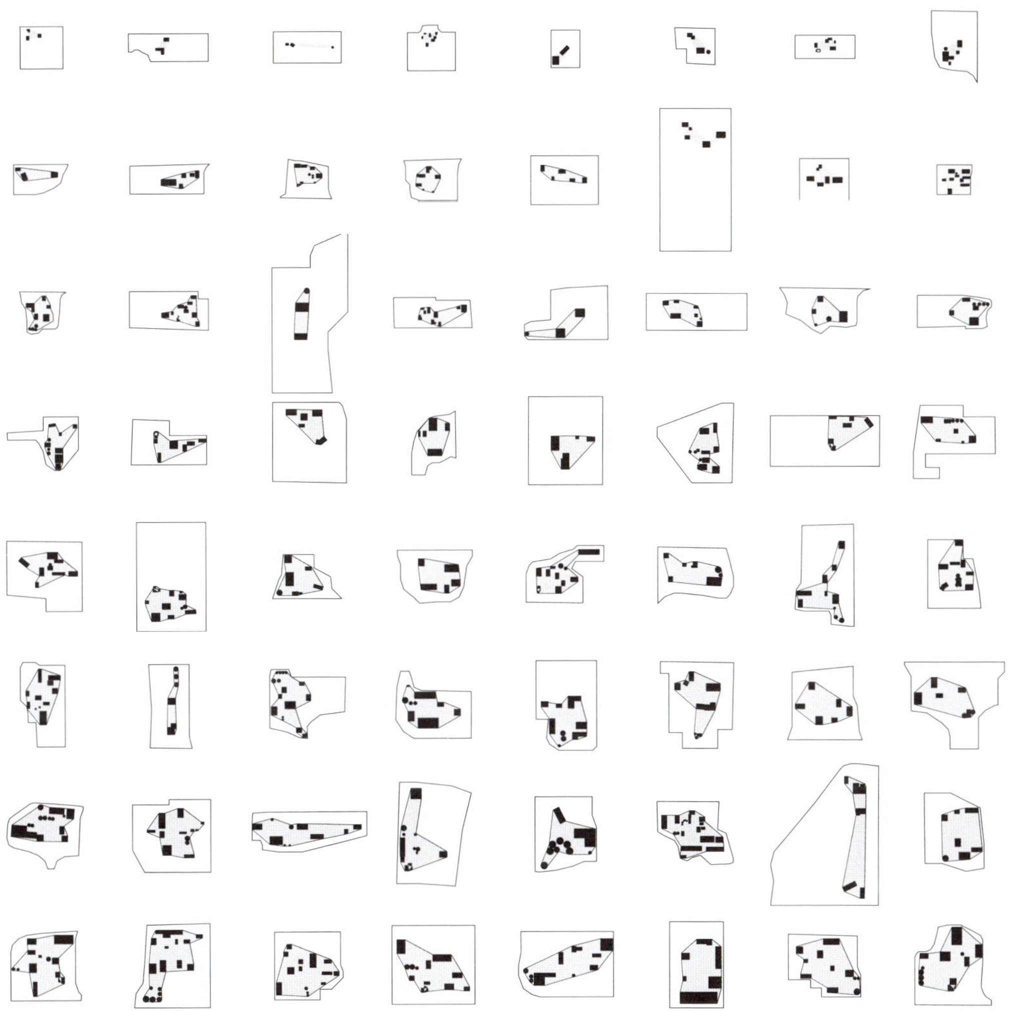

Region: American Midwest
System: Inhabitation
Diagram: Cases organized according to surface areas of urbanized areas
Type: Urbanized and non-urbanized areas
Drawing: Plan
Author: Tao Tao

Region: American Midwest
System: Inhabitation
Diagram: Variations of fenced urbanized areas and levels of connectivity between units
Type: Urbanized and non-urbanized areas
Drawing: Plan
Author: Tao Tao

Region: American Midwest
System: Inhabitation
Diagram: Cases organized according to fencing lengths
Type: Urbanized and non-urbanized areas
Drawing: Plan
Author: Tao Tao

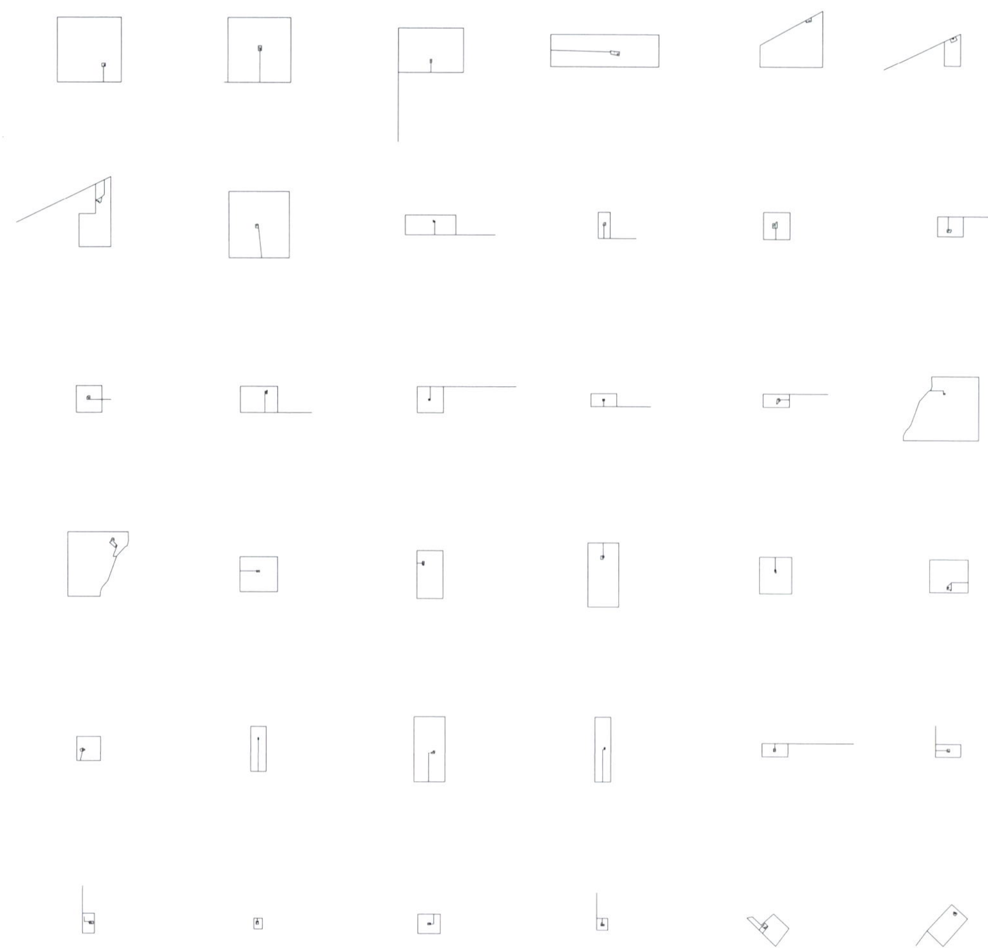

Region: Argentine Pampas
System: Inhabitation
Diagram: Case study survey
Type: Urbanized and non-urbanized areas
Drawing: Plan
Author: Guillermo Aporszegi

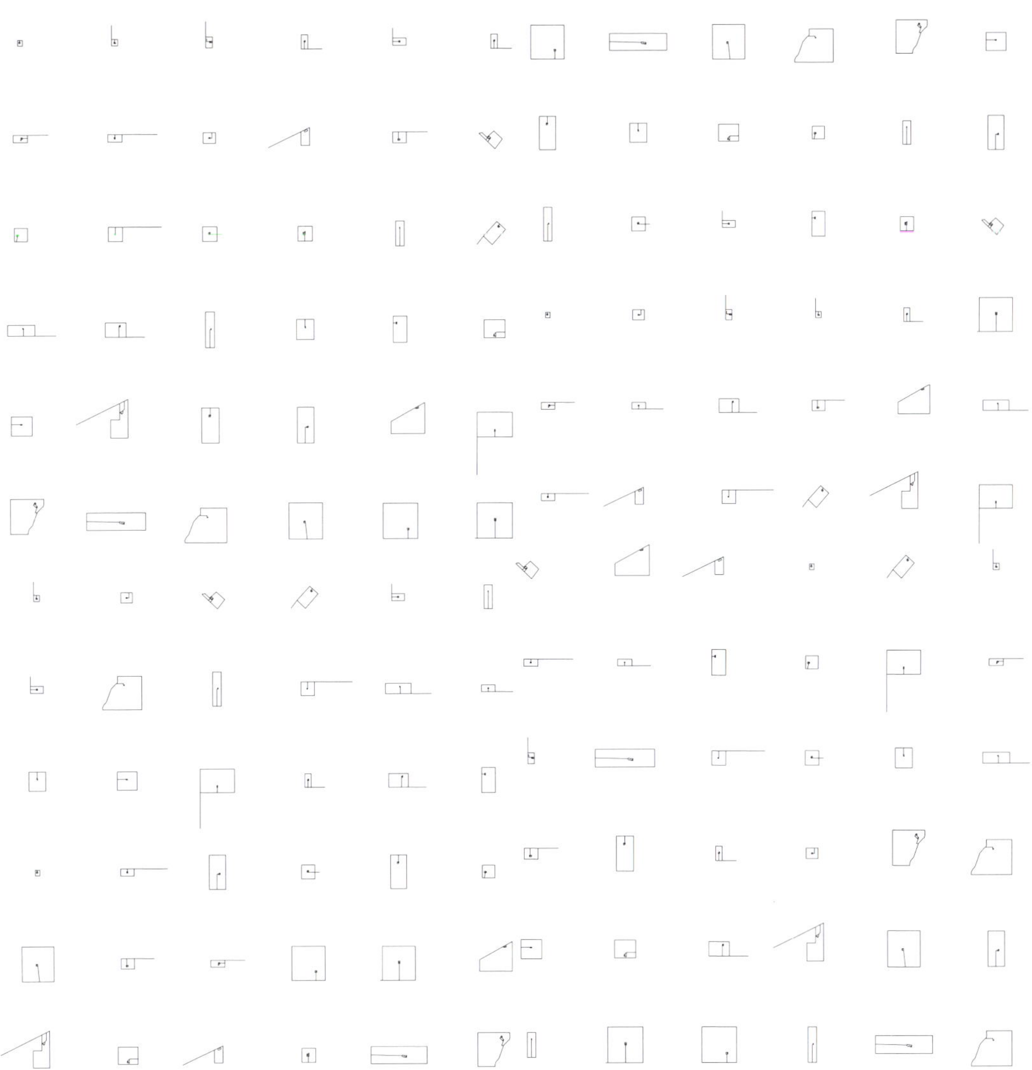

Region: Argentine Pampas
System: Inhabitation
Diagram: Cases organized according to plot dimensions, distance to roads, urbanized area dimensions, distance of access to urbanized area
Type: Urbanized and non-urbanized areas
Drawing: Plan
Author: Guillermo Aporszegi

Region: Argentine Pampas
System: Inhabitation
Diagram: Cases organized according to plot dimensions, distance to roads, urbanized area dimensions, distance of access to urbanized area, subsystems
Type: Urbanized and non-urbanized areas
Drawing: Plan
Author: Guillermo Aporszegi

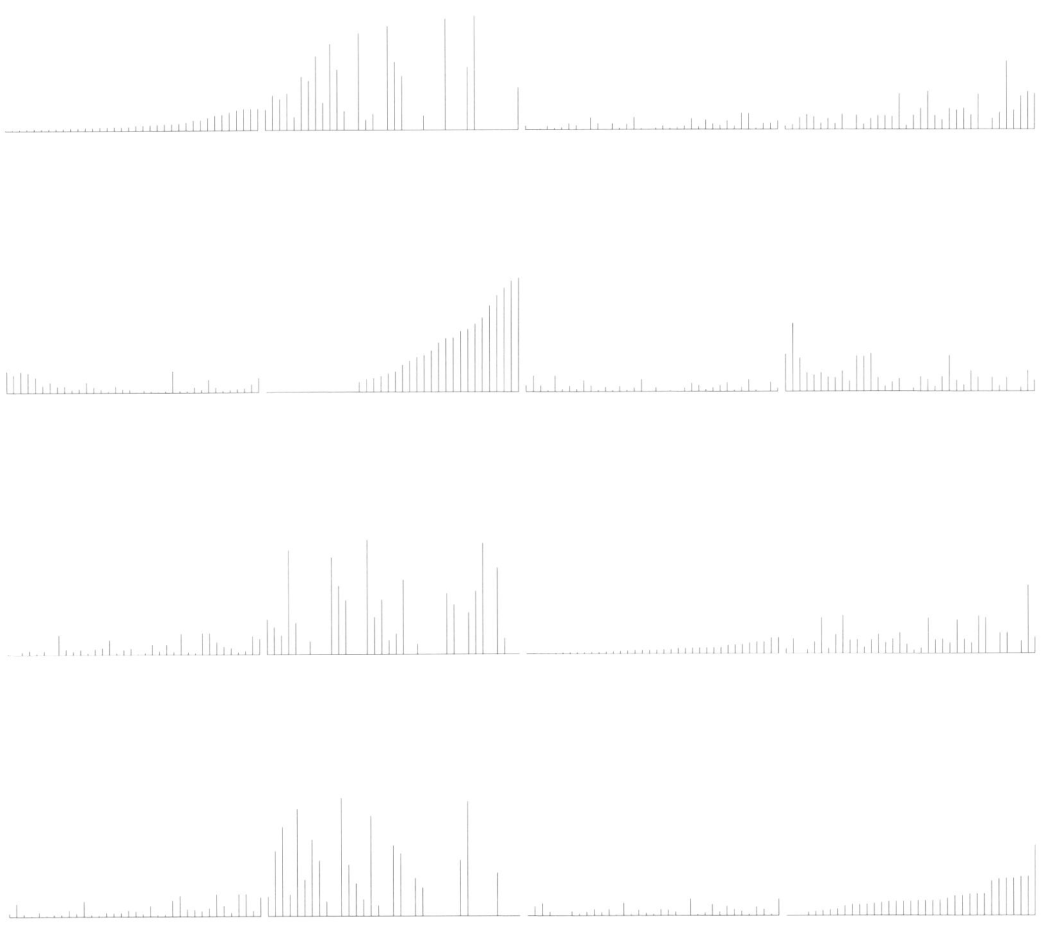

Region: Argentine Pampas
System: Inhabitation
Diagram: Cases organized according to plot dimensions, distance to roads, urbanized area dimensions, distance of access to urbanized area, measurements
Type: Urbanized and non-urbanized areas
Drawing: Chart
Author: Guillermo Aporszegi

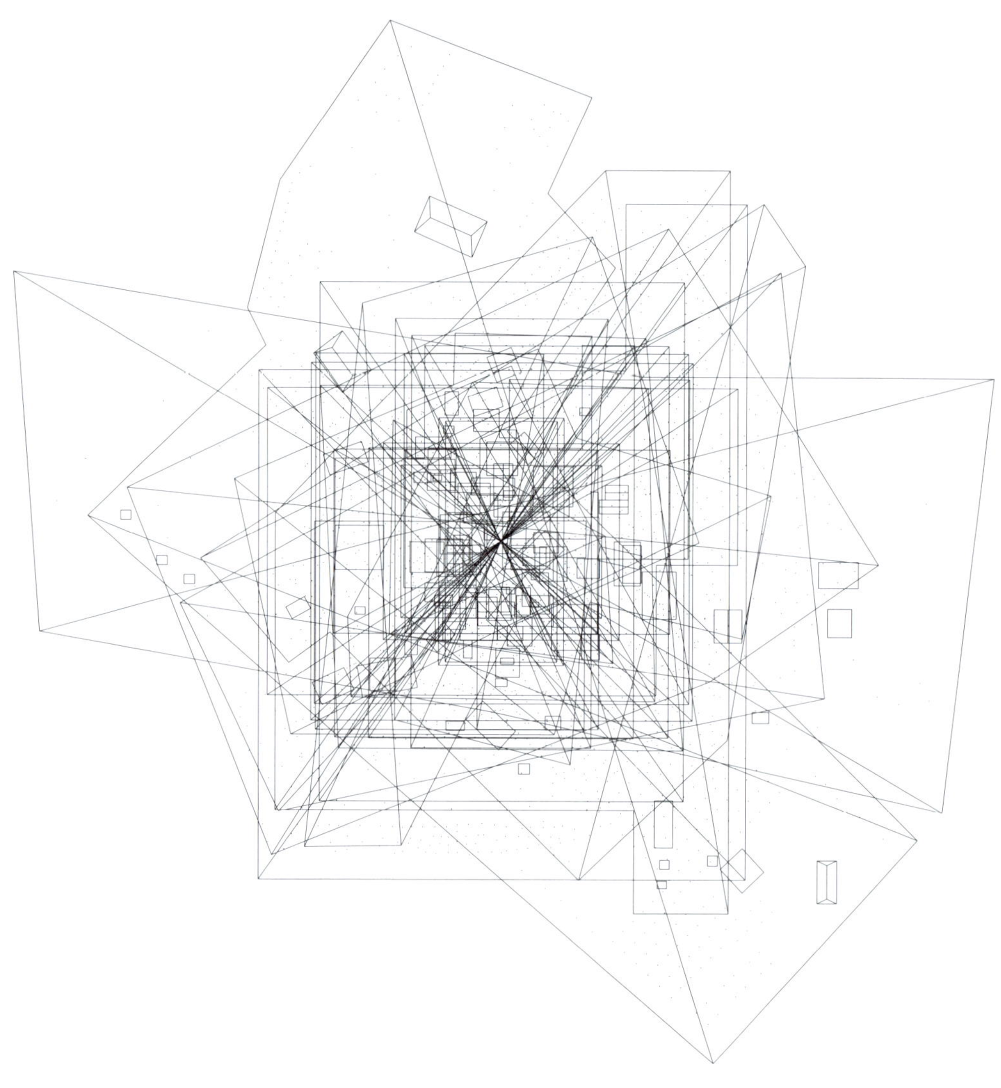

Region: Argentine Pampas
System: Inhabitation
Diagram: Superimposition of cases
Type: Urbanized and non-urbanized areas
Drawing: Plan
Author: Guillermo Aporszegi

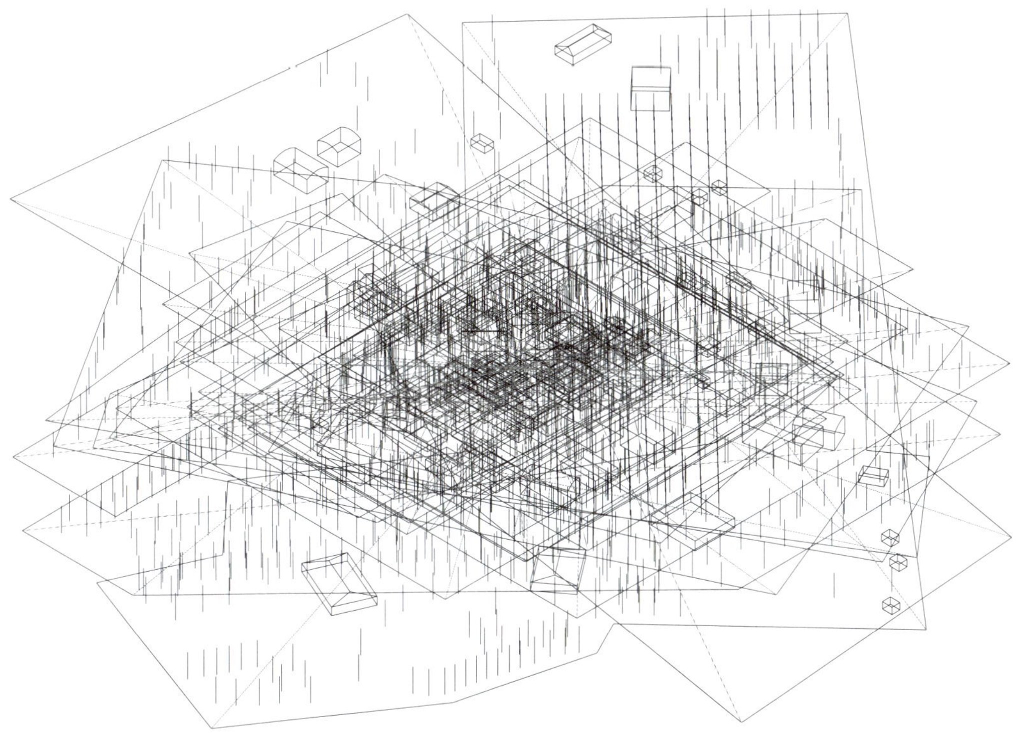

Region: Argentine Pampas
System: Inhabitation
Diagram: Superimposition of cases
Type: Urbanized and non-urbanized areas
Drawing: Axonometric
Author: Guillermo Aporszegi

CATTLE MANAGEMENT

AMERICAN MIDWEST / ARGENTINE PAMPAS

Singular and discrete linear organizations that enable the counting, checking, differentiation and distribution of specimens, and the health management of rural animals for the control of birth and growth, the running of routines of cleaning and vaccination, and the organization of cattle production.

Model / Cattle funneling, queuing, filtering, obstructing, trapping, confining, and management organized along circulatory lines, branches, circular detours, and stoppages, gates and cages for the total or partial mobilization and immobilization of animals and the control of movement of animal parts.

Operations / Funneling, enclosing, cornering, fencing, trapping, sequencing, segregating, nesting, orthogonal, radial, non-regular branching, rotating, turning, partial and total immobilizing, squeezing, visual controlling, distance controlling, quantity controlling, stress managing, ramping up and down.

Systems / Barns, bunks, feedlots, parlors, fences, gates, alleys, catwalks, cages, chutes, head gates, yards, bumpers, buffers, docks, walkways, pens, racks, lifts, ramps, spreaders, pushers, circular pitches, confinements, circulatory platforms, temporary roofs, grades, steps, seats, benches, walks, locks, snares.

Dynamics / Several processes of local and regional management and migration of animals, involving animal surveys and evaluations, health control, birth and growth supervision, reproduction control, feeding balance, segregation, distribution, selection, movement, transportation, slaughtering.

Performances / Increase or reduction of cattle productivity, variable insularity, regularity of changes through animal migration resulting from grass consumption, water availability, soil erosion, segregation or mix of specimens and species, care-taking, health protection, activation of time-based production.

Effects / Multi-scalar patches and grids, linear striations, branching structures, arrays and patchworks, clusters, aggregations, building singularities, funnels and corridors, overlaps of activities, mosaics of eroded and muddy patches, small-grain patterns of enclosures, pitches and service infrastructures.

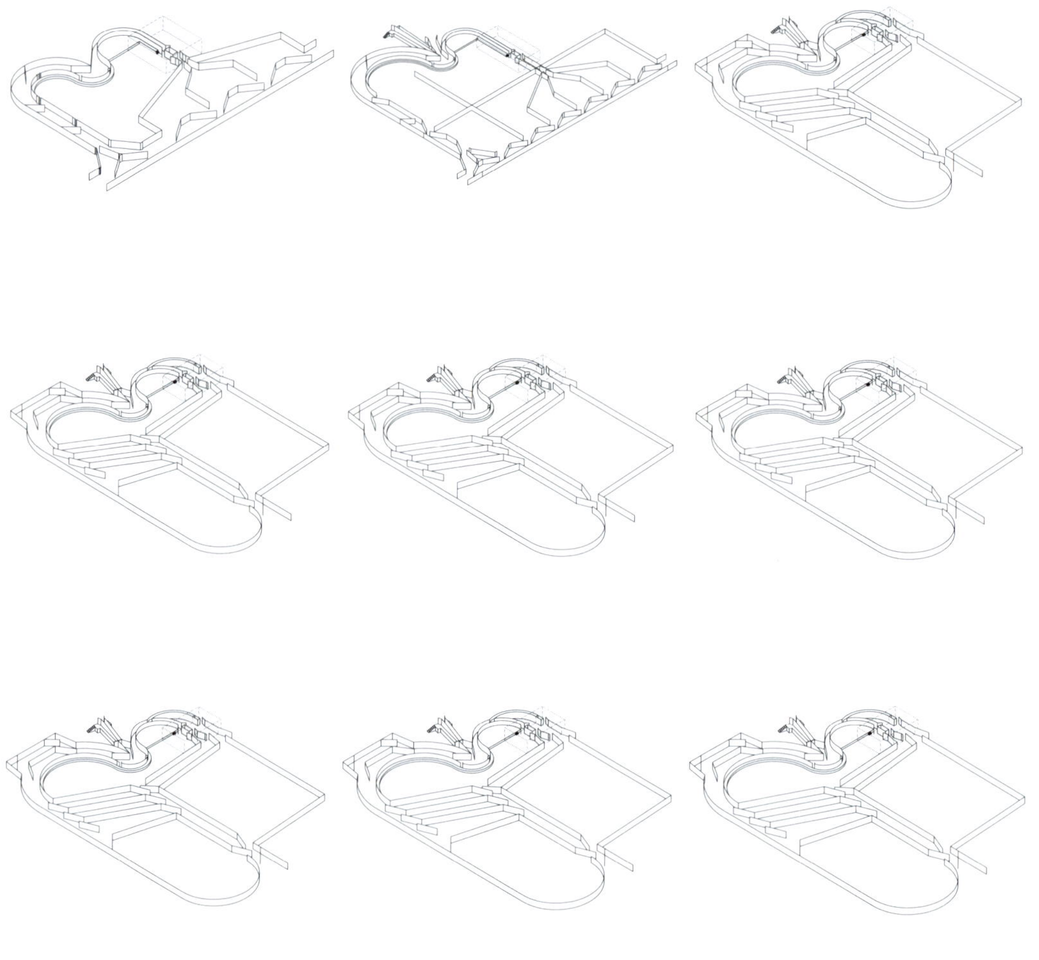

Region: American Midwest
System: Cattle Management
Diagram: Variations of dimensions and complexity
Type: Corral for cows and calves
Drawing: Axonometric
Author: Samuel Tanis

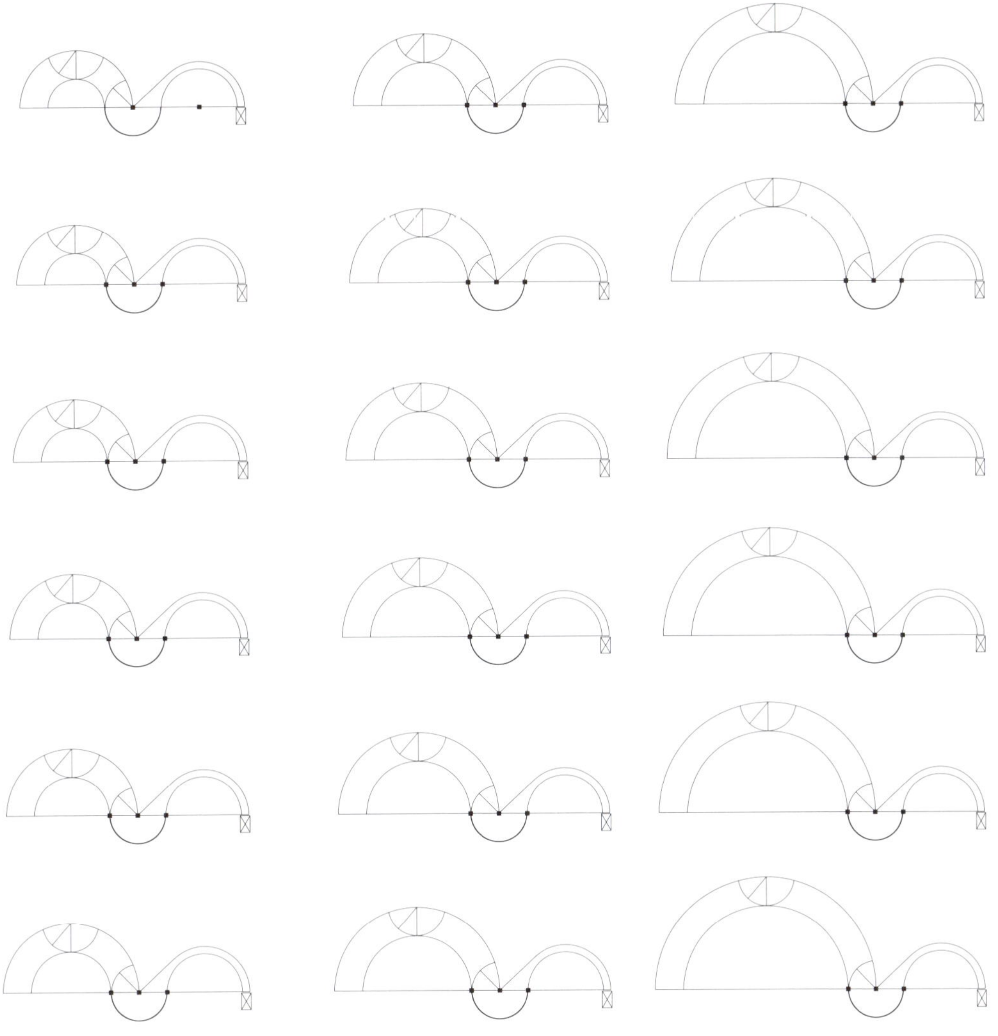

Region: American Midwest
System: Cattle Management
Diagram: Variations of dimensions and complexity
Type: Basic curved corral system
Drawing: Plan
Author: Samuel Tanis

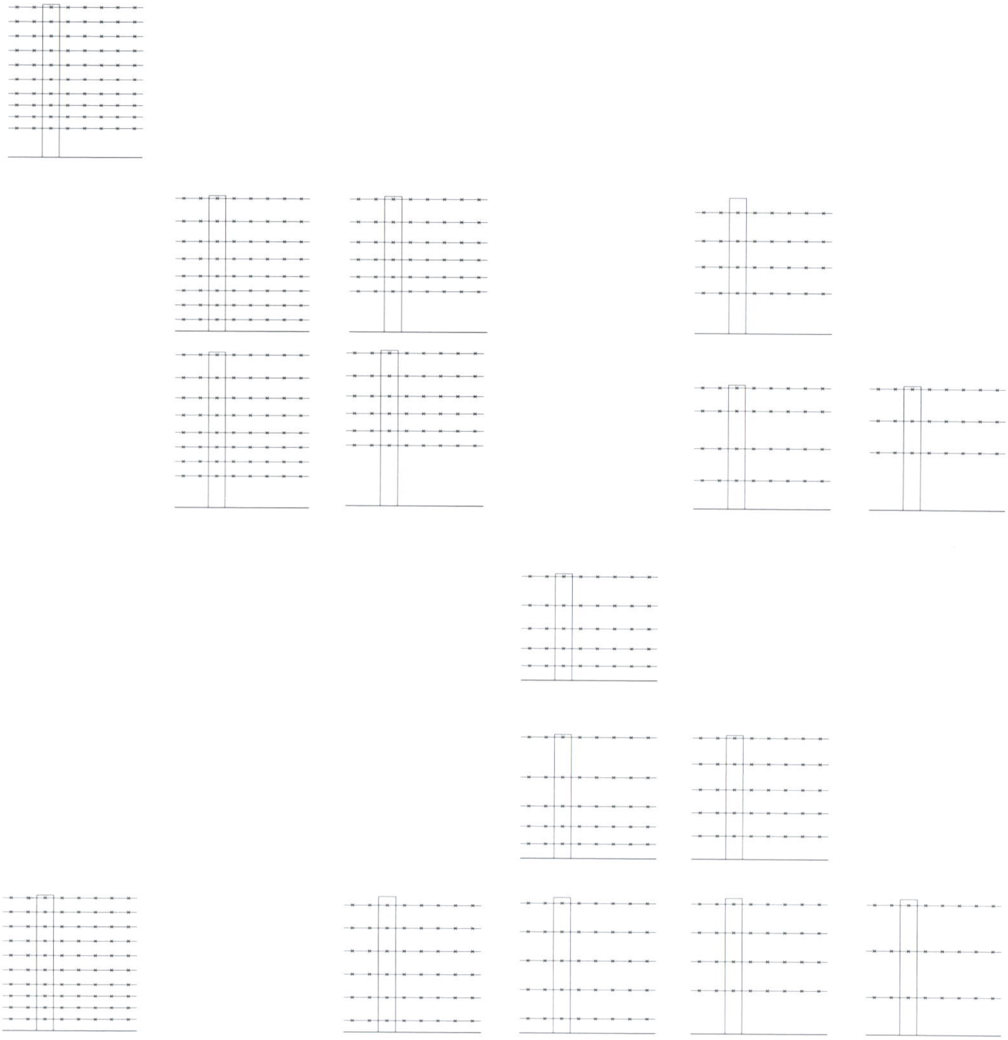

Region: American Midwest
System: Cattle Management
Diagram: Degrees of variability
depending on types of cattle
Diagram: Barbed wire fencing
Drawing: Elevation
Author: Samuel Tanis

Region: American Midwest
System: Cattle Management
Diagram: Degrees of variability depending on types of cattle
Diagram: Smooth wire fencing
Drawing: Elevation
Author: Samuel Tanis

Region: Argentine Pampas
System: Cattle Management
Diagram: Superimposition of variations per type
Type: Cattle, calf, sheep and lamb immobilizing mechanisms, cattle full immobilizing mechanisms, cattle fixed and mobile pens, sheep fixed and mobile pens
Drawing: Elevation
Author: Andrew Pringle

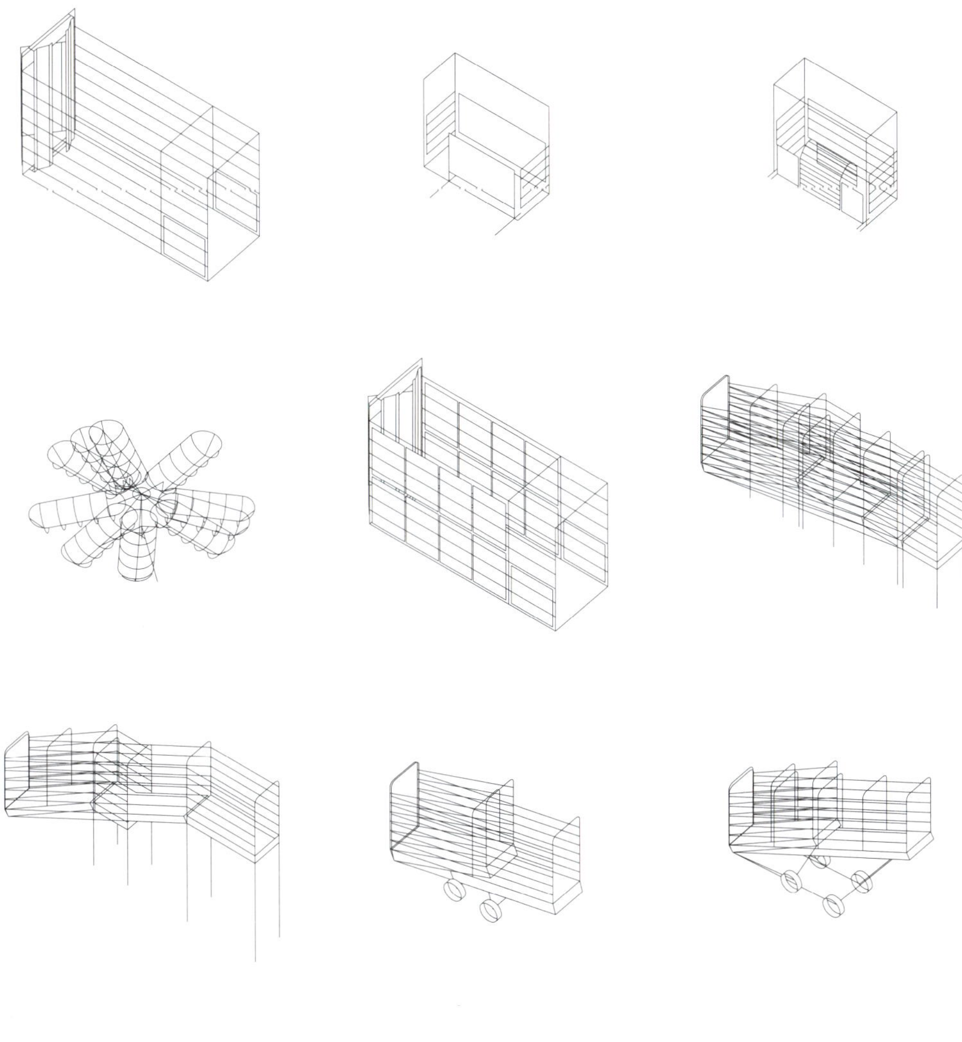

Region: Argentine Pampas
System: Cattle Management
Diagram: Superimposition of variations per type
Type: Cattle, calf, sheep and lamb immobilizing mechanisms, cattle full immobilizing mechanisms, cattle fixed and mobile pens, sheep fixed and mobile pens
Drawing: Axonometric
Author: Andrew Pringle

Region: Argentine Pampas
System: Cattle Management
Diagram: Superimposition of variations per type
Type: Sheep double pens, cattle fixed pens, cattle handling pens of two, three and four exits
Drawing: Elevation
Author: Andrew Pringle

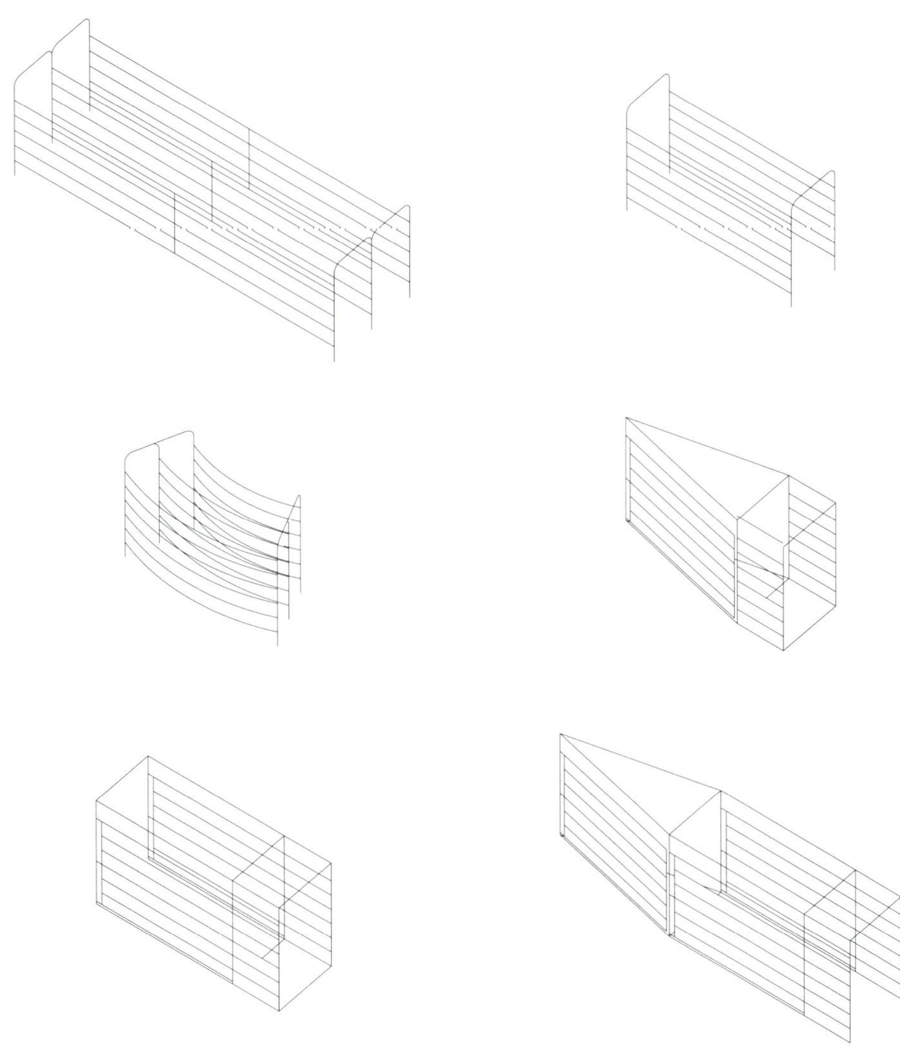

Region: Argentine Pampas
System: Cattle Management
Diagram: Superimposition of variations per type
Type: Double sheep pens, fixed cattle pens, cattle handling pen of two, three and four exits
Drawing: Axonometric
Author: Andrew Pringle

Region: Argentine Pampas
System: Cattle Management
Diagram: Superimposition of variations per type
Type: Horse trailers, cattle corral modules, sheep corral modules, cattle circular handling and sorting, sheep circular handling and sorting
Drawing: Elevation
Author: Andrew Pringle

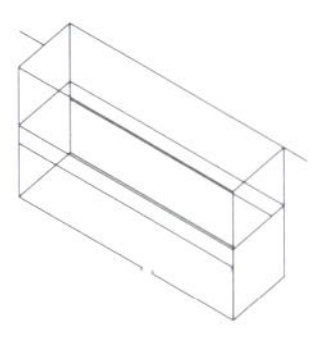
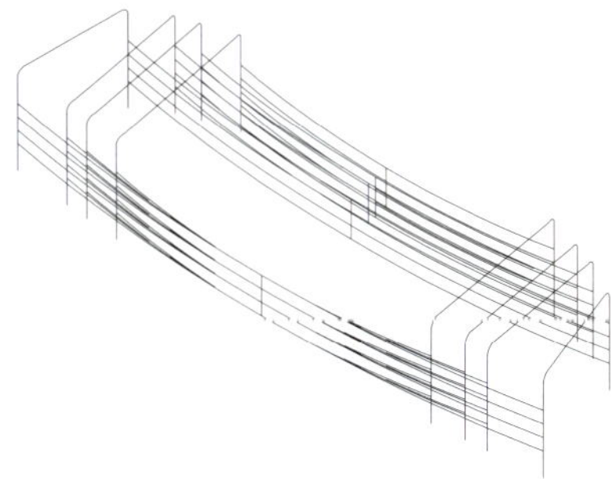
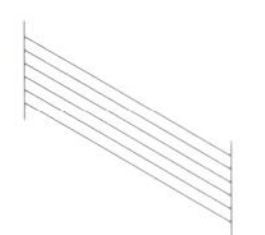
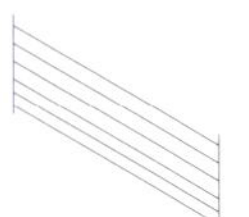
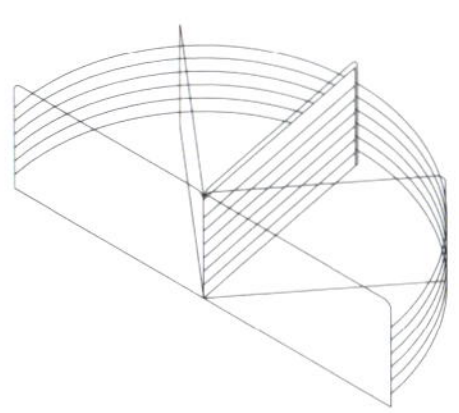
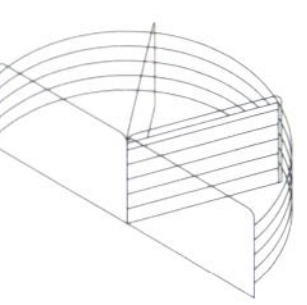

Region: Argentine Pampas
System: Cattle Management
Diagram: Superimposition of variations per type
Type: Horse trailers, cattle corral modules, sheep corral modules, cattle circular handling and sorting, sheep circular handling and sorting
Drawing: Axonometric
Author: Andrew Pringle

SOCIALIZATION

AMERICAN MIDWEST / ARGENTINE PAMPAS

Clusters of centralized, repetitive and singular open-air and interior organizations of multiple scales of human socialization that accommodate people, goods, supplies, vehicles, machines and animals in short term events, including markets, exhibitions, ferias, rodeos, festivals, and sport fields and facilities.

Model / Concentric organizations around arenas, polycentric sets of open-air fields, distributed clusters of market stalls, linear repetitions of ephemeral displays and informal structures, kiosks, orthogonal grids of corrals, casual circulations, provisional enclosures, migrating objects and small constructions.

Operations / Networking, branching, creating nodes, arraying, repeating, aggregating, connecting, segregating animal and human territories, creating contiguities, demarcating domains, distributing rentable space, services, equipment, circulation, parking, internal networking, varying tree densities.

Systems / Pole tents, arenas, pitches, sport fields, circulatory corridors, circulatory platforms, temporary roofs, grades, steps, seats, benches, tables, walks, lifts, ramps, billboards, charts, maps, signage, stalls, kiosks, displays, chutes, gates, panels, schedules, vehicles, trucks, motorhomes, portable corrals, boxes.

Dynamics / Several processes of activation of local nodes and regional networks through the instigation of people exchange, goods exchange, social gathering and temporary occupation, usually by means or accompanied by social settings, entertainments, attractions, commercial activities and sport events.

Performances / Social exposure and interaction, exchange and consumption, entertainment and celebration, playful exchange between systems, enhancement of industrialization, automatization, and accountability of production, development of new and consolidation of existing lifestyle standards.

Effects / Multi-scalar networks and grids, linear striations, branching structures, arrays and patchworks, clusters, aggregations, building singularities, overlaps of activities, parking surfaces, mosaics of eroded and muddy patches, small-grain patterns of terraces, enclosures, pitches and service infrastructures.

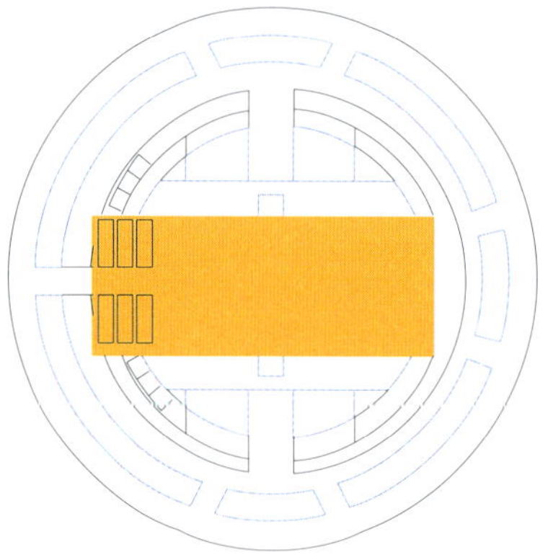

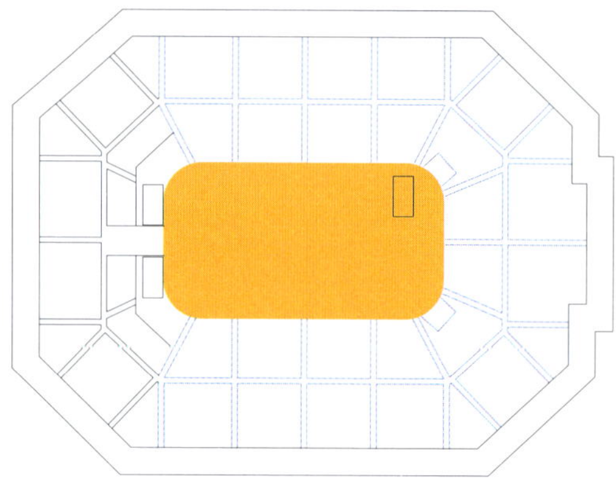

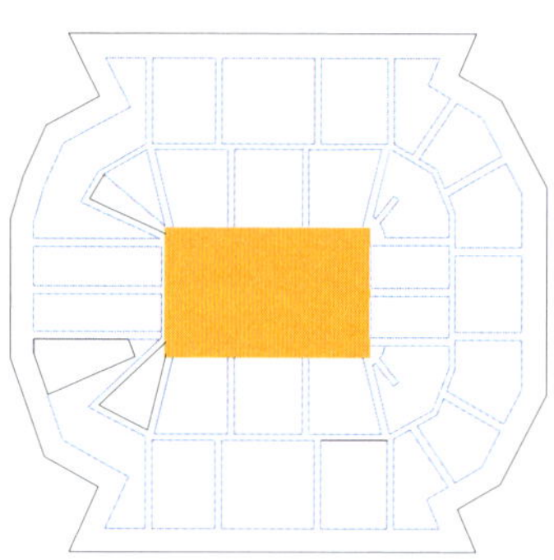

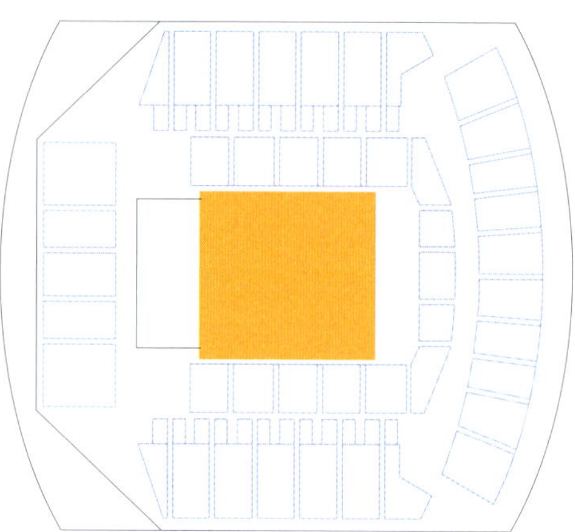

Region: American Midwest
System: Socialization
Diagram: Case study survey
Type: Rodeos, Alliant Energy Center-Coliseum, Madison (Wisconsin), Allstate Arena, Rosemont (Illinois), Bismarck Civic Center, Bismarck (North Dakota), JQH Arena, Springfield (Missouri)
Drawing: Plan
Author: Taylor Holloway

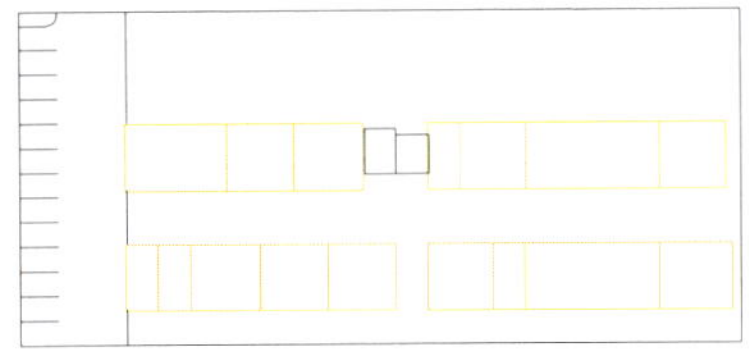

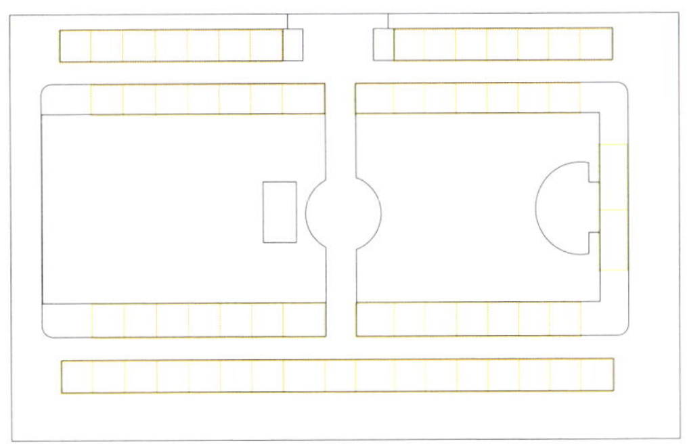

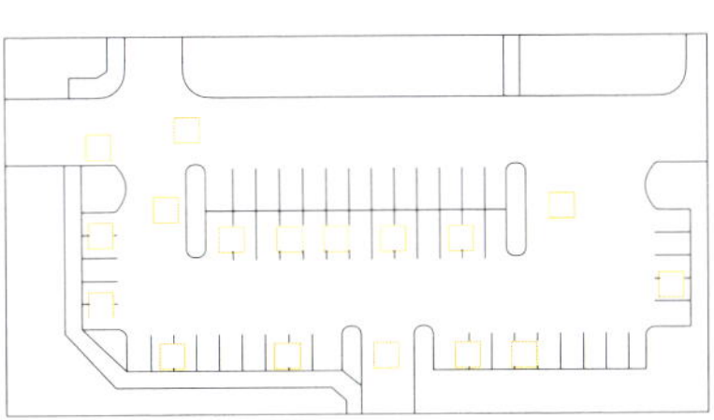

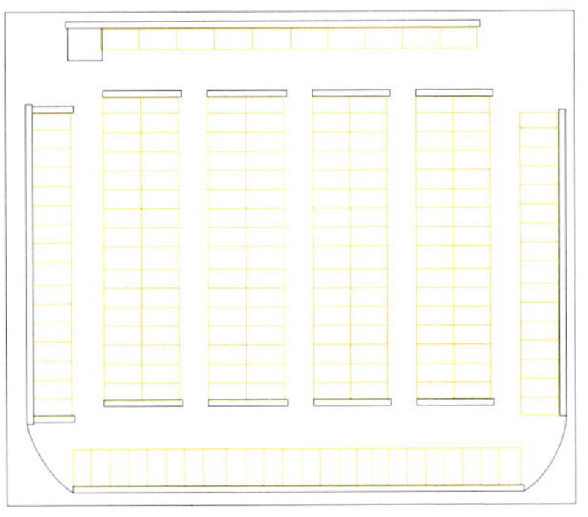

Region: American Midwest
System: Socialization
Diagram: Case study survey
Type: Farmer markets vendor booths: Bettendorf (Iowa), Carmel (Indiana), Urbana (Illinois), Schaumburg (Illinois)
Drawing: Plan
Author: Taylor Holloway

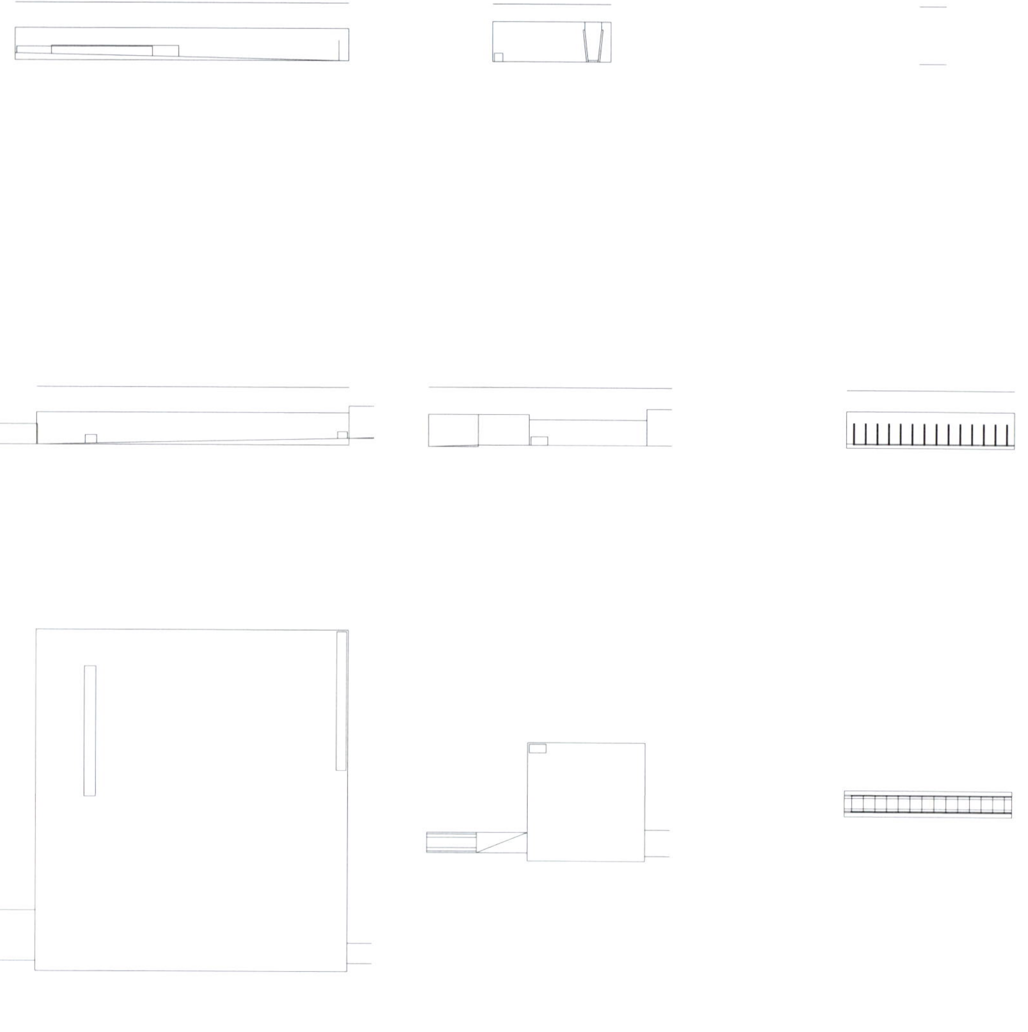

Region: Argentine Pampas
System:Socialization
Diagram: Case study survey
Type: Slaughterhouse, arrival corral, observation and clamping corral, bathing
Drawing: Plan, elevation
Author: Rosario Vaquer Melo

Region: Argentine Pampas
System: Socialization
Diagram: Case study survey
Type: Slaughterhouse, septic area, intermediate area, clean area
Drawing: Plan, elevation
Author: Rosario Vaquer Melo

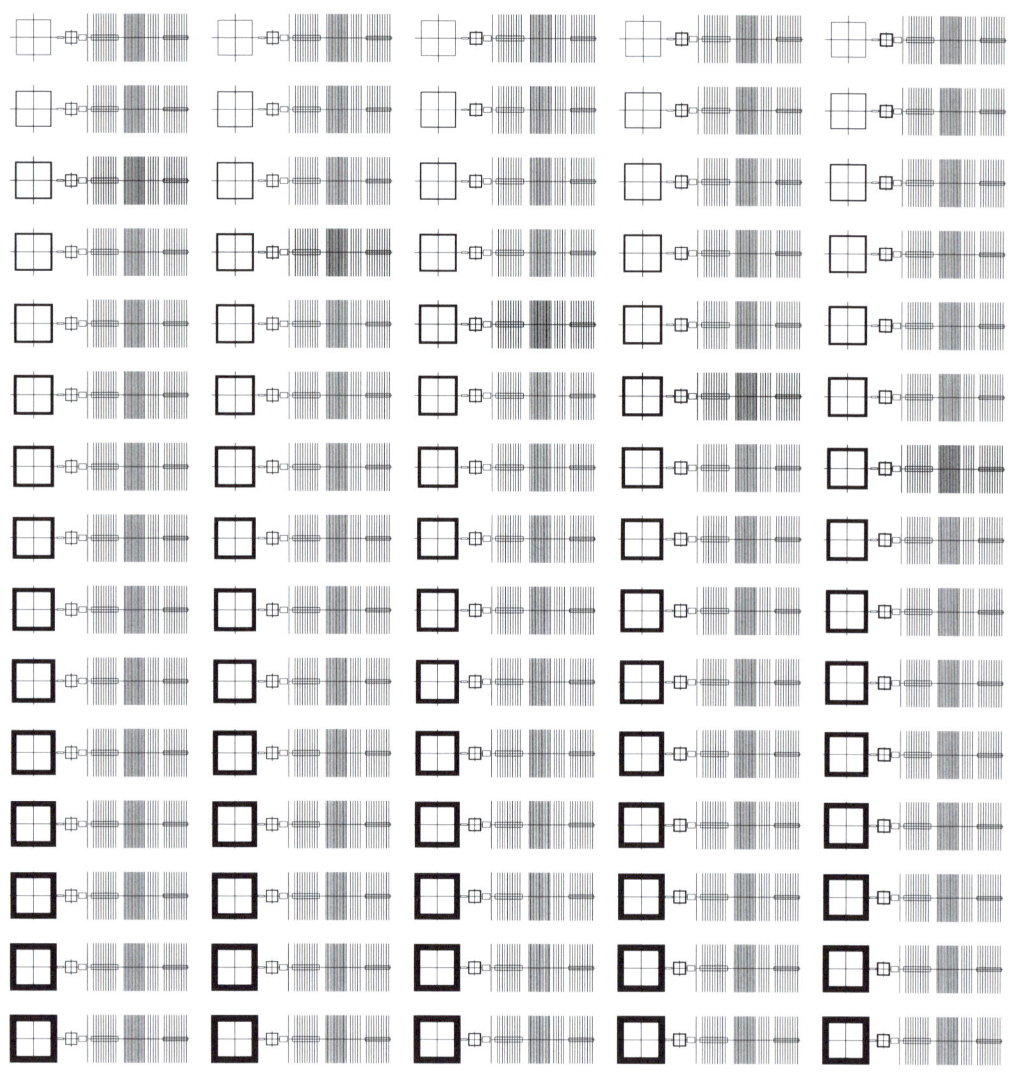

Region: Argentine Pampas
System: Socialization
Diagram: Superimposition of variations
Type: Slaughterhouse, cases organized according to type and amount of animals
Drawing: Plan
Author: Rosario Vaquer Melo

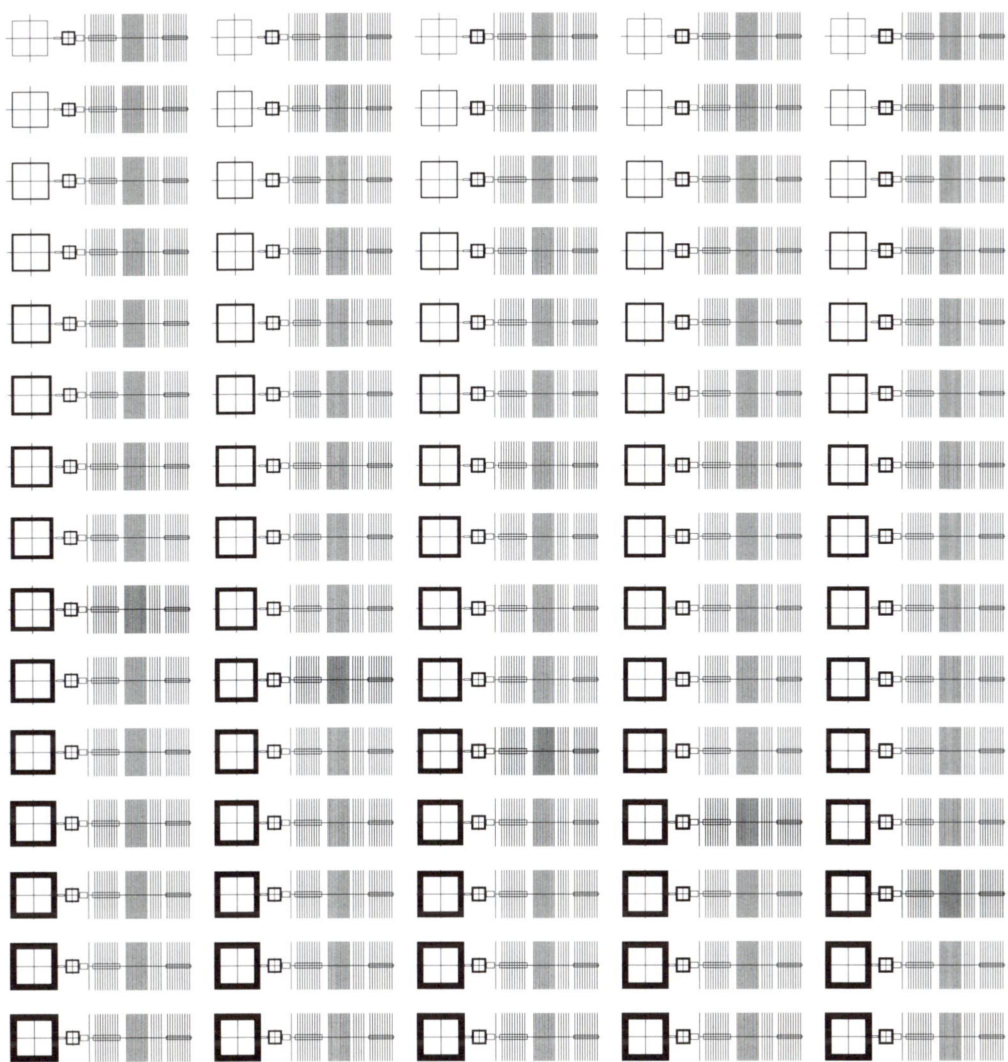

Region: Argentine Pampas
System: Socialization
Diagram: Superimposition of variations
Type: Slaughterhouse, cases organized according to type and amount of animals
Drawing: Plan
Author: Rosario Vaquer Melo

LUMBER CO.

77TH DAYTON CHAMPIONSHI
WOODRUFF
ELECTRIC
POET
CALL TODAY FOR ALL YOUR
CORN MARKETING NEEDS
NEW
COOPERATIVE INC.
Sparky
one stop

3
4
5
6

STORAGE

AMERICAN MIDWEST / ARGENTINE PAMPAS

Clusters of singular and discrete or repetitive open-air and interior organizations for accumulating, regulating and storing goods, supplies, vehicles, machines, harvests, animals, and products to be employed, consumed, or commercialized across seasons, stages of production and market fluctuations.

Model / Long-span and extra-large spatial continuums, enclosed cylindrical, spherical, conic volumes, horizontally repetitive structures, blank buildings, extended roofs, extruded envelopes and flexible fabrics, connected to each other through tubes, buckets, bags, carriages, carts, trucks and wagons.

Operations / Networking, branching, creating nodes, arraying, repeating, connecting, internal networking, building densities, parking extension, circulatory bundling, creating contiguities, segregating, elevating, delimitating domains, distributing installations, defining accessibilities.

Systems / Barns, bunkers, silos, silo-bags, bags, containers, cages, crates, gins, hoppers, dryers, staves, cranes, conveyors, tanks, trucks, carriages, carts, platforms, tubes, ducts, buckets, stacks, heaps, ladders, elevators, grain elevators, long-span sheds, shelters, embankments, parking and maneuvering areas.

Dynamics / Several processes of regulation, synchronization and control of production, handling, treating, exchange, transportation and consumption through the storing of raw and semi-raw materials, the protection and drying of grains, and the management of by-products for prescribed periods of time.

Performances / Regulation of flows between fields with different levels of stability, regularity of changes through collection, harvest, storage, handling, processing, redistribution, sale, consumption and profit balance, management of seasonal productivity, activation and deactivation of exchanges of goods.

Effects / Multi-scalar patches and grids, linear striations, branching structures, arrays and patchworks, clusters, aggregations, building singularities, overlaps of activities, hard surfaces, mosaics of eroded and muddy patches, small-grain patterns of enclosures, pitches and service infrastructures.

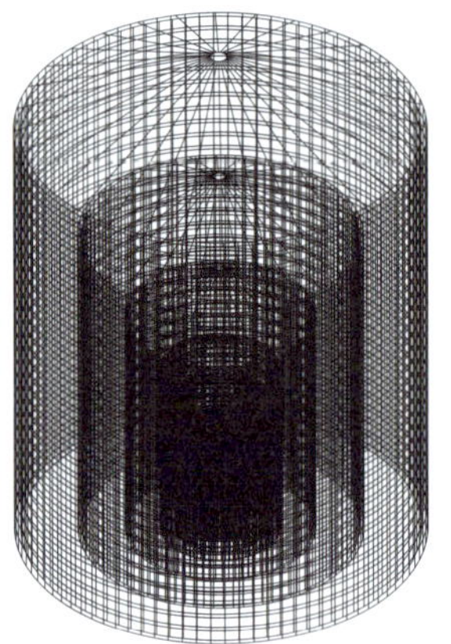

Region: Argentine Pampas
System: Storage
Diagram: Variability by superimposition of variations
Type: On site concrete silo
Drawing: Axonometric
Author: Tomás Rowinski

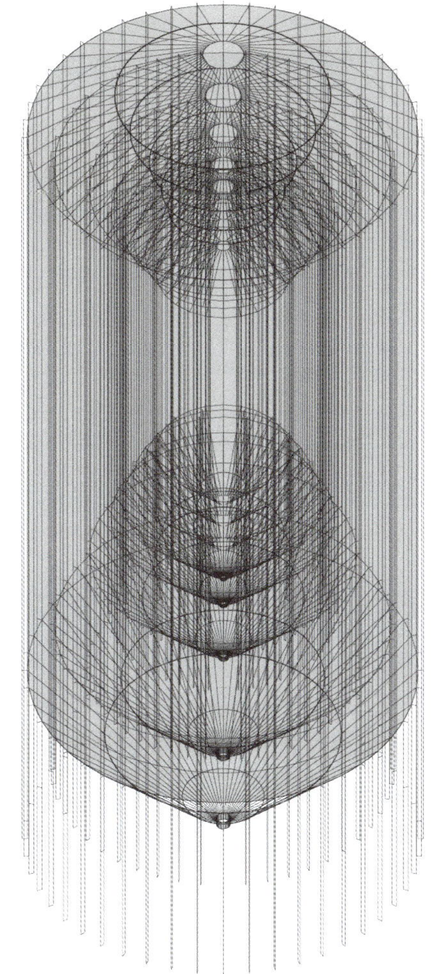

Region: Argentine Pampas
System: Storage
Diagram: Variability by superimposition of variations
Type: Metal silo, aerial
Drawing: Axonometric
Author: Tomás Rowinski

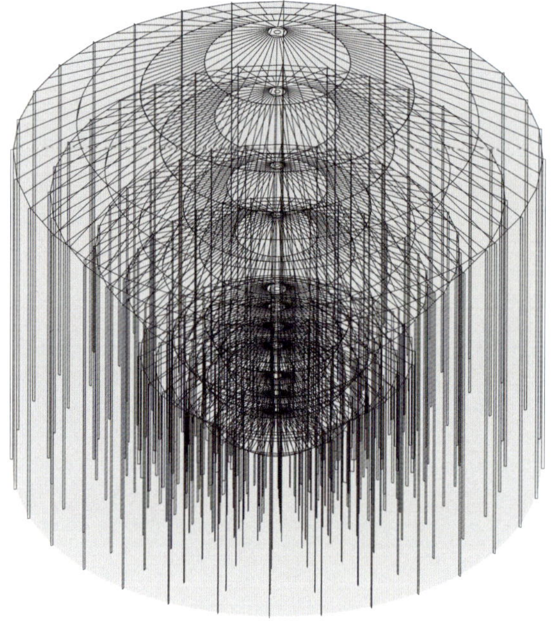

Region: Argentine Pampas
System: Storage
Diagram: Variability by superimposition of variations
Type: Metal silo, fixed
Drawing: Axonometric
Author: Tomás Rowinski

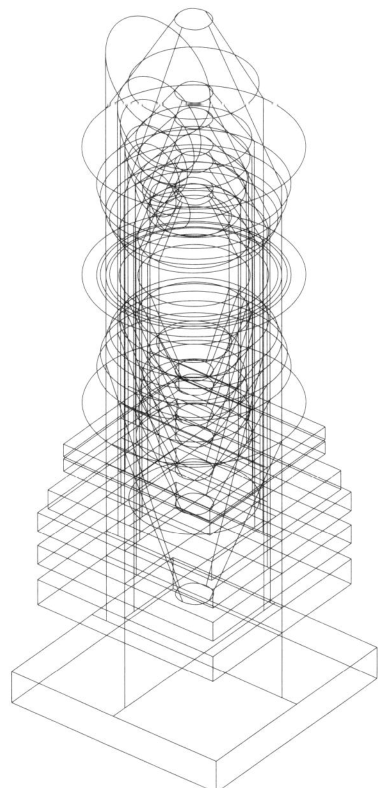

Region: Argentine Pampas
System: Storage
Diagram: Variability by superimposition of variations
Type: Fiberglass silo
Drawing: Axonometric
Author: Tomás Rowinski

Region: Argentine Pampas
System: Storage
Diagram: Variability by superimposition of variations
Type: Shed of metal porticos supported by concrete basement walls
Drawing: Axonometric
Author: Tomás Rowinski

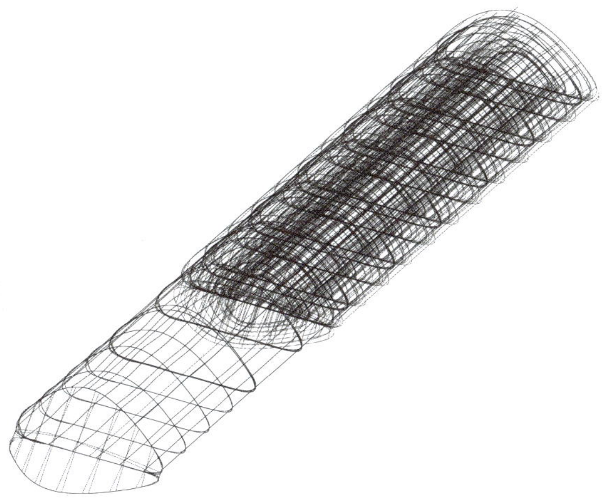

Region: Argentine Pampas
System: Storage
Diagram: Variability by superimposition of variations
Type: Silo-bag
Drawing: Axonometric
Author: Tomás Rowinski

TRA FER
TRA FER

VISIONS OF THE SUPRARURAL COSMOPOLIS

The following projects are, on the one hand, rigorous yet playful experimentations of assembly of rural protocols in differential urban-territorial prototypes, and on the other, visions of a Suprarural Cosmopolis that use the rural as both an inertial and a tendentious medium. They are constructed by using the Architectural Atlas of Rural Protocols of the American Midwest and the Argentine Pampas as a manual of design techniques. The projects are based on the same systems as the manuals: transport infrastructure, land subdivision, agricultural production, water management, irrigation and fumigation, inhabitation, cattle management, socialization, storage. One or more of these systems are used to configure a virtual substrate onto which urban determinations are embedded and urban components are incorporated. This process of integration is enabled through the understanding of protocols as abstract relationships.

Protocols behave as engines of design. They do not close questions or illustrate existing ideas about the rural but generate feedback on the performance of systems, requiring a constant redefinition of the extent, range, relevance and rationality of their rules. In this sense, the project outcomes use systems as forces, and empower them back through architectural definitions. Yet, although faithful to the machinic organization of the protocols, the projects do not operate within their given logics of causality, grounded on established forms of know-how, and systems are not used to generate rapid conclusions and efficacies but rather the opposite: they are the vehicles by which positive feedback loops are triggered. The designer here constantly breeds existing systemic relationships and establishes new ones through evaluations, from which the architectural qualities generated take the form of a paradoxically down-to-earth vision.

These feedback loops break the dichotomy between the factuality of the architectural object and the history of its process, as the process becomes useful at an operative level but unnecessary as a ground of validation, and insufficient to justify the project and fully understand the history and the machinery behind its making. The project itself becomes a process, without for this reason melting down in a self-fulfilling prophecy. And, vice versa, the process becomes a project, that is, in a medium where to unfold an architectural agenda on practice, yet it neither claims to be the only possible project nor does it stand as practice per se. The question then becomes how to approach this material without falling into the misunderstanding of it as a tautological structure. In the Suprarrural project, procedure and vision become one and the same thing such that the systematic contingency of one engenders the essential vagueness and openness of the other.

How else can the territory become, literally, a matter of architecture, if not through the full embracement of its repressed uncertainties, as if they were the crucial factor of architecture's creativity? The Suprarural embraces the territorial by means of its most earthly, earnest techniques, rural protocols, and assumes that these are embedded with artistic potential by default, avoiding an attitude of exclusion and, equally, the slightest mystification. The Suprarural is, in this sense, far from accruing a new surrealist ethics into the recent history of the discipline. This is precisely why it does not adopt montage as a technique for the sudden encounter of the diverse in view to the thinking of the new. No matter how effective, these techniques have demonstrated that they have a short life span, given their intrinsic reliance on shock as procedure. Rather, Suprarural visions are closer to what can be seen as a super-realist operation, where total embedding in the normative leads to a joyful form of constructing the sublime.

Consequently, what if the rural world actualized itself as a Suprarural Cosmopolis? New urban hierarchies, grounded and nurtured by archaic territorial orders, would turn into extensive and imaginative organizational regimes, where old-time efficiencies of the rural, some of them persistent today purely through inertia and repetition of the same, and more recent ones, based on the ruthless deployment of biological, ecological and technological experiments across the territory, would meet, mutually reciprocate, and be purposely qualified through visionary design statements and operative relationships. These visions, evidently present but apparently inexistent, would be nothing but defiant glimpses into surprisingly close yet far-fetched forms of a future, which, without revisiting the old radical and transformative ambitions of utopian architecture or the soft social concerns and political claims of nowadays, would start up architectural engines for projective speculation and forward-looking forms of play.

If projects are, to a large extent, drawings, they perform effectively as pure documentation, in which the memory of past regulations is upgraded into regimes of what would otherwise remain as a sheer fact or as a latent potential. If this potential is processed through an ongoing diagram that absorbs, assembles and revolves around certain protocols, any document that registers or controls a performance, no matter how banal, is immediately confronted with the vertigo of becoming the virtual substrate of an urban organization. Both the historical illustration and the abstract simulation of dynamic processes might run short of the real capacity of a regime of protocols to unfold an active design mind with a joyful form of intelligence, grounded in basic sources of knowledge. Rural documents, here, become the tools at hand for the designer, and are simultaneously traversed by the general logics of architectural expertise. The game board through which the territory becomes an artistically open field capable of activating unprecedented organizations is set up.

Unlike many of its contemporary acquaintances, the Suprarural Cosmopolis does not imply a regression into the good old futures of the recent past in order to instill a politically correct framework in the insatiable contemporary world. Neither is it a robust new megastructural form, capable of dealing with complex conditions and of enduring. It is not another nostalgia of an ironic city form that can comment on the real through a narrative. It is not a slick form of post-corporate modernism, driven to organize and profiting from what otherwise appears fragmented and disperse. It is not a new form of cartoonish dystopia that celebrates the loss of the real. It is not the ghost of a degraded form of ideological critique, trying to install order by means of overtly simplistic forms, which degrade all knowledge about form. With no reliance on past forms of optimism, be they refreshed as if they were new, the Suprarural is simply an amoral glimpse, neither positive nor negative, into what may come next. Earnestness is its main risk.

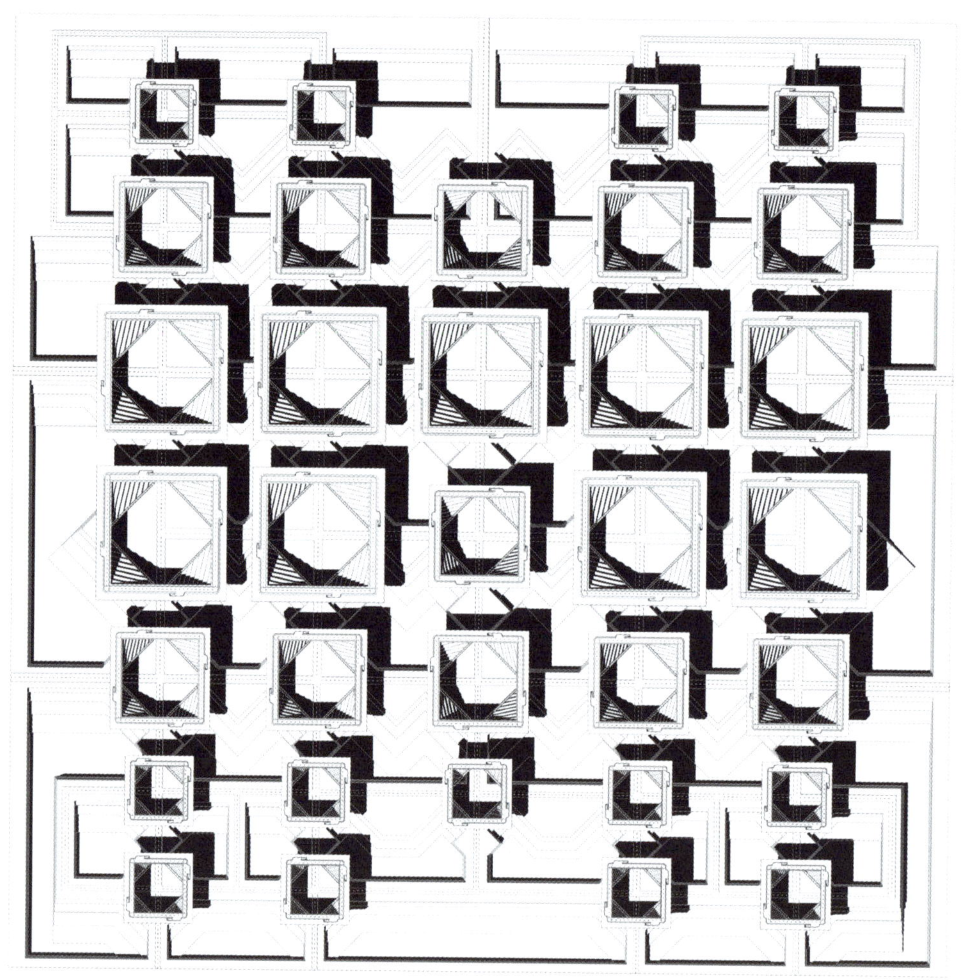

Region: American Midwest
System: Transport Infrastructure
Project: Vertical Land Ordinance
Specifications: Circulatory terraced grid, terraced housing superblocks, terraced crops diagonal grid
Drawing: Plan
Author: Travis Kalina

Region: American Midwest
System: Transport Infrastructure
Project: Vertical Land Ordinance
Specifications: Circulatory terraced grid, terraced housing superblocks, terraced crops diagonal grid
Drawing: Plan of building type
Author: Travis Kalina

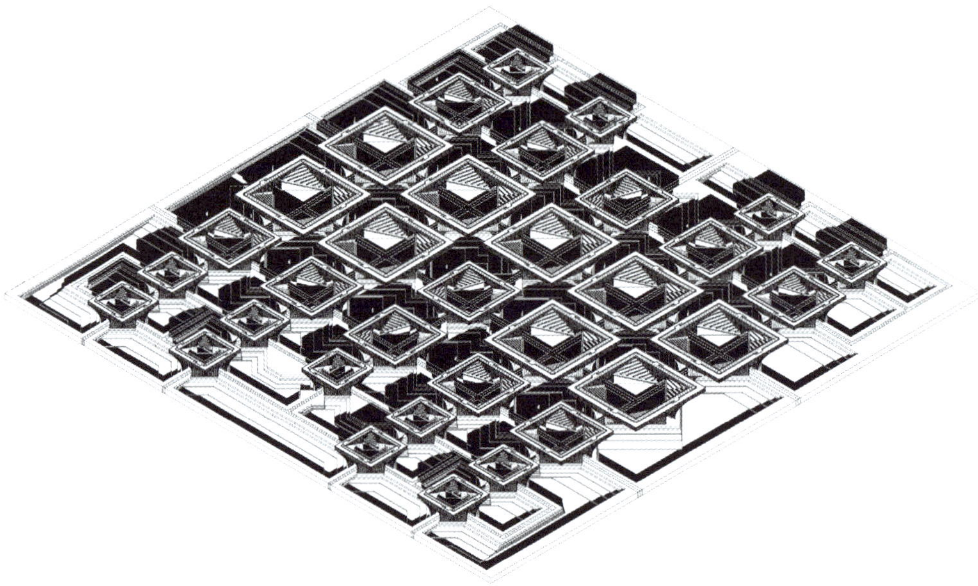

Region: American Midwest
System: Transport Infrastructure
Project: Vertical Land Ordinance
Specifications: Circulatory terraced grid, terraced housing superblocks, terraced crops diagonal grid
Drawing: Axonometric
Author: Travis Kalina

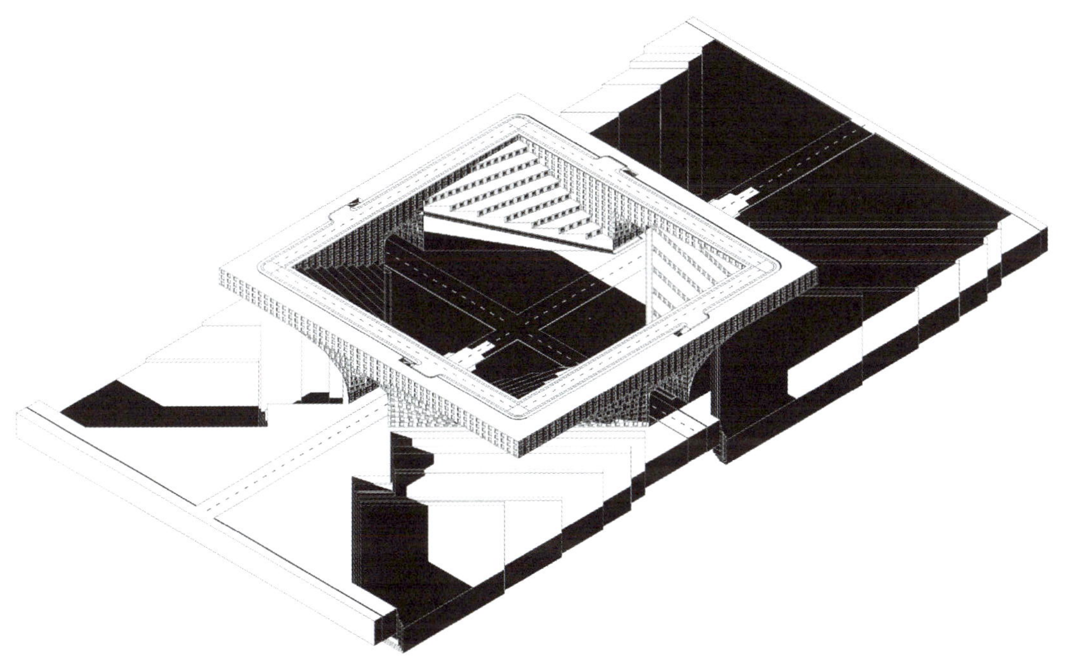

Region: American Midwest
System: Transport Infrastructure
Project: Vertical Land Ordinance
Specifications: Circulatory terraced grid, terraced housing superblocks, terraced crops diagonal grid
Drawing: Axonometric
Author: Travis Kalina

Region: American Midwest
System: Transport Infrastructure
Project: Vertical Land Ordinance
Specifications: Circulatory terraced grid, terraced housing superblocks, terraced crops diagonal grid
Drawing: Axonometric of building type
Author: Travis Kalina

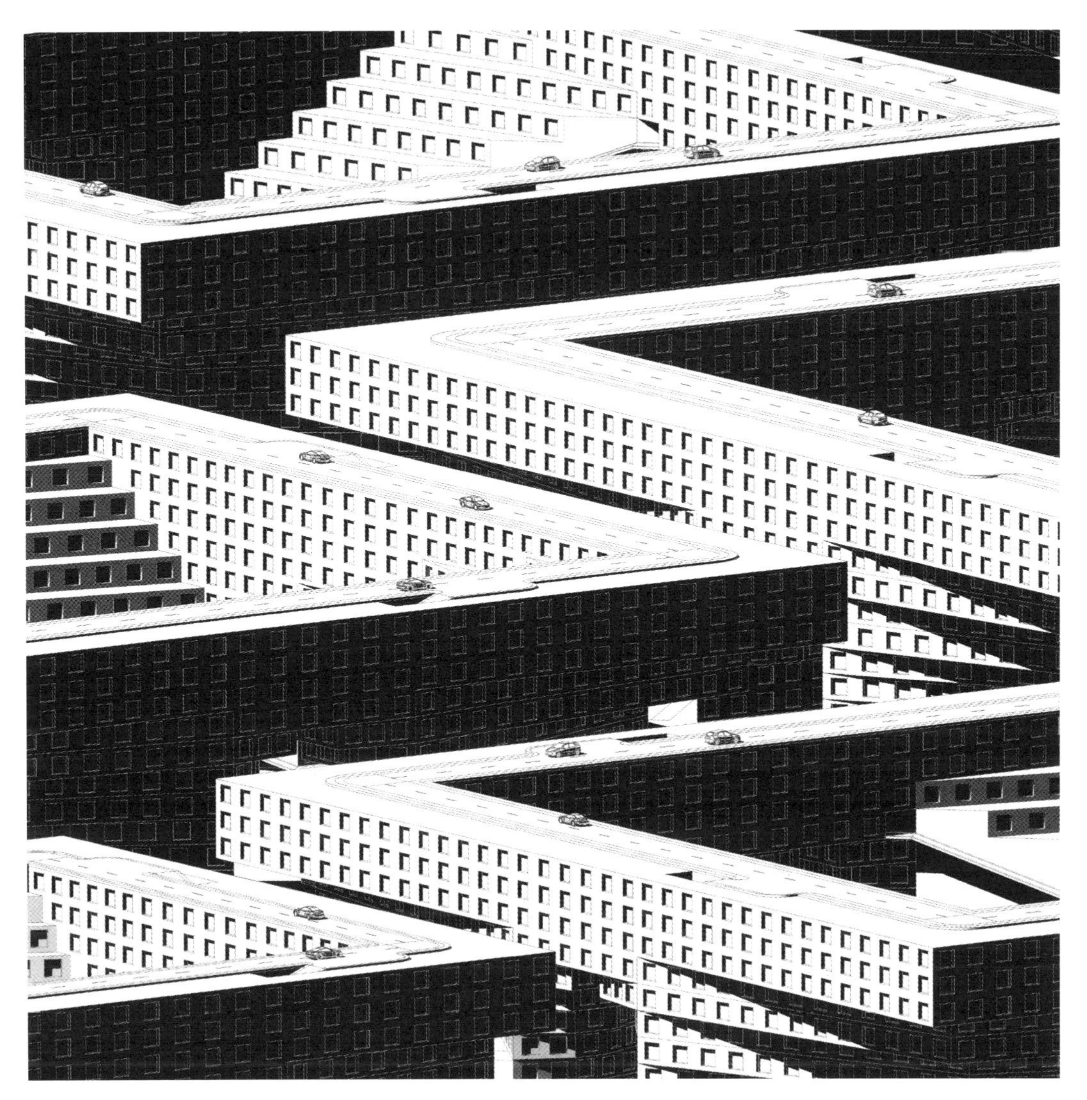

Region: American Midwest
System: Transport Infrastructure
Project: Vertical Land Ordinance
Specifications: Circulatory terraced grid, terraced housing superblocks, terraced crops diagonal grid
Drawing: Perspective
Author: Travis Kalina

Region: American Midwest
System: Land Subdivision
Project: Field of Domes
Specifications: Domes of social events and water management
Image: Model plan
Author: Kim Hibben

Region: American Midwest
System: Land Subdivision
Project: Field of Domes
Specifications: Domes of social events and water management
Image: Model plan
Author: Kim Hibben

Region: American Midwest
System: Agricultural Production
Project: Rotation Towers
Specifications: Furrows organized according to seasonal variations, low density built and crop areas
Drawing: Plan
Author: Jason Mould

Region: American Midwest
System: Agricultural Production
Project: Rotation Towers
Specifications: Furrows organized according to seasonal variations, low density built and crop areas
Drawing: Plan
Author: Jason Mould

Region: American Midwest
System: Agricultural Production
Project: Rotation Towers
Specifications: Furrows organized according to seasonal variations, low density built and crop areas
Image: Model plan
Author: Jason Mould

Region: American Midwest
System: Agricultural Production
Project: Rotation Towers
Specifications: Furrows organized according to seasonal variations, low density built and crop areas
Image: Model perspective
Author: Jason Mould

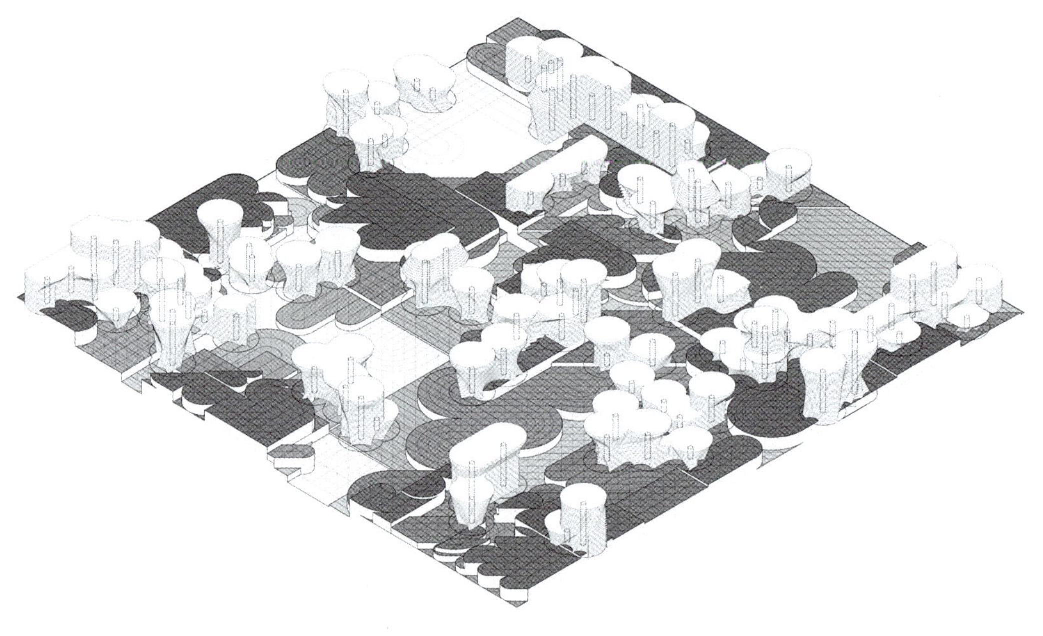

Region: American Midwest
System: Agricultural Production
Project: Rotation Towers
Specifications: Furrows organized according to seasonal variations, low density built and crop areas
Drawing: Axonometric
Author: Jason Mould

Region: American Midwest
System: Agricultural Production
Project: Rotation Towers
Specifications: Built mass, subtractions according to crop rotation patterns
Image: Model perspective
Author: Jason Mould

Region: American Midwest
System: Water Management
Project: Rolling Stones
Specifications: Housing towers and spiraled crop mounds
Image: Model plan
Author: Paola Gómez-Piñeiro

Region: American Midwest
System: Water Management
Project: Rolling Stones
Specifications: Housing towers and spiraled crop mounds
Image: Model of a building type, perspective
Author: Paola Gómez-Piñeiro

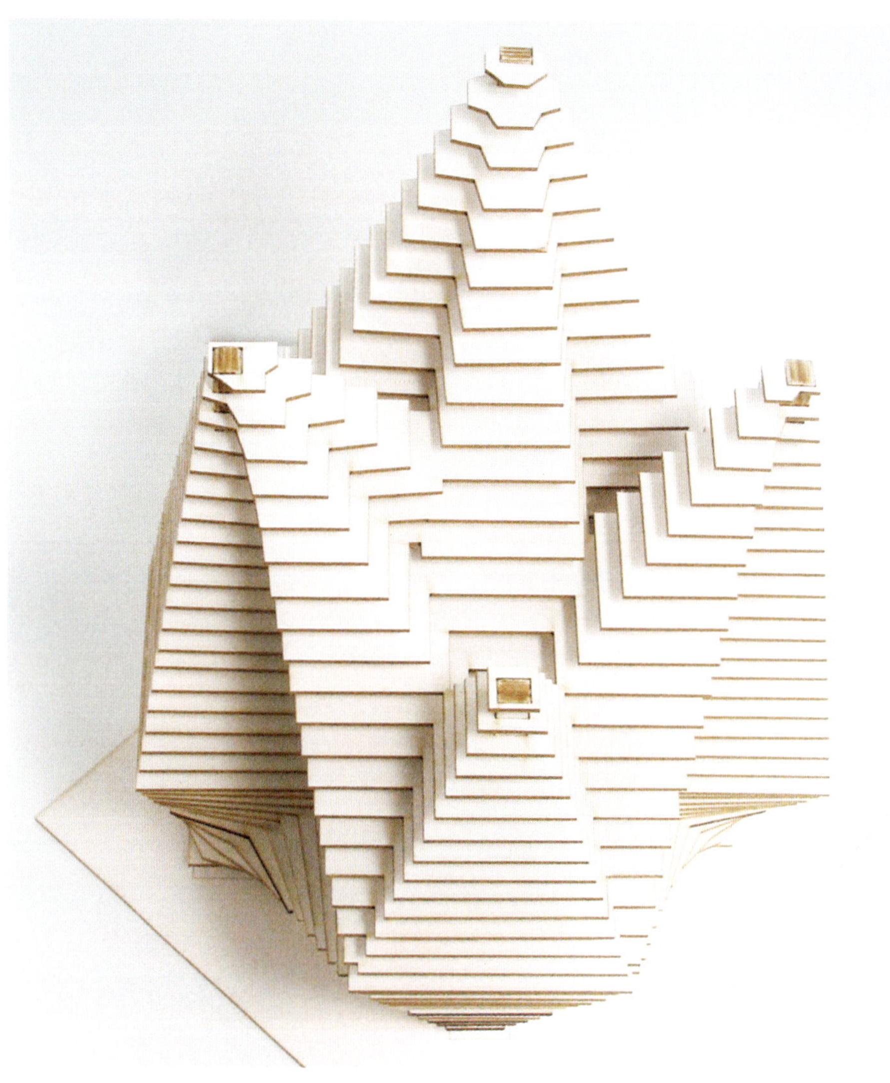

Region: American Midwest
System: Water Management
Project: Rolling Stones
Specifications: Housing towers and spiraled crop mounds
Image: Model of a building type, perspective
Author: Paola Gómez-Piñeiro

Region: American Midwest
System: Water Management
Project: Rolling Stones
Specifications: Housing towers and spiraled crop mounds
Image: Model of a building type, perspective
Author: Paola Gómez-Piñeiro

Region: American Midwest
System: Irrigation and Fumigation
Project: Sprinkler Towers
Specifications: Housing towers, circulation paths, irrigation patterns
Drawing: Plan
Author: John Sohn

Region: American Midwest
System: Irrigation and Fumigation
Project: Sprinkler Towers
Specifications: Housing tower type organized according to irrigation patterns
Image: Model perspective
Author: John Sohn

Region: American Midwest
System: Irrigation and Fumigation
Project: Sprinkler Towers
Specifications: Housing towers, circulation paths, irrigation patterns
Image: Model plan
Author: John Sohn

Region: American Midwest
System: Irrigation and Fumigation
Project: Sprinkler Towers
Specifications: Housing tower type organized according to irrigation patterns
Image: Model perspective
Author: John Sohn

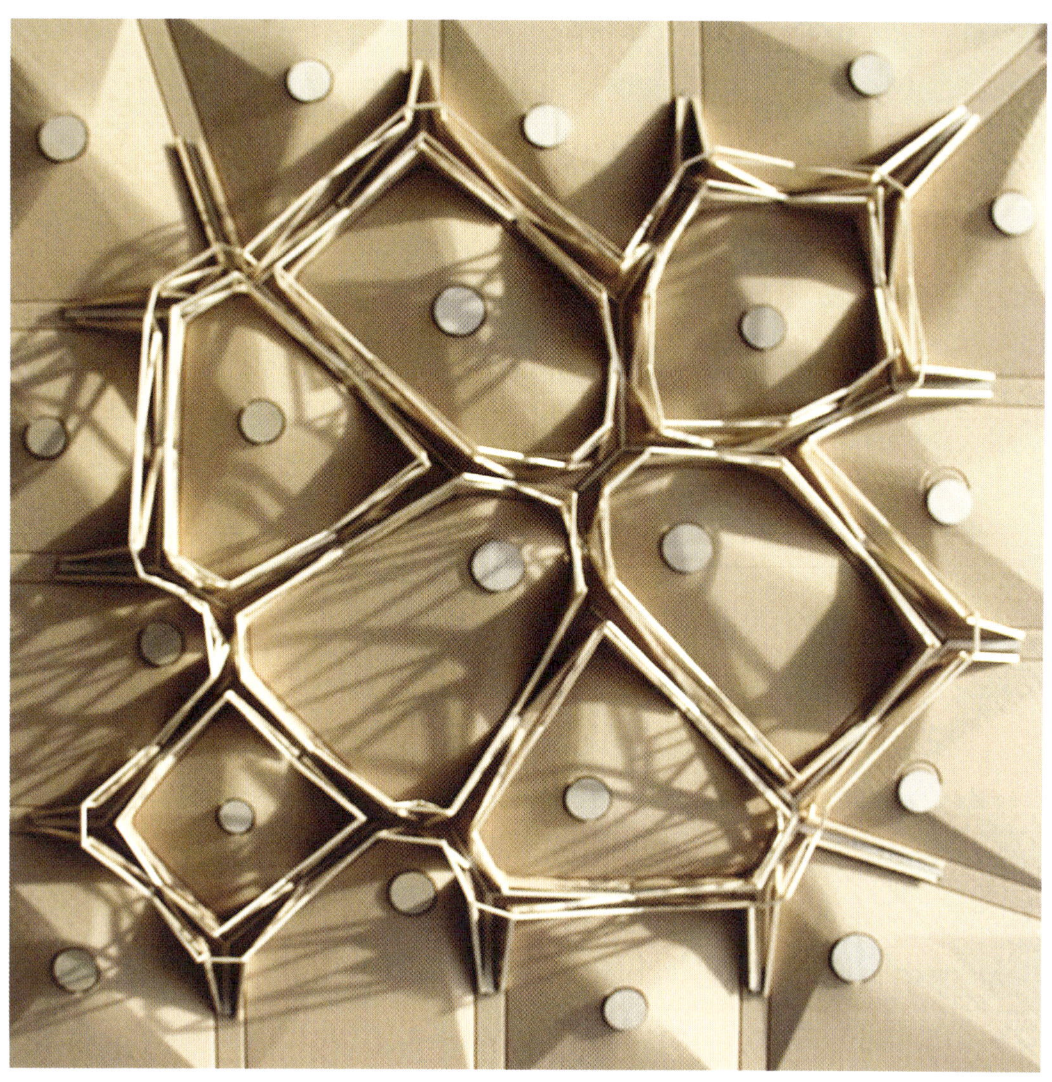

Region: American Midwest
System: Inhabitation
Project: Layerland
Specifications: Circulatory network and cellular territorial subdivision
Image: Model plan
Author: Tao Tao

Region: American Midwest
System: Inhabitation
Project: Layerland
Specifications: Circulatory network and cellular territorial subdivision
Image: Model perspective
Author: Tao Tao

Region: American Midwest
System: Cattle Management
Project: Transfer City
Specifications: Cropping areas, cattle management platforms, lagoons and curved corrals
Image: Model plan
Author: Samuel Tanis

Region: American Midwest
System: Cattle Management
Project: Transfer City
Specifications: Cropping areas, cattle management platforms, lagoons and curved corrals
Image: Model perspective
Author: Samuel Tanis

Region: American Midwest
System: Socialization
Project: Starbovis
Specifications: Event towers, water management grounds, circulatory roads, crop areas
Drawing: Plan
Author: Taylor Holloway

Region: American Midwest
System: Socialization
Project: Starbovis
Specifications: Event towers, water management grounds, circulatory roads, crop areas
Image: Model plan
Author: Taylor Holloway

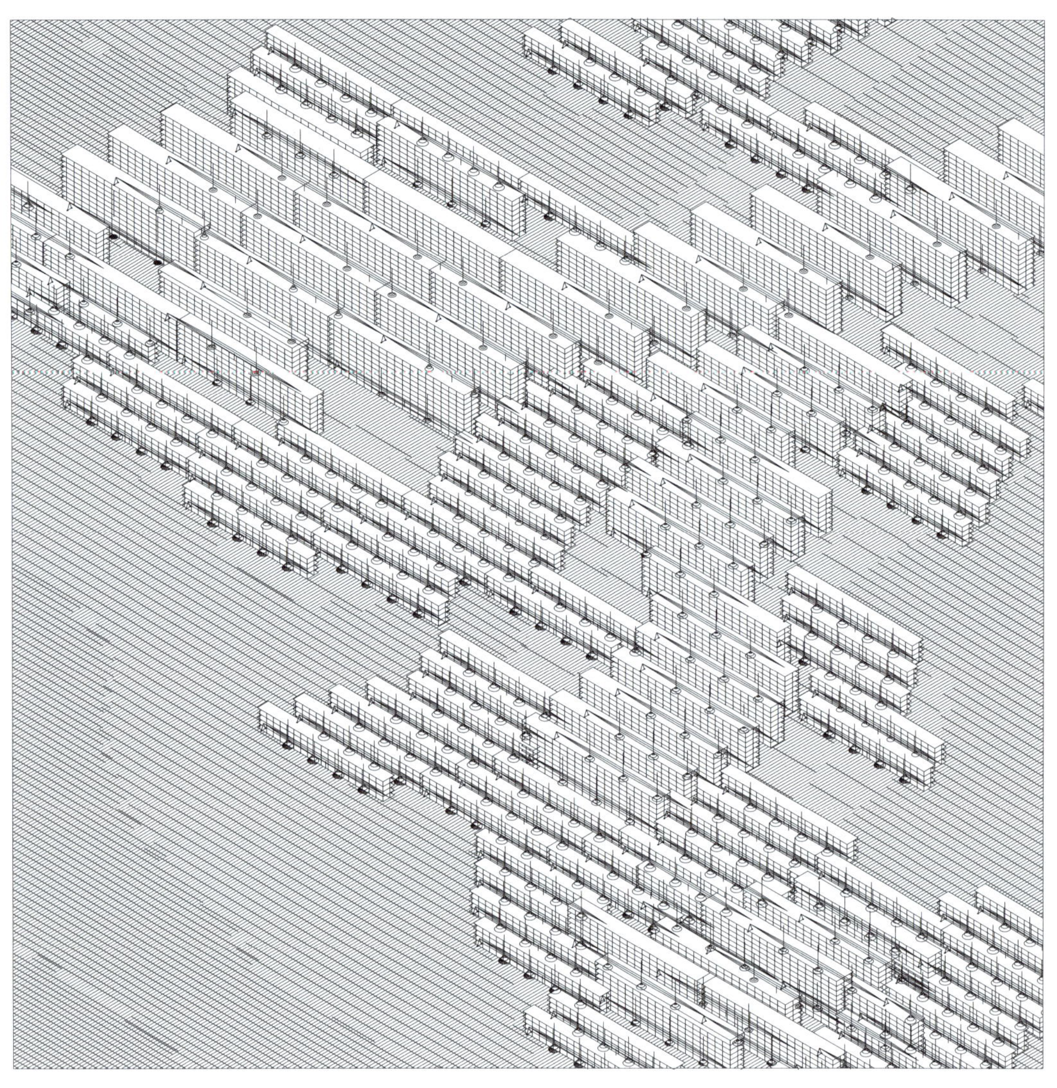

Region: Argentine Pampas
System: Irrigation and Fumigation
Project: Ville Irrigation, The Modern City as an Agricultural System
Specifications: Integrated organization of housing bars of varying density over irrigation structures and crop patterns
Drawing: Axonometric
Author: Paula Maidana

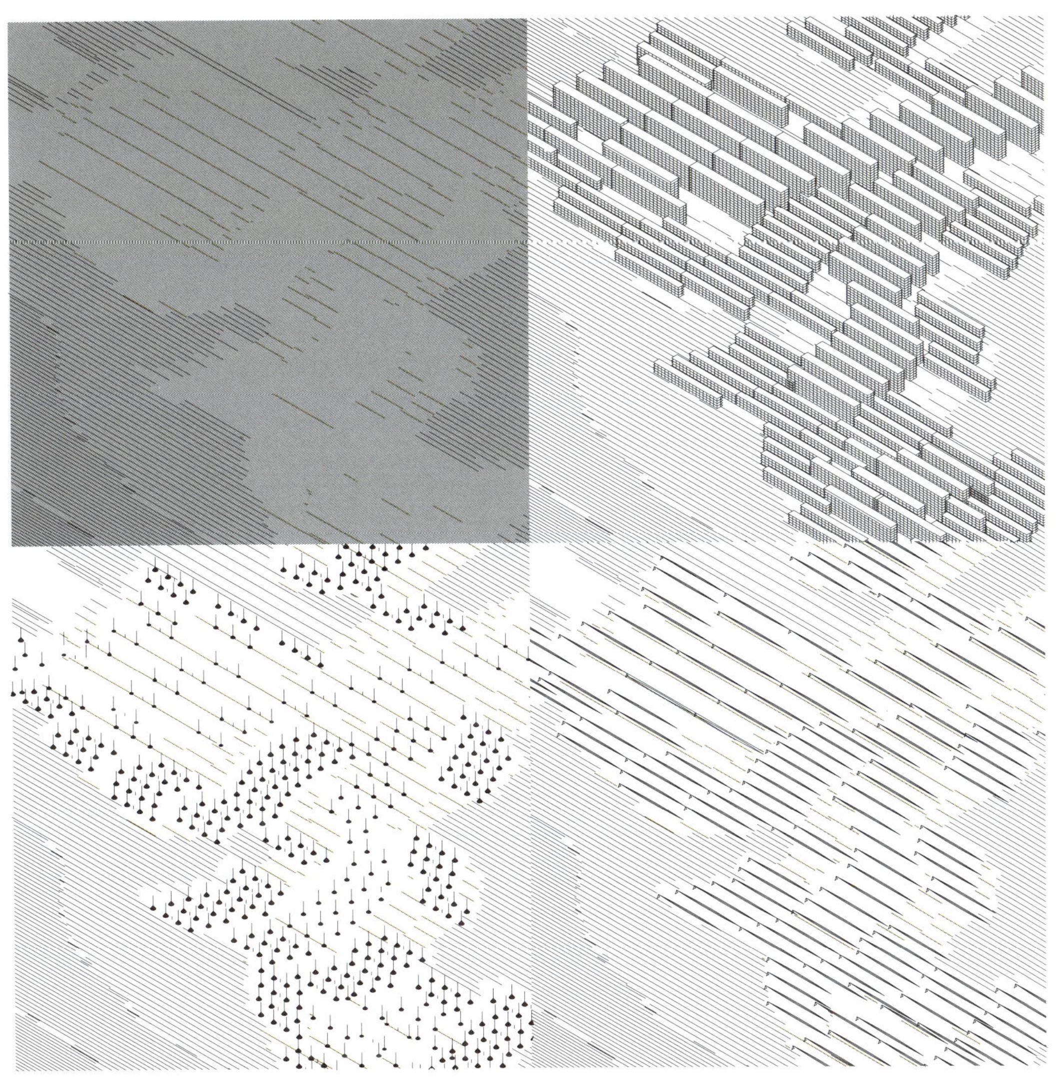

Region: Argentine Pampas
System: Irrigation and Fumigation
Project: Ville Irrigation, The Modern City as an Agricultural System
Specifications: Subsystems, crop patterns, crop patterns and housing bars of varying density, crop patterns and irrigation cones, crop patterns and irrigation structures
Drawing: Axonometric
Author: Paula Maidana

Region: Argentine Pampas
System: Irrigation and Fumigation
Project: Ville Irrigation, The Modern City as an Agricultural System
Specifications: Integrated organization of housing bars of medium density over irrigation structures, areas for horticulture, covered irrigated areas for controlled crops, covered non irrigated areas for general circulation
Drawing: Plan, sector
Author: Paula Maidana

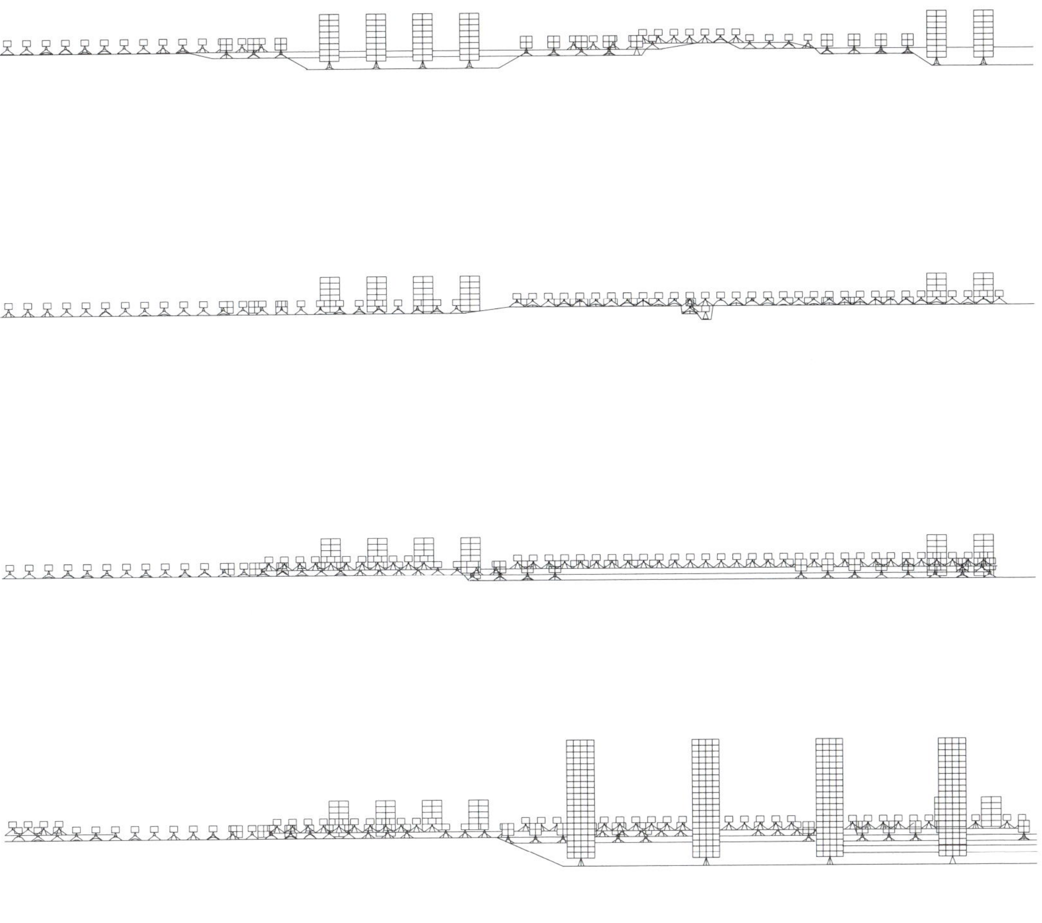

Region: Argentine Pampas
System: Irrigation and Fumigation
Project: Ville Irrigation, The Modern City as an Agricultural System
Specifications: Integrated organization of housing bars of medium density over irrigation structures, areas for horticulture, covered irrigated areas for controlled crops, covered non irrigated areas for general circulation
Drawing: Section, every 400 meters
Author: Paula Maidana

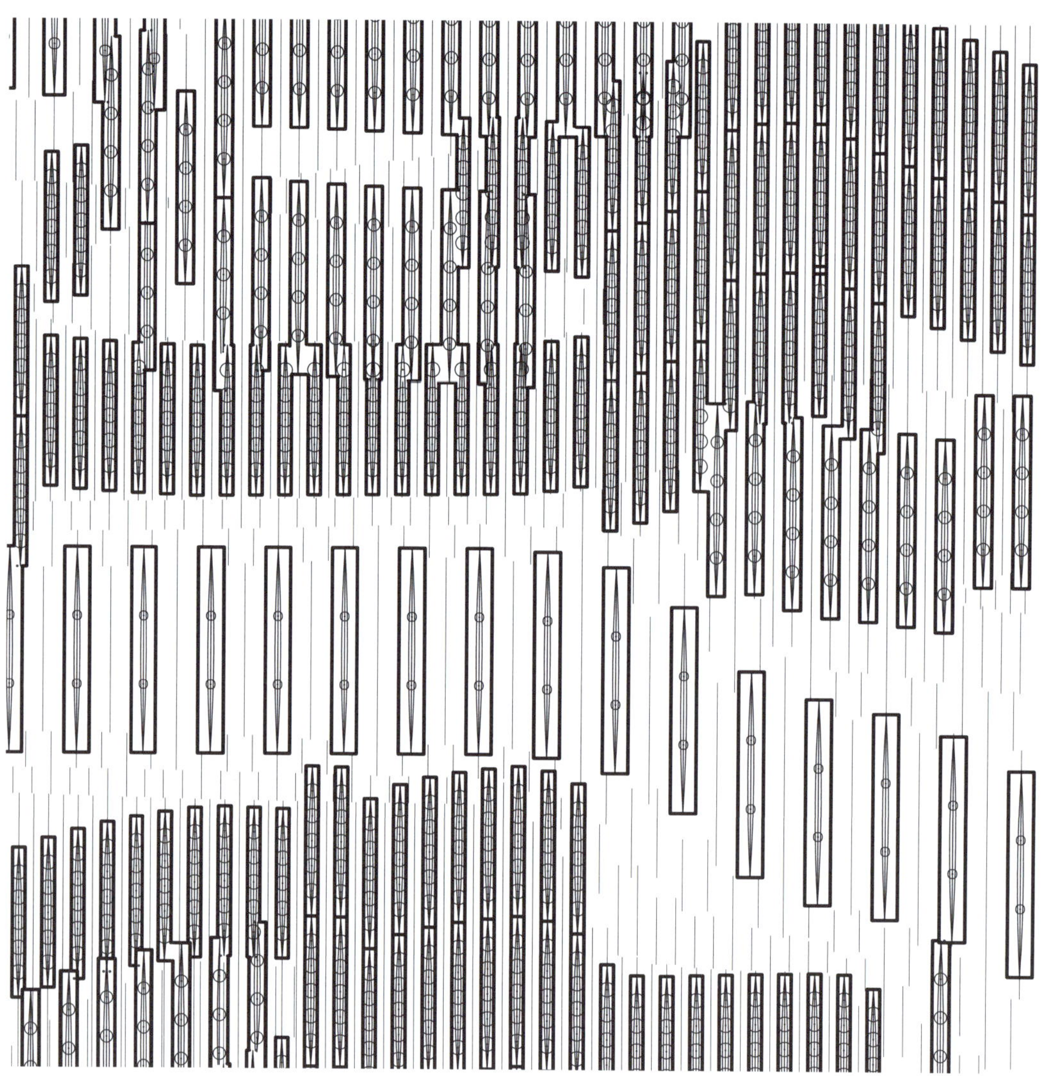

Region: Argentine Pampas
System: Irrigation and Fumigation
Project: Ville Irrigation, The Modern City as an Agricultural System
Specifications: Integrated organization of housing bars of high density over irrigation structures, areas for horticulture, covered irrigated areas for controlled crops, covered non irrigated areas for general circulation
Drawing: Plan, sector
Author: Paula Maidana

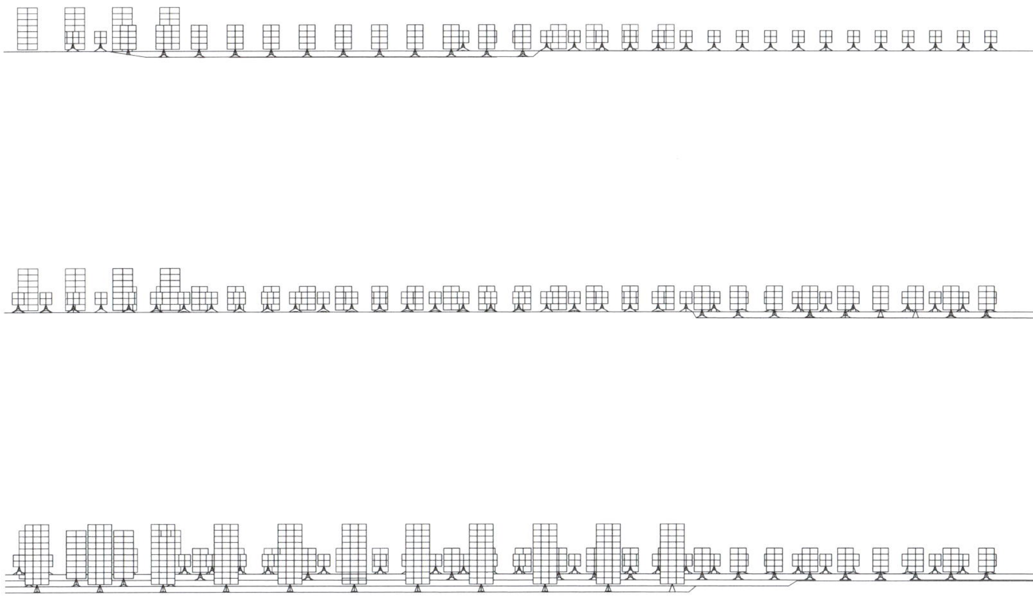

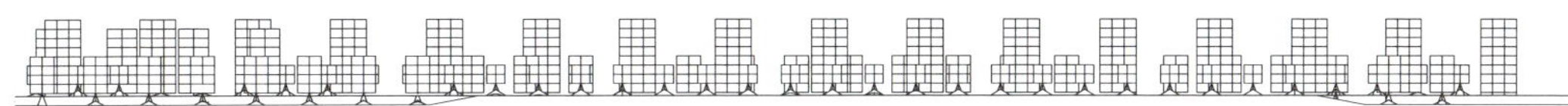

Region: Argentine Pampas
System: Irrigation and Fumigation
Project: Ville Irrigation, The Modern City as an Agricultural System
Specifications: Integrated organization of housing bars of high density over irrigation structures, areas for horticulture, covered irrigated areas for controlled crops, covered non irrigated areas for general circulation
Drawing: Section, every 400 meters
Author: Paula Maidana

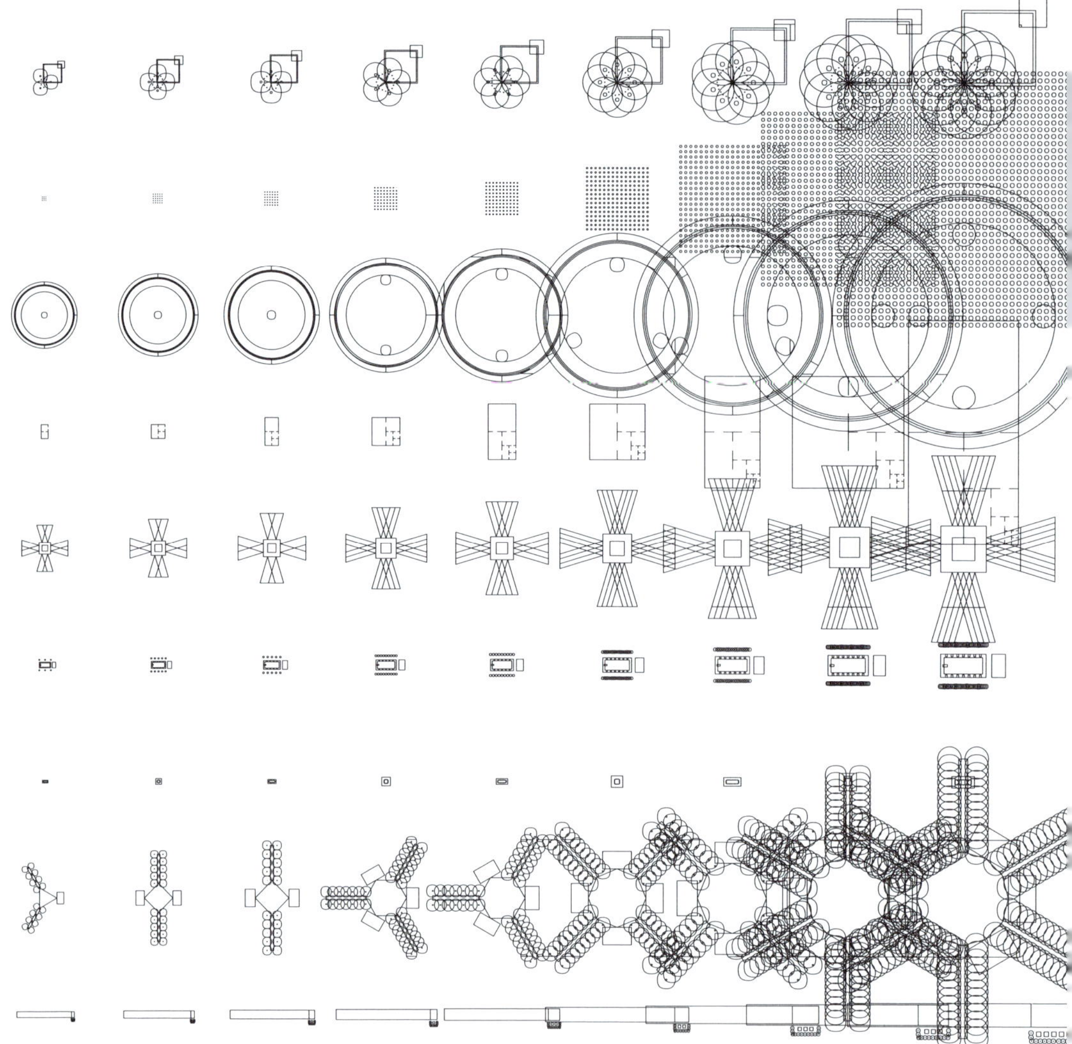

Region: Argentine Pampas
System: Inhabitation
Project: Grid Games, or the Hedonist Territory
Specifications: Linear variations of open-air recreational typologies, lunch area under the trees, walk under the geometric forest, boat ride in the artificial pond, deer breeding, skeet shooting, swimming jump contest, board games at the main house, ceremonies at the central garden, and playground at the runway
Drawing: Plan
Author: Martina Rossi

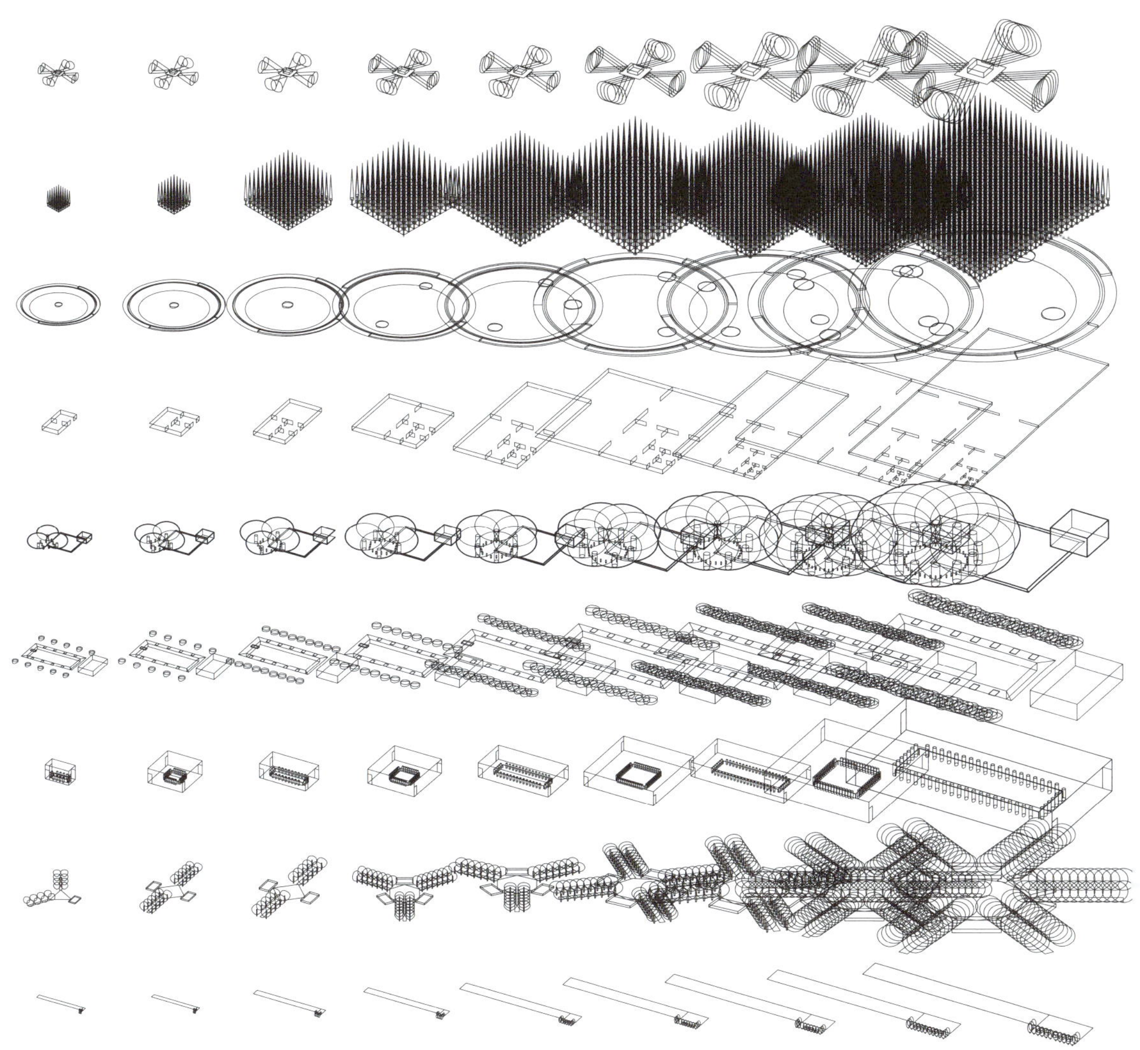

Region: Argentine Pampas
System: Inhabitation
Project: Grid Games, or the Hedonist Territory
Specifications: Linear variations of open-air recreational typologies, lunch area under the trees, walk under the geometric forest, boat ride in the artificial pond, deer breeding, skeet shooting, swimming jump contest, board games at the main house, ceremonies at the central garden, and playground at the runway
Drawing: Axonometric
Author: Martina Rossi

5	7				4	5	6	2	3	4	2	3											7	7	6	5
1	8		1	9	2	7	8	6		9			7			5		2	4		4	6		9	7	
67		2				2	6	5	12											1	8		8	9		8
			11		3	11		1	2	3				4						7	73		9	8	1	5
6	7		89			4	8		39			2	6		5	4		7			6	6		9	5	8
3		9	39			38		2	2	5	4	6		4			6	3		5	97			9	5	3
					4		2			11		4	5	3	8	8	3			7	76		7			8
6	9		44			6	5		55			5	8	4	98			7	12		5	2		8	2	
		9			5			9			9	5	1	6	21		4	8	2		99					3
	3		3	2			2			7			8			9	5		2	8	5	5	2	4	4	1
2	7		5	1	3	3			5			9	5		4	77		9	3		3	2		9		1
		5	6		7			7			7			7			2			6	8		6	7		5
	4			8			7	7		1	2		6	7		8	6	2	4	5	4	5		6	7	3
9			7	2		6			6			3			7			6		1	5		5	8		
		8			9			9			7						1	1	2		7	9	3	4	1	7
	4			8	93					1	6			12	4	5			5	5				4	5	9
5			7			4	11		8	1		8	3		83				3		3	6		7	4	
		6			5			8			4				7		5	2	4	4			6	4	3	7
							9	8		8			9	5			1			9		3				
3			5			8			8	5		6	1		1				2		1	3		1	4	
		8			8			8		8	11		9	4									33			
		8			9			8	9	9	2	9	9	3	5	7	1	1	5	6		3				
1			2			2	4		9	8	9	4	3	7	4			4			5			2		
									8	7	2	4	6	66	1	3	8									3
	2				9		6	8		9	4	6	7		1	2	6			4			6			
2			4	3		6	6		3	6		7			1						1			2	2	
		4						1			2	5	4	1	1		2			4			33			

Region: Argentine Pampas
System: Inhabitation
Project: Grid Games, or the Hedonist Territory
Specifications: Distribution of linear variations of open-air recreational typologies according to variations of territorial properties
Drawing: Plan
Author: Martina Rossi

Region: Argentine Pampas
System: Inhabitation
Project: Grid Games, or the Hedonist Territory
Specifications: Gradient and distribution pattern of linear variations of open-air recreational typologies
Drawing: Plan
Author: Martina Rossi

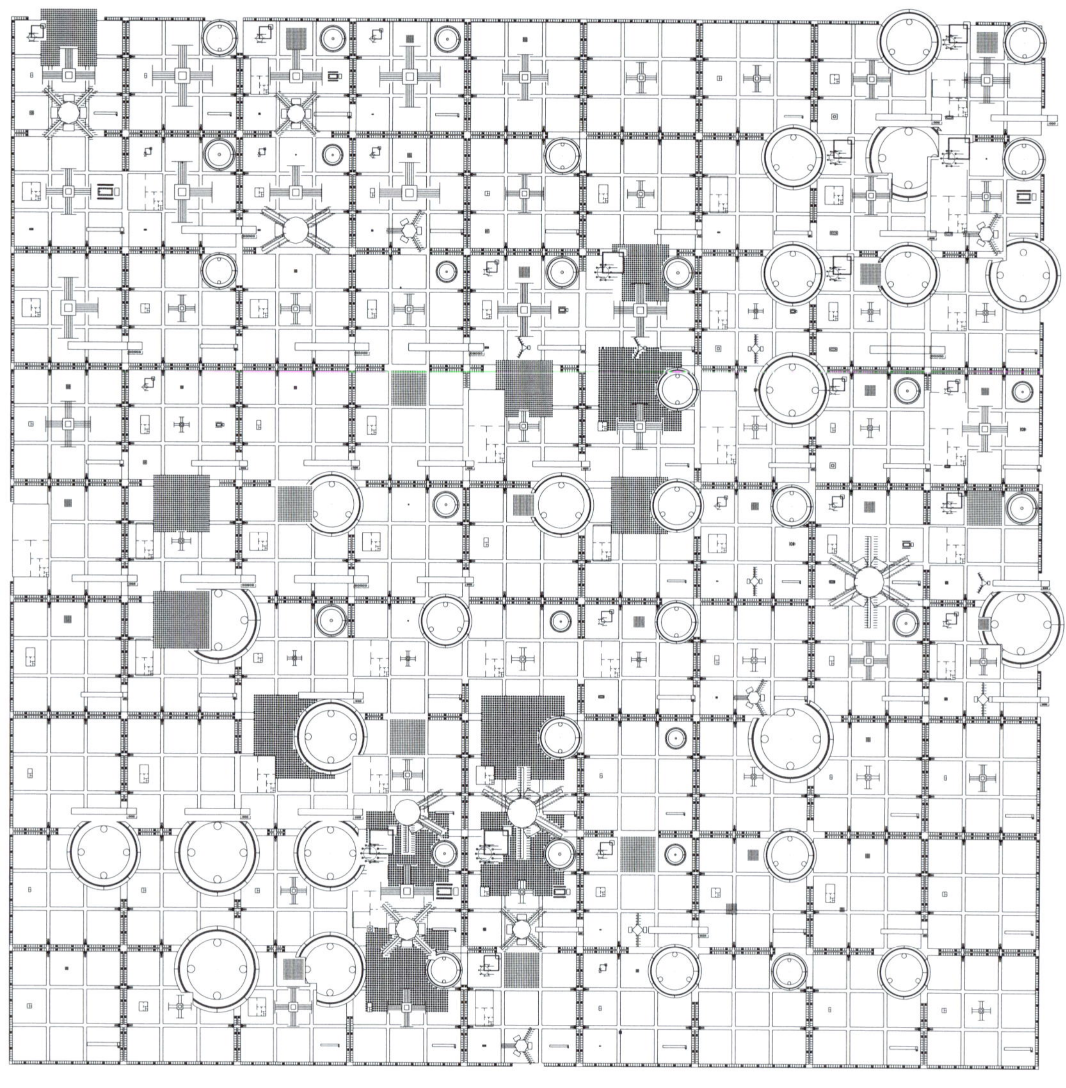

Region: Argentine Pampas
System: Inhabitation
Project: Grid Games, or the Hedonist Territory
Specifications: Integrated organization of cloister buildings with open-air recreational typologies gradually distributed
Drawing: Plan
Author: Martina Rossi

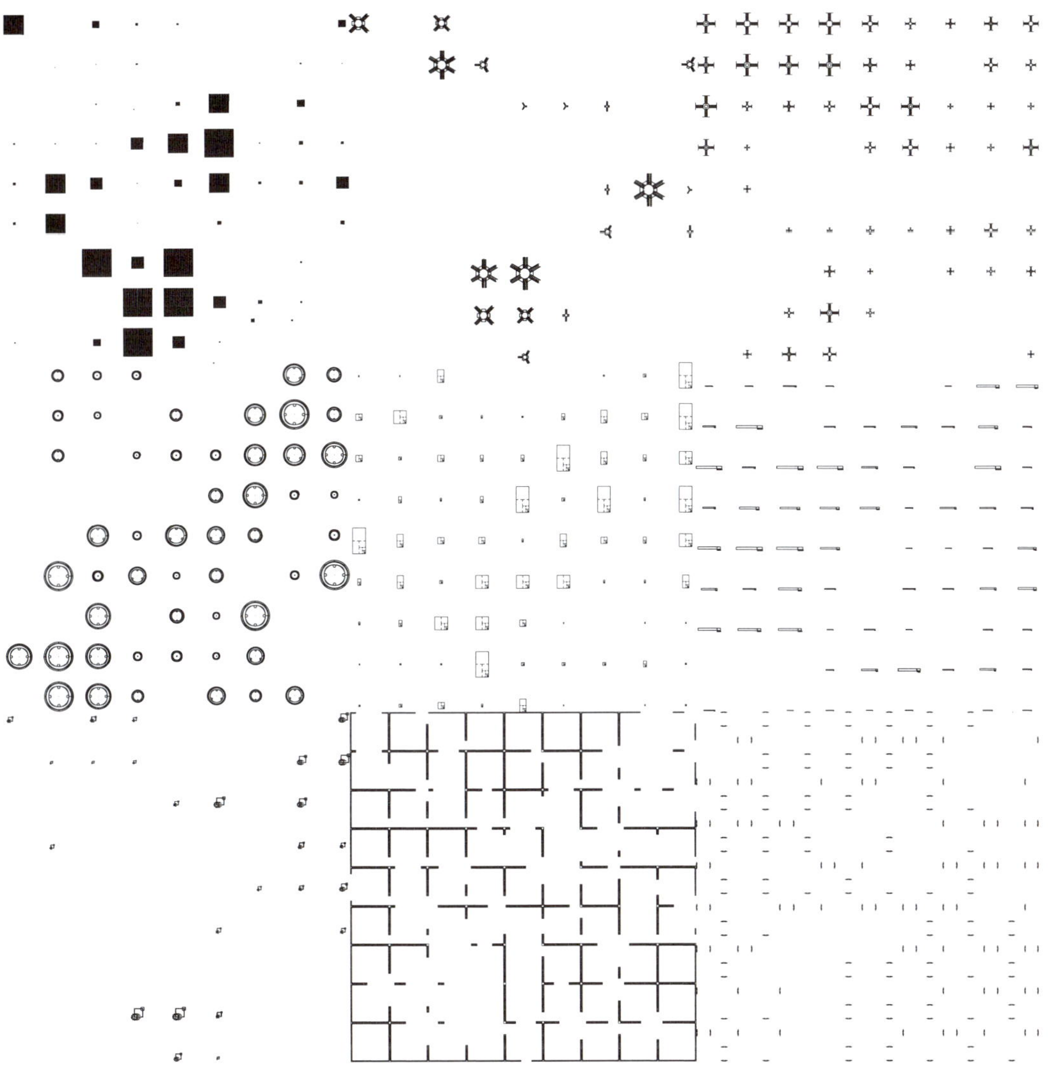

Region: Argentine Pampas
System: Inhabitation
Project: Grid Games, or the Hedonist Territory
Specifications: Subsystems of open-air recreational typologies, walk under the geometric forest, ceremonies at the central garden, skeet shooting, boat ride in the artificial pond, deer breeding, playground at the runway, lunch area under the trees, housing bars, and vertical circulation
Drawing: Plan
Author: Martina Rossi

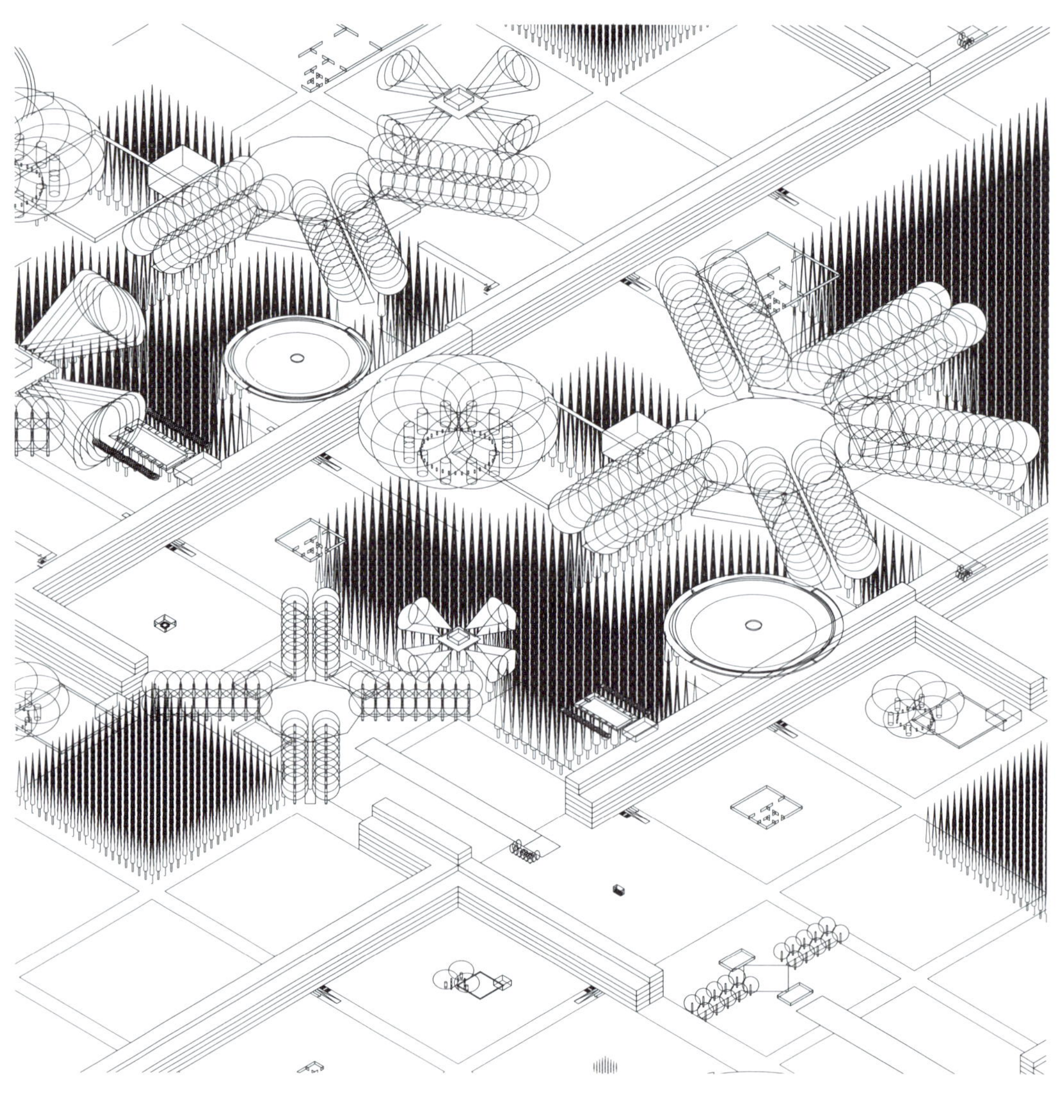

Region: Argentine Pampas
System: Inhabitation
Project: Grid Games, or the Hedonist Territory
Specifications: Integrated organization of cloister buildings with open-air recreational typologies gradually distributed
Drawing: Axonometric, sector
Author: Martina Rossi

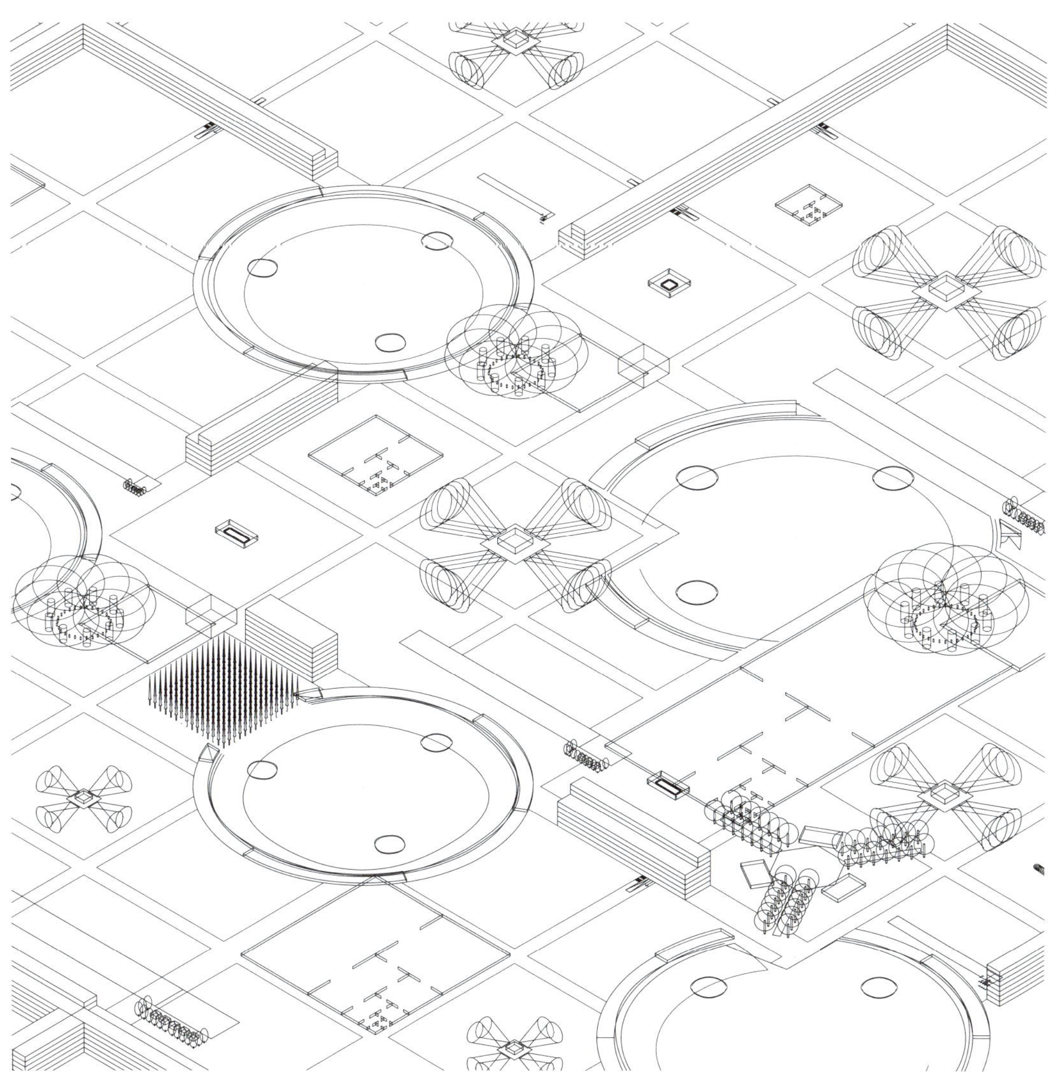

Region: Argentine Pampas
System: Inhabitation
Project: Grid Games, or the Hedonist Territory
Specifications: Integrated organization of cloister buildings with open-air recreational typologies gradually distributed
Drawing: Axonometric, sector
Author: Martina Rossi

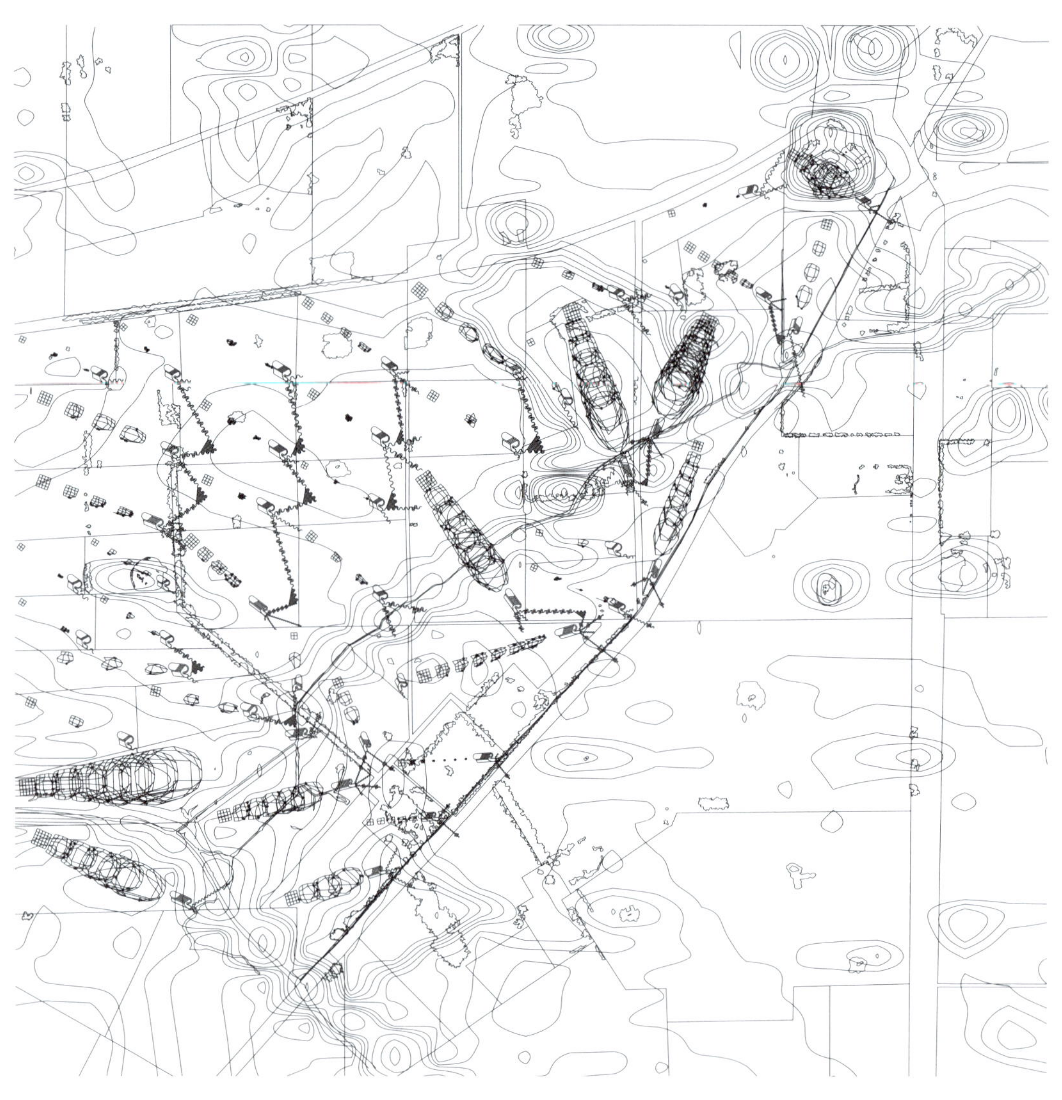

Region: Argentine Pampas
System: Cattle Management
Project: Cattle Mall, Vertical Handling Machines
Specifications: Integrated organization of variations of built mass, cattle handling, and lot dimension
Drawing: Plan
Author: Juan Cruz Rio

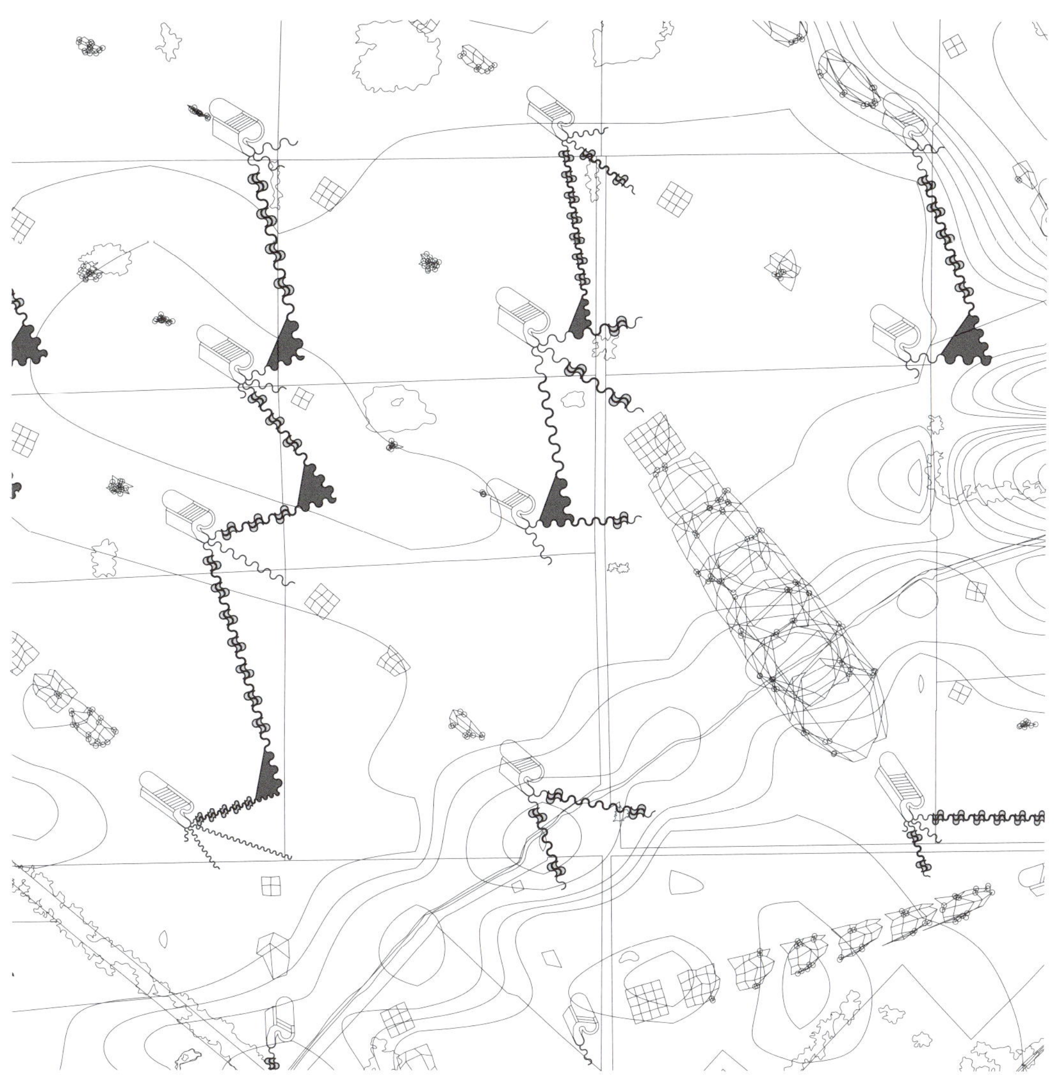

Region: Argentine Pampas
System: Cattle Management
Project: Cattle Mall, Vertical Handling Machines
Specifications: Integrated organization of variations of built mass, cattle handling, and lot dimension
Drawing: Plan, sector
Author: Juan Cruz Río

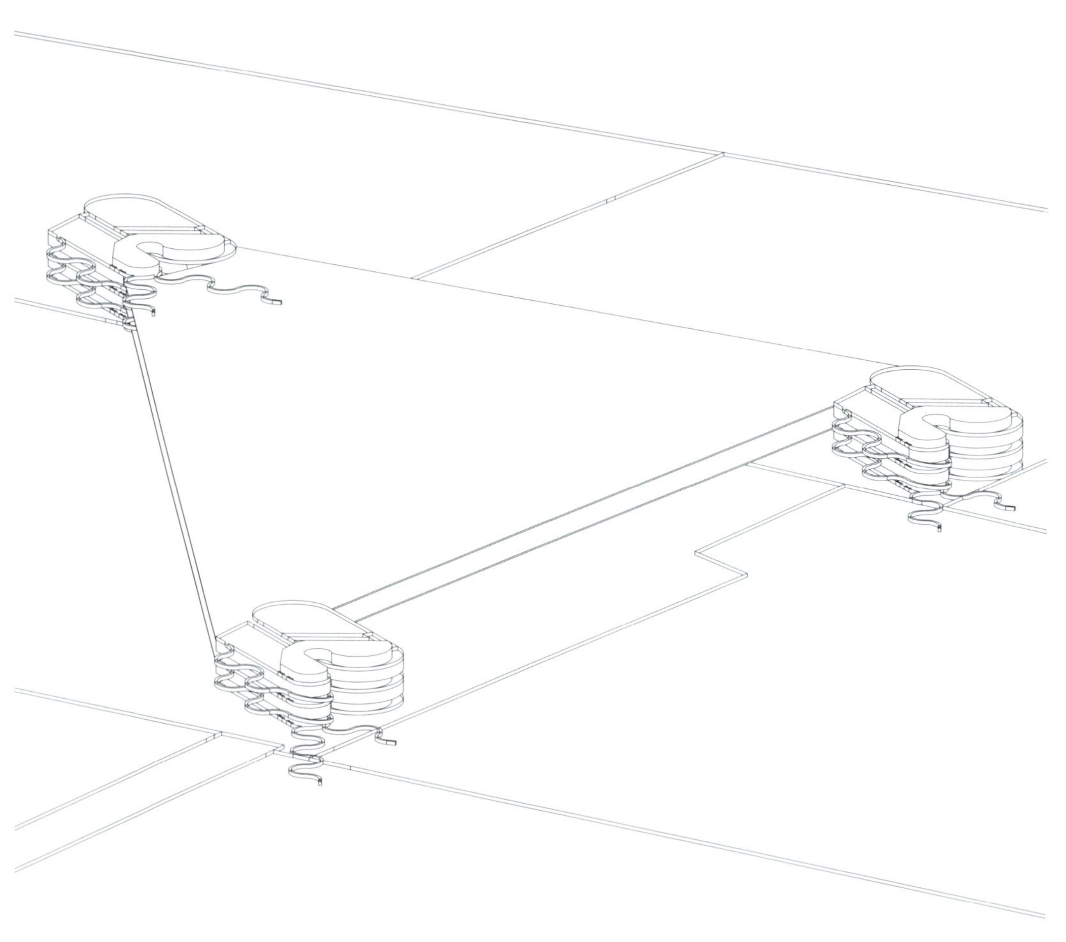

Region: Argentine Pampas
System: Cattle Management
Project: Cattle Mall, Vertical Handling Machines
Specifications: Integrated organization of variations of built mass, cattle handling, and lot dimension
Drawing: Axonometric, sector
Author: Juan Cruz Río

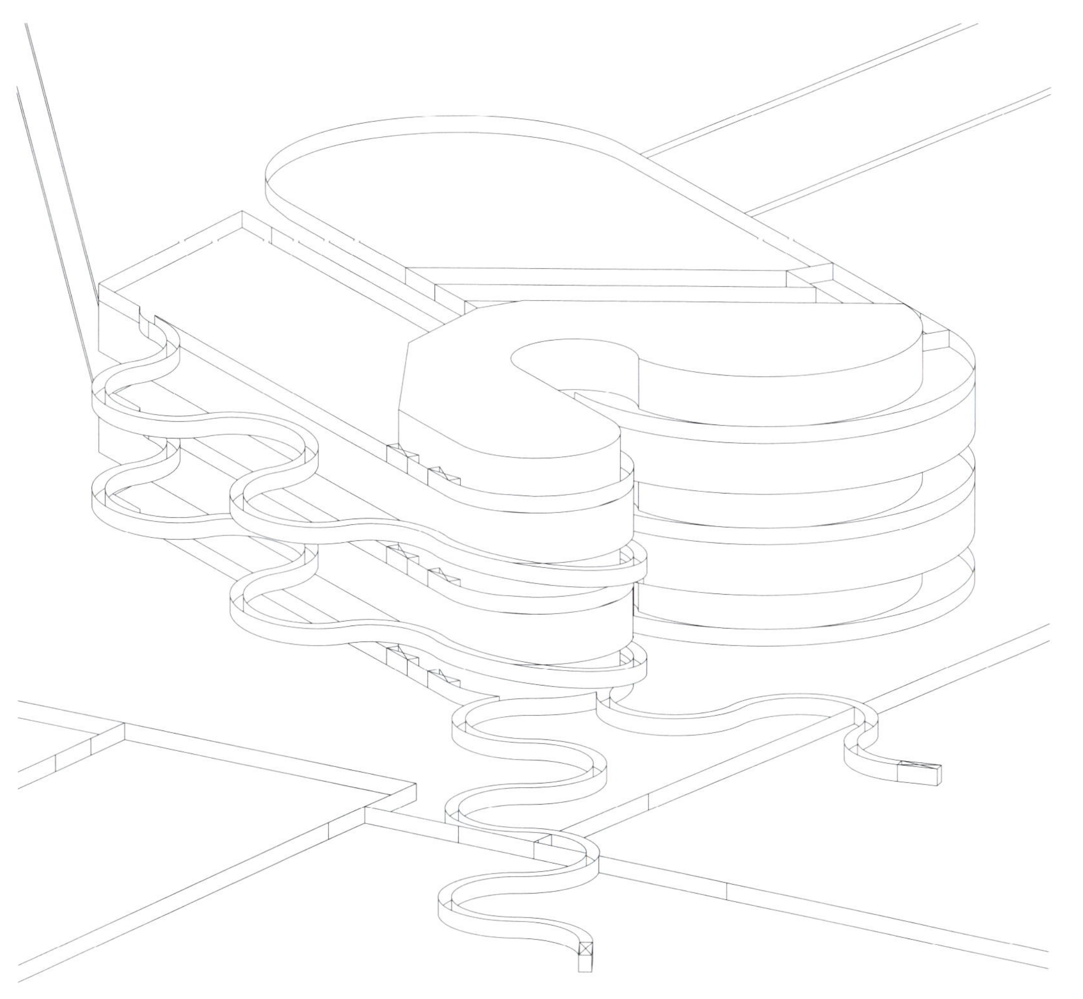

Region: Argentine Pampas
System: Cattle Management
Project: Cattle Mall, Vertical Cattle Handling Machines
Specifications: Cattle handling standard type
Drawing: Axonometric, building type
Author: Juan Cruz Rio

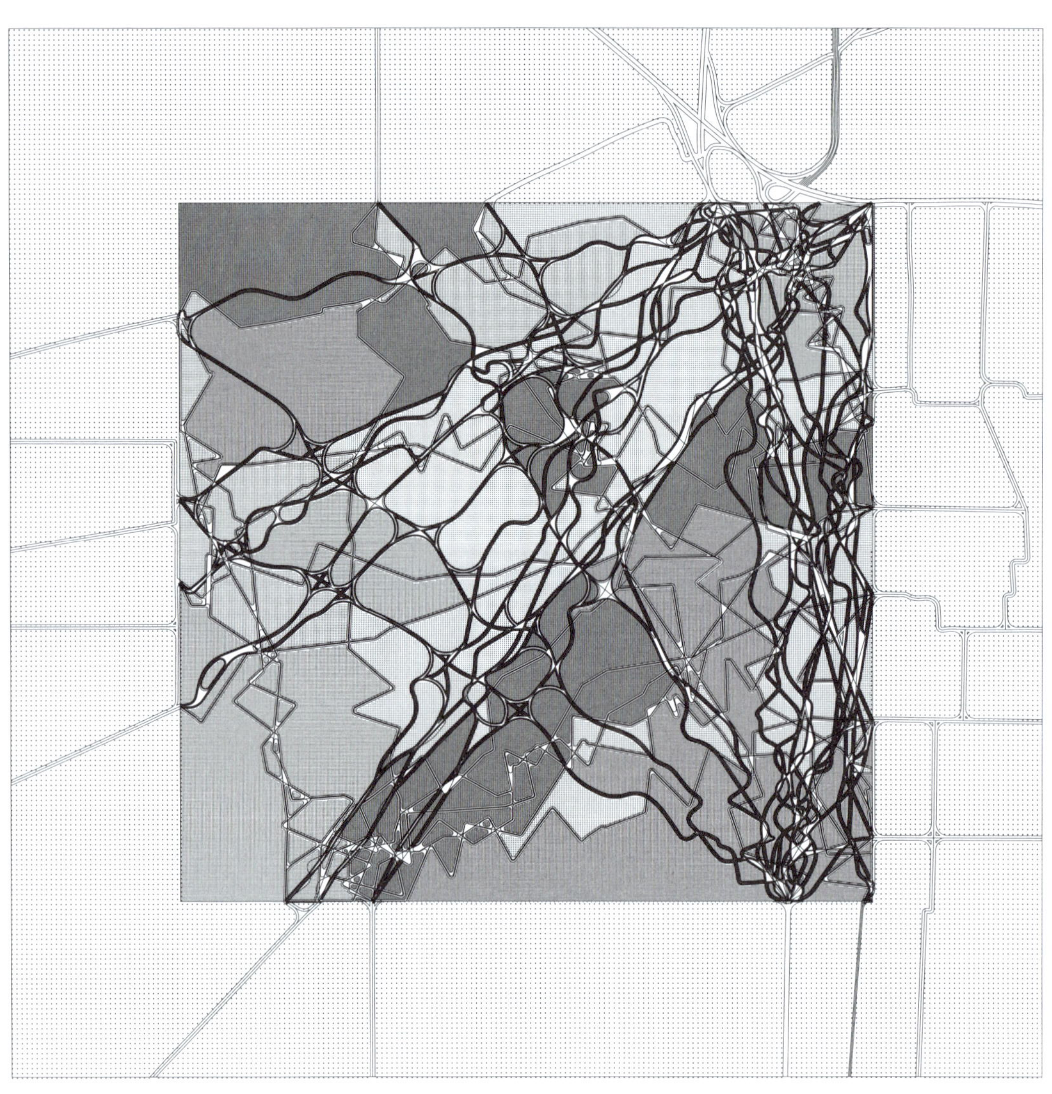

Region: Argentine Pampas
System: Transport Infrastructure
Project: Silo-roads, Agro-productive Urbanism
Specifications: Integrated organization of various types of circulatory routes and storage corridors, varying according to speed of transport
Drawing: Plan
Author: Andrew Pringle

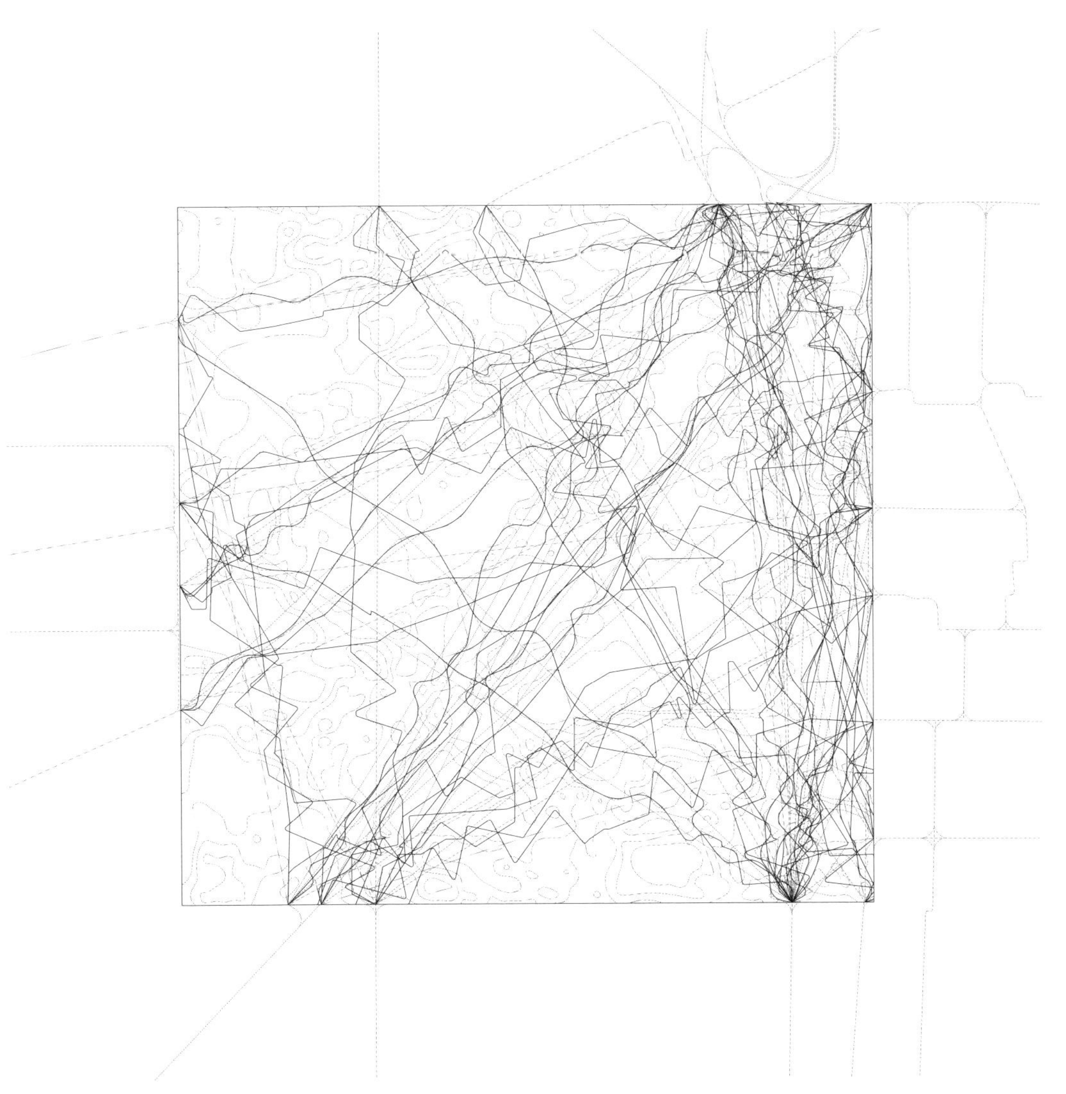

Region: Argentine Pampas
System: Transport Infrastructure
Project: Silo-roads, Agro-productive Urbanism
Specifications: Process of mutual feedback between circulatory routes and storage corridors, varying according to speed of transport
Drawing: Plan
Author: Andrew Pringle

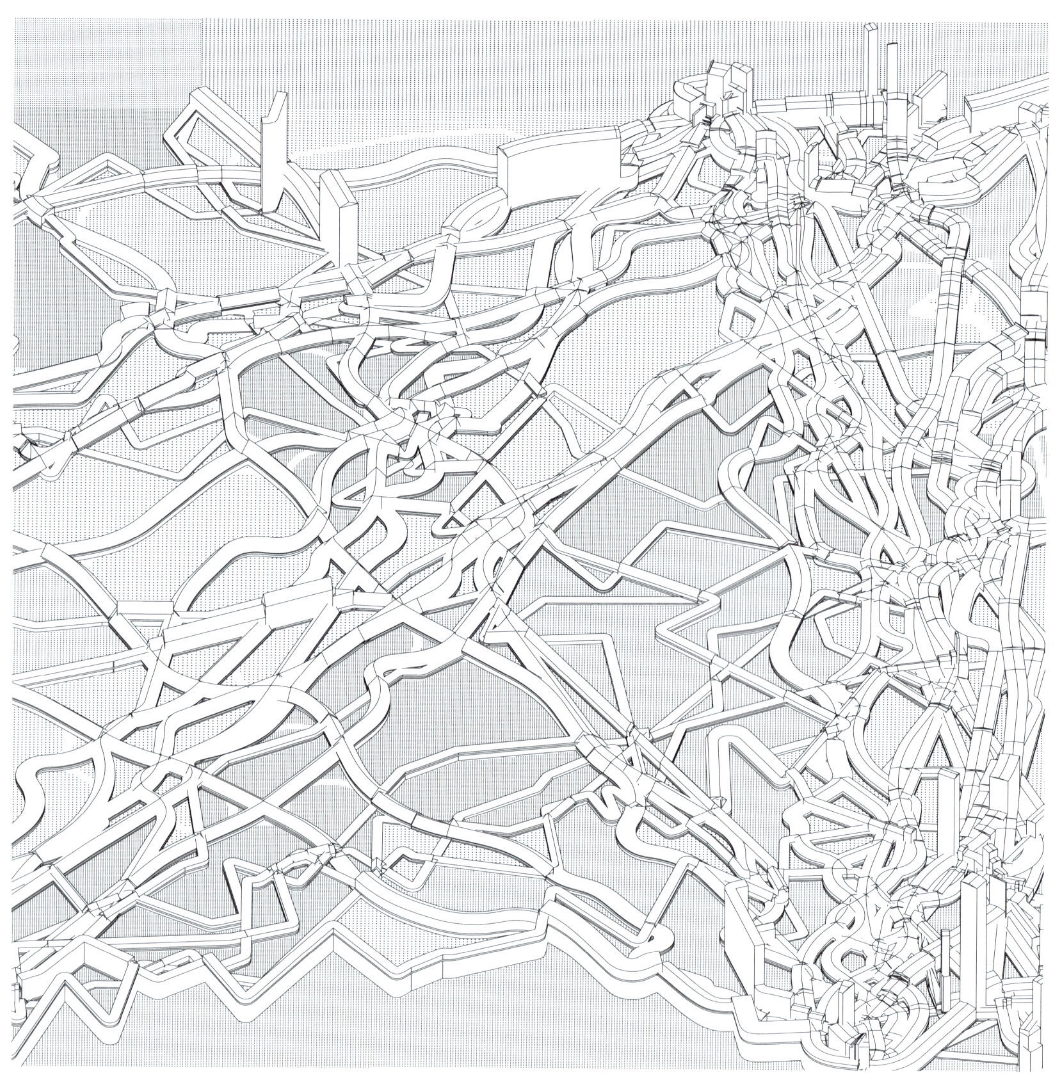

Region: Argentine Pampas
System: Transport Infrastructure
Project: Silo-roads, Agro-productive Urbanism
Specifications: Integrated organization of various types of circulatory routes and storage corridors, varying according to speed of transport
Drawing: Axonometric
Author: Andrew Pringle

Region: Argentine Pampas
System: Transport Infrastructure
Project: Silo-roads, Agro-productive Urbanism
Specifications: Integrated organization of various types of circulatory routes and storage corridors, varying according to speed of transport
Drawing: Section, every 200 meters
Author: Andrew Pringle

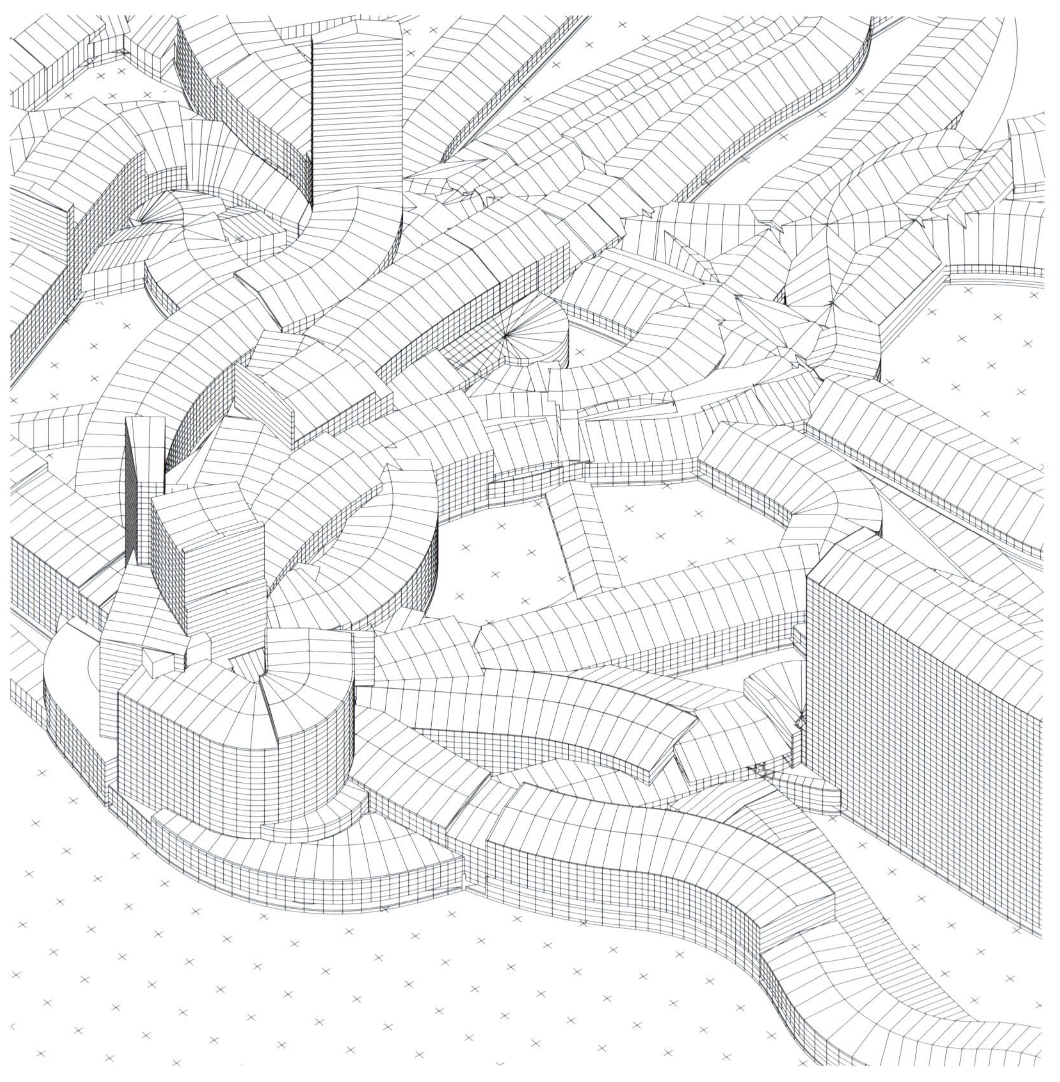

Region: Argentine Pampas
System: Transport Infrastructure
Project: Silo-roads, Agro-productive Urbanism
Specifications: Integrated organization of various types of circulatory routes and storage corridors, varying according to speed of transport
Drawing: Axonometric, sector
Author: Andrew Pringle

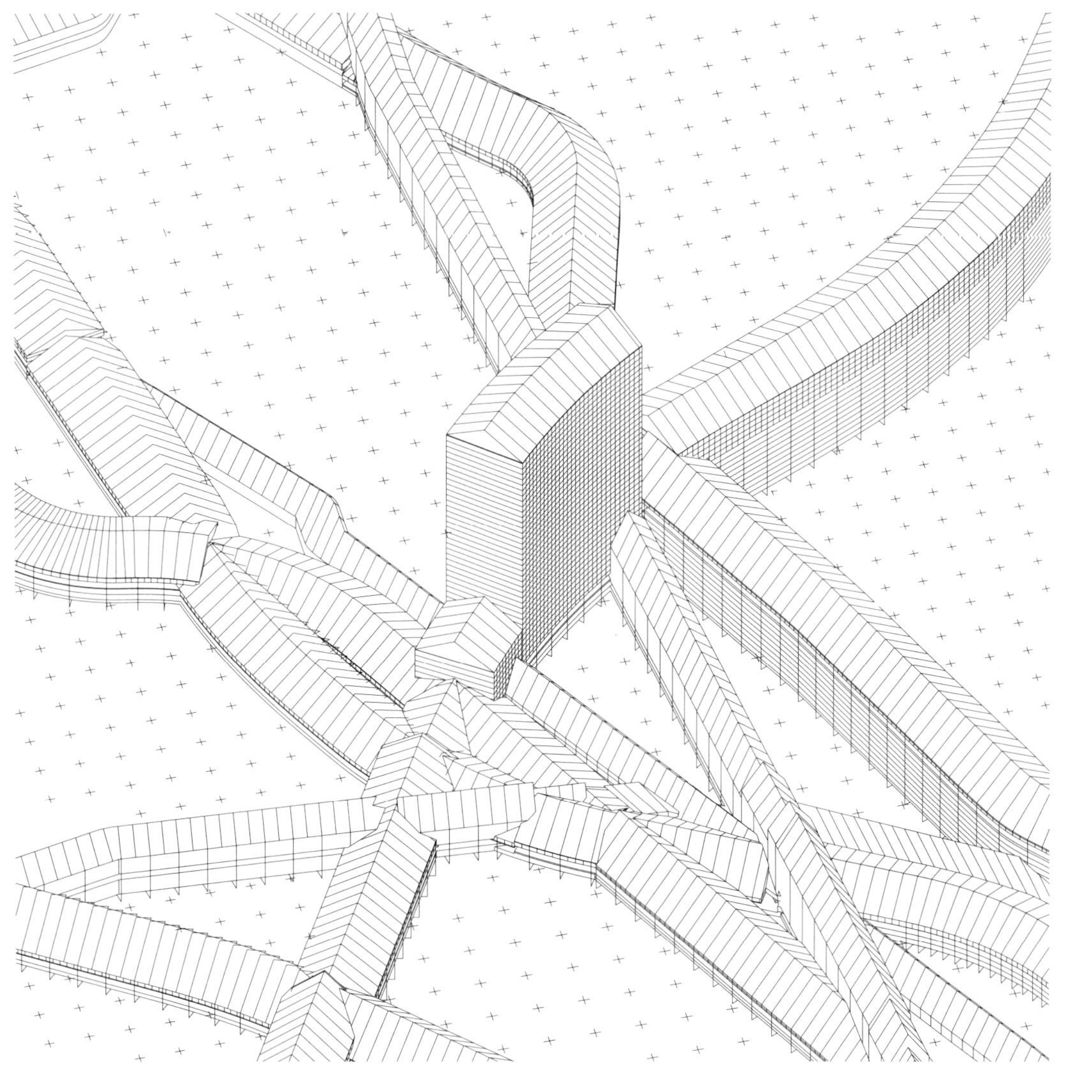

Region: Argentine Pampas
System: Transport Infrastructure
Project: Silo-roads, Agro-productive Urbanism
Specifications: Integrated organization of various types of circulatory routes and storage corridors, varying according to speed of transport
Drawing: Axonometric, sector
Author: Andrew Pringle

Biographies

Ciro Najle is an architect, researcher and educator. He studied Architecture at the Universidad de Buenos Aires, and is Master of Science in Advanced Architectural Design, Columbia University (GSAPP). Dean at the School of Architecture and Urban Studies and Professor at the Universidad Torcuato Di Tella (Buenos Aires), Visiting Professor at the Harvard University Graduate School of Design (Cambridge, Massachusetts), co-founder and former Director of the Landscape Urbanism Graduate Design Master Program and Diploma Unit Master at the Architectural Association (London), he has taught at various architectural institutions, including Cornell University (Ithaca, New York), Columbia University (New York), the Berlage Institute (Rotterdam), the Universidad Federico Santa María (Valparaíso) and the Universidad de Buenos Aires. Director of GDB General Design Bureau, architectural office and multidisciplinary laboratory of research in Buenos Aires, and previously of MLab Machinic Laboratory, material research laboratory in Valparaíso, and of MID, Young Architect of the Year Second Prize (London, 2001), his work has been exhibited in cultural venues including the Museum of Contemporary Art in Denver, Le Laboratoire in Paris, the Prague Biennale of Art, and he was the curator of the London Pavilion at the Beijing Biennale of Architecture. His theoretical and professional work has been published in the magazines *Plot, Quaderns d'Arquitectura i Urbanisme, Architectural World, Oris, UR, Egg, Esquire, Praxis* and *Summa+*. Author of the introductions to the Barcelona based 2G monographs on Foreign Office Architects/FOA (2000), MGM Morales-Gilles-Mariscal (2009) and Adamo-Faiden (2013), he was the researcher and designer for the book *Tokyo Bay Experiment* (Columbia University, New York, 1994) and co-editor of *Landscape Urbanism: A Manual for the Machinic Landscape* (Architectural Association, London, 2004, with Moshen Mostafavi). He has recently co-edited with Anna Font and Julián Varas the books *Modos de práctica* and *Culturas digitales* at the Universidad Torcuato Di Tella, and is currently working on the book *The Generic Sublime*, to be published by Harvard University GSD.

Lluís Ortega is an architect, researcher and educator. He studied Architecture at the Barcelona School of Architecture (ETSAB/UPC) and is Master of Science in Advanced Architectural Design, Columbia University (GSAPP), Diploma in Philosophy, Universitat de Barcelona, and PhD at the ETSAB/UPC. At present he is Assistant Professor at the University of Illinois at Chicago (UIC) and Visiting Professor at the Universidad Torcuato Di Tella in Buenos Aires. Previously he has taught at the ETSAB (Barcelona), the Universidad de Alicante, the Harvard University Graduate School of Design (Cambridge, Massachusetts) and the

Akademie der bildenden Künste (Vienna). He co-founded F451arquitectura in 2000, rebranded as Sio2arch in 2014, an internationally awarded and exhibited collaborative practice with Santiago Ibarra, Xavier Osarte and Esther Segura. He was the director of *Quaderns d'Arquitectura i Urbanisme* (Barcelona, 2003-2005) and he worked as an editor on *2G* magazine no. 16 (Foreign Office Architects, Barcelona, 2000) and on the co-edition of Josep Llinàs's writings *Saques de esquina* (Pre-Textos, Valencia, 2002, with Moisés Puente) and *Platform GSD 2008* (GSD/Actar, Barcelona, 2008). He published the reader *La digitalización toma el mando* [Digitalization Takes Command] (Editorial Gustavo Gili, Barcelona, 2009) and was Adjunct Curator and main designer of the Spanish Pavilion at the Venice Architecture Biennale 2014.

Anna Font studied architecture at the Universitat Ramon Llull (Barcelona) and has a Master's from the Harvard University Graduate School of Design (GSD). She is currently an associate architect with the GDB Design Bureau, a Buenos Aires office focusing on architecture, design and urban planning. She is a professor at the School of Architecture and Urban Studies at the Universidad Torcuato Di Tella (Buenos Aires), where she coordinates the publication archives. She is also the editor of *Archivos 01/Modos de Práctica*. She is currently collaborating on the edition of the book series *The Generic Sublime*, to be published by Harvard University. She has published articles in the journals *Archivos, Plot* and *Notas*.

Paul Andersen founded Indie Architecture in 2009. He is a professor at the University of Illinois at Chicago and the Universidad Torcuato di Tella (Buenos Aires); he has also been a professor at the Harvard University Graduate School of Design (GSD) and Cornell University (Ithaca). He has served as guest curator for the Museum of Contemporary Art Denver and the Biennial of the Americas, and he is author of the books *The Architecture of Patterns* (W. W. Norton & Co., New York, 2010; with David Salomon) and *The Monuments Power the Cars* (Actar, New York, 2015; with Adam Lerner). His work has been named as a finalist for the MoMA/PS1 Young Architects Award and he is a Fulbright Specialist in Architecture.

Francisco Cadau studied architecture in the Faculty of Architecture, Design and Urbanism at the Universidad de Buenos Aires (UBA) and is director of his own architecture studio. He is a professor and coordinator of the postgraduate program "Architecture and Technology" for the School of Architecture and Urban Studies at the Universidad Torcuato Di Tella, assistant professor at the Faculty of Architecture, Design and Urbanism at the UBA, and has been a guest professor at the Architectural Association (London), the Royal Danish Academy (Copenhagen), Cornell University (Ithaca) and the Pontifícia Universidade Católica of Rio de Janeiro. His work has been included in biennials and exhibitions in Argentina, Brazil, Colombia, Austria, the Netherlands and Italy.

David Salomon holds a PhD in architecture from the program in Critical Studies in Architecture Culture at the University of California, Los Angeles (UCLA). He is currently a professor of Architectural Design, History and Theory at Ithaca College. He is the author of *The Architecture of Patterns* (W. W. Norton & Co., New York, 2010; with Paul Andersen) and his work has been published in journals such as *Grey Room, Log, Harvard Design Review, Architectural Design, Places, The Journal of Architectural Education* and *The Journal of Architecture*. His current research is focused on the aesthetic efficiency of architecture and the intersections between art, technology and the suburbs in the 1960s.

Axel Cherniavsky is a researcher with the CONICET and holds a PhD from the Université de Paris I Panthéon-Sorbonne and the Universidad de Buenos Aires. He is a professor in the areas of Contemporary Philosophy and Metaphysics for the Faculty of Philosophy and Letters at the Universidad de Buenos Aires and the author of *Temps et langage chez Bergson* (Harmattan, Paris, 2009) and *Concept et méthode. La conception de la philosophie de Gilles Deleuze* (Publications de la Sorbonne, Paris, 2012).

Ramon Faura holds a PhD from the Barcelona School of Architecture (ETSAB). He is an assistant professor in the History of Art and Architecture at the Reus School of Architecture (EAR) and a professor at the Elisava School, Barcelona. He has been a guest professor at the ETSAB and the Universidad Torcuato Di Tella (Buenos Aires). Between 2003 and 2006 he was editor-in-chief of the magazine *Quaderns d'Arquitectura i Urbanisme*. He served as co-curator of the exhibition *Architectures without Place* (Centre d'Art Santa Mònica, Barcelona, 2009). He is the author of *Louis XIV in Royal Costume: The Decapitation of the Mystical Body* (EAR, Reus, 2010) and is a regular contributor to the magazine *Nativa*.

Teresa Galí-Izard is the co-director of Arquitectura Agronomía (with Jordi Nebot) and head of the Landscape Architecture Department at the University of Virginia. In her studio she explores new languages and forms while working with living systems such as land, water and plant-life, based on a contemporary approach to dynamics and management. She is the author of *The Same Landscapes: Ideas and Interpretations* (Editorial Gustavo Gili, Barcelona, 2005) and editor of the book *Jacques Simon. Les autres paysages. Idées et réflexions sur le territoire* (Editorial Gustavo Gili, Barcelona, 2012; with Daniela Collafranceschi). She is currently involved in projects in the UK, Venezuela, Switzerland, Spain, Ukraine, Lebanon and Algeria.

Lluís Viu Rebés studied architecture at the Barcelona School of Architecture (ETSAB) and earned his degree from the Architectural Association (London). He was a collaborator with Foreign Office Architects for a year and in 2005 he founded the studio Max de Cusa in Barcelona (with Jordi Pagés). Between 2001 and 2005 he was a professor at the Architectural Association. He has collaborated with the Institute for Advanced Architecture of Catalonia (IaaC, Barcelona) and is currently a professor of architectural design for the School of Architecture and Urban Studies at the Universidad Torcuato Di Tella (Buenos Aires).

Julián Varas holds a degree in Architecture from the Universidad de Buenos Aires and a Master's degree from the Architectural Association (London). He has been a guest professor at the Architectural Association (London), the ETH (Zurich), Cornell University (Ithaca), the Universidad de Buenos Aires, and the Pontificia Universidad Católica (Santiago de Chile). He is currently a professor at the School of Architecture and Urban Studies at the Universidad Torcuato Di Tella (Buenos Aires), where he coordinates the Center for Studies in Contemporary Architecture and is director of the Master's program "Architectural History and Culture and the City." He contributed to the book *Archipelagos: A Manual for Peripheral Buenos Aires* (ETH/Universidad de Palermo, Zurich/Buenos Aires, 2011) and is currently working on the manuscript for his doctoral dissertation *In the Name of the User: Postwar Public Housing and the Project of Architectural Heterogeneity*.

Pablo Gerson earned his degree in architecture from the Universidad de Buenos Aires, where he has been a professor since 2003. He also teaches an Introduction to Expressive Media course at the School of Architecture and Urban Studies at the Universidad Torcuato Di Tella (Buenos Aires). As a photographer, he studied at the International Center of Photography in New York; his work has been exhibited and published in different media on a number of occasions and he is an habitual collaborator with the magazine *Plot*. In 2005 he founded Estudiox (EX), a film and television production company focusing on educational and historical content. Since 2013 he has been a founding partner at 153C, an organization devoted to documenting, producing and distributing disciplinary content.

Acknowledgements

This book was supported by a grant from the Graham Foundation for Advanced Studies in the Fine Arts. Its research was developed simultaneously in studios and seminars taught at the School of Architecture and Urban Studies of the Universidad Torcuato Di Tella in Buenos Aires (UTDT) and at the School of Architecture of the University of Illinois at Chicago (UIC). Aside from these institutions, we would like to extend our gratitude to Anna Font for her continuous work on the project and the book, to Iñaki Ábalos and Robert Somol for their support for the project; and to Paul Andersen, David Salomon, Teresa Galí-Izard, Ramon Faura, Julián Varas, Francisco Cadau, Lluís Viu, Axel Cherniavsky, Pablo Gerson and Diego Camats for their generous contributions. To Paula Maidana, Andrew Pringle, Juan Cruz Río, Martina Rossi, Guillermo Aporszegi, Julia D'Alotto, Santiago Mussi, Josefina Nano, Andrew Pringle, Fernanda Raimondi, Tomás Rowinski, Rosario Vaquer Melo and Máximo Sánchez Granel, students from at UTDT; and to Paola Gómez-Piñeiro, Kim Hibben, Taylor Holloway, Travis Kalina, Jason Mould, John Sohn, Sam Tanis and Tao Tao, students from at UIC, who so dedicatedly participated in the research. To Julia Capomaggi for her insights and constant support; to Kim Hibben and Jason Mould for their help in editing drawings; and to Ramon Prat, Ricardo Devesa, Moisés Puente, Angela Bunning, Sara Sánchez Buendía and Paul Hammond for their editorial support and editing feedbacks.

Credits

Universidad Torcuato Di Tella in Buenos Aires
School of Architecture and Urban Studies
Professor Ciro Najle
Assistant Anna Font
Students Paula Maidana, Andrew Pringle, Juan Cruz Río, Martina Rossi, Guillermo Aporszegi, Julia D'Alotto, Santiago Mussi, Josefina Nano, Andrew Pringle, Fernanda Raimondi, Tomás Rowinski, Rosario Vaquer Melo and Máximo Sánchez Granel
Courses dictated in 2012 and 2013

University of Illinois at Chicago
School of Architecture
Professor Lluís Ortega
Students Paola Gómez-Piñeiro, Kim Hibben, Taylor Holloway, Travis Kalina, Jason Mould, John Sohn, Sam Tanis and Tao Tao
Courses dictated in 2012 and 2013

Published by
Actar Publishers, New York,
www.actar.com
Authors Ciro Najle and Lluís Ortega
Edited by Ciro Najle, Lluís Ortega and Anna Font
Translation Angela Bunning
Copy-editing Paul Hammond
Photography Pablo Gerson
Graphic Design Ramon Prat

ISBN 978-1-940291-54-3

Distributed by
Actar D
151, Grand Street, 5th Floor
New York, NY 10003 USA
Phone +1 212 966 2207
salesnewyork@actar-d.com
eurosales@actar-d.com
www.actar-d.com

Also available in Spanish
Suprarrural
ISBN 978-1-940291-77-2